Teacher Evaluation:
Educative Alternatives

CONTEMPORARY ANALYSIS IN EDUCATION SERIES
General Editor: Philip Taylor, University of Birmingham, UK.

Contemporary Analysis in Education Series

Teacher Evaluation: Educative Alternatives

Andrew Gitlin and John Smyth

The Falmer Press
(A member of the Taylor & Francis Group)
New York . Philadelphia . London

UK   The Falmer Press, Falmer House, Barcombe, Lewes, East Sussex, BN8 5DL

USA   The Falmer Press, Taylor & Francis Inc., 242 Cherry Street, Philadelphia, PA 19106-1906

© A. Gitlin and J. Smyth 1989

First published 1989

British Library Cataloguing in Publication Data

Smyth, John
Teacher Evaluation: critical educative and transformative
alternatives. — (Contemporary analysis in education series).
1. Teachers. Assessment
I. Title. II. Gitlin, Andrew
371.1′44
ISBN 1-85000-522-2
ISBN 1-85000-523-0 (pbk.)

Typeset in 10/12 Garamond by
Alresford Typesetting & Design, Alresford, Hants

Jacket design by Leonard Williams

Printed in Great Britain by Taylor & Francis (Printers) Ltd, Basingstoke

Contents

General Editor's Preface

Accountability and the application of forms of quality control over the processes of education are not new. The Education Act of 1870, piloted through the British Houses of Parliament by Robert Lowe, led to the infamous, and in the end ineffective, system of payments by results. This early version of teacher assessment was followed later by the use of inspection for the same purpose. Both failed, not because they were unworkable, but because they were intolerable in an open society, the very openness of which depends on the quality of education it provides for its citizens.

Current moves toward teacher evaluation may fail for the same reasons. It is the virtue of this book that it both argues and illustrates why and how this need not be. It represents the most systematic exploration of the nature of teacher evaluation yet undertaken and does so with erudition and poise. But it does more than this. It offers ways ahead through which teacher evaluation, about which almost everyone in the education service is agreed, including teachers, can contribute to the improvement of the quality of educational life lived in schools and classrooms. In short, it can be turned to educative ends.

The authors are to be congratulated on the twin achievements of this book. It deserves to be widely read and debated not only for its clarification but also for its practical proposals.

Philip Taylor
August, 1988

Authors' Preface[1]

In recent times, public schooling has come in for constant criticism. The supposed failing of schools has led to a rush of proposed reforms, and although these vary, from one country to another, for the most part they focus on the alleged inadequacies of teachers; specifically, teachers are viewed as being deficient and in need of help. Whether the need is in respect of content, skill development, or the latest in management techniques, the proposed reforms appear as a delivery of a service from those who know about 'good' teaching (the experts), to those who are regarded as not meeting up to expected standards (teachers and students). In this book we raise some serious questions about the efficacy of the underlying presumption that teachers are somehow the primary cause of the economic and social malaise afflicting western democracies. In our view, if the fundamental presumption is wrong, or at least highly problematic, then the centralized, prescriptive, and sanction-ridden courses of action that are being proposed and enacted are highly questionable to say the least. The hardening of the educational arteries around the world, as educational systems develop more and more sophisticated systems of teacher surveillance and appraisal, is tangible evidence of that faulty thinking. There is a dual dimension at work here. On the one hand, there is the overt (and highly publicized) agenda of improving the technicalities of teaching through more rigorous forms of teacher evaluation[2], but at the same time there is the more subtle covert agenda of the ideological forces at work that serve to maintain and legitimate the cultural and social status quo. These schemes set 'standards' by using rating schemes which reflect a particular constrained notion of good teaching, these standards being communicated to teachers through the distribution of rewards based on their performance on selected criteria. In this way, teacher evaluation schemes become a means by which expert notions of good teaching are used purportedly to change teacher behaviour in desired ways.

Teacher evaluation processes predicated on this type of thinking also affect the way teachers approach their teaching. For example, teachers tend to become dependent on others to analyze the strengths and weaknesses of their classroom practices. This is particularly problematic in an occupation that is itself preoccupied with the assessment of the educational experiences of students. The effect is that the emphasis on evaluating teachers is reproduced in teachers' own unconscious and unquestioned acceptance of externally imposed practices of assessing students. In effect, evaluation becomes a way of ensuring compliance among students, in much the same way as external agencies ensure teacher compliance through evaluation. Teachers become discouraged from adopting an enquiring approach to their classrooms, diverting their energies instead into meeting minimalist standards of outside experts. The tragedy of this is that students themselves become co-opted into the meritocratic process of grade-performance exchange. There are as well crucial but largely unanswered questions about the distribution of power involved here. The moral and ethical worth of what teachers are attempting to do through their teaching is completely ignored in evaluation schemes designed to get teachers 'to lift their game'.

Evaluation of this kind amounts to a 'delivery system' that rests uneasily with teachers working autonomously towards helping one another, while striving towards a critical consciousness of the circumstances of their teaching. Having schools that are enquiring places in which students adopt a critically informed view of the world around them requires, at minimum, a situation in which teachers work with other teachers so they can clarify what is 'good' teaching, what is happening in the classroom, why and with what effect. In sum, we need an approach that encourages change based on dialogue, rather than on monologue delivered by outside experts and received in an unquestioned fashion by those inside schools.

However, for this alternative to occur it is essential to think non-hierarchically so as to encourage and foster dialogue. Simply replacing 'external' forms of evaluation with 'internal' processes, that require teachers to assess the extent to which colleagues meet up to externally determined standards, will not suffice either. What is required instead are ways in which teachers can collaborate with one another so as to understand their teaching in its historically and socially embedded context, while engaging in collective change based on a careful examination of an array of taken-for-granted assumptions which define teaching in narrow and oppressive ways.

We believe that this book will have a multiple audience. It will be relevant to pre-service teacher education students who themselves have a wealth of personal knowledge about what it means to be on the receiving end of 'evaluation' during their elementary and secondary education. For these readers, the critique section of this book enables them to see behind processes that they have been a part of as students themselves in schools, and provides them with a way of asking questions about the nature of social control and power implicit in existing dominant schemes of teacher appraisal. The alternative possibilities addressed in the second part of the book supply living examples of how the critique may be worked through in practice. For experienced teachers, and those who work with them in various capacities such as consultants, in-service co-ordinators and staff developers, this section illustrates how to move from habituated approaches to teaching, to ones that have a much more problematic perspective. It is a perspective that causes them to ask questions about why past practices in teacher evaluation have shaped teaching in the way they have, and provides them with examples of the 'lived' practices of other teachers who have begun to raise questions about the social and political context of their work.

For reasons of manageability the book falls into two parts, although intellectually there is continual traffic between the sections in terms of ideas. While the first part of the volume is given over to a critique of the widespread impositional (or 'dominant') mode of teacher evaluation—what it represents, and where it has come from—the second part presents two alternative forms of teacher evaluation (which we label as 'educative') that have their roots in an entirely different philosophical viewpoint.

Chapter 1 commences by briefly sketching out what an educative model of teacher evaluation might look like, a model that attempts to give teachers *more* rather than *less* control over their teaching lives. By regarding their teaching and the contexts within which it occurs problematically, and by engaging in dialogue with one another about that teaching, we argue that this model enables teachers to examine a whole range of habitual and taken-for-granted issues about pedagogical processes and school structures. By way of contrast to this less impositional mode, we lay out the features of the dominant view of teacher evaluation and show that it is not only hierarchical and dehumanizing, but it also has a misplaced faith in the capacity of scientific forms of research on teaching to deliver definite knowledge about the nature of teaching. Through some brief historical glimpses of how teacher evaluation came to be in England, USA and Australia, we see how a view of teacher competency based exclusively upon technical rationality has come to be used primarily as a way of reproducing existing social relations and cultural capital. By a gradual process of de-skilling teachers through a social division of labour that vests control through surveillance in the hands of an inspectorial (or managerial) class, teachers are progressively denied access to the methodologies and the resources necessary to make sense of their own teaching. In place of an empowering paradigm based upon dialogue, reason and discussion, what we have instead is a commodified view of the 'right' way to teach that involves a heavy monitoring, detecting and enforcing of what are deemed to be 'correct' pedagogical practices. The voices of teachers, students and others who have a legitimate stake in expressing a viewpoint about the way teaching might be, while not completely silenced, are at least muted as they are relegated to marginalized forms of resistance.

Authors' Preface

Tackling the issues of how to replace the polluted dominant forms of teacher evaluation with 'better' alternatives requires, first, that we have a clear understanding of the ways in which the mainstream view has become contaminated. It is not that we are proposing that there is no place for teacher evaluation schemes in schools—rather, our claim is that existing mainstream views have become fundamentally distorted as they have lost sight of their own espoused ideals. In Chapter 2 we look at the manner in which dominant forms of teacher evaluation have become narrowed; through their separation of 'knowing' from 'doing' in teaching; through a dogmatic view of what constitutes a 'scientific' rendering of teaching; through a pre-occupation with evaluation as a technique; by dissociating teachers and teaching from their cultural politics and history; through a reliance on edicts and monologue instead of debate and dialogue; and through encouraging an individualistic and competitive (as distinct from a collective and collaborative) agenda in the sense-making process in schools.

How the notion of domination embodied in the surveillance model of teacher evaluation is actually played out is the subject of discussion in Chapter 3. In large part, the continuing widespread acceptance of this mode rests upon the unquestioned acceptance of both its naturalness and its rightfulness. Once we begin to contest aspects of this model that have intruded into shaping the technical nature of teachers' work through textbooks, rationalized curricula, national testing of students and the like, then we begin to develop a sense of the way in which teachers' work has been intensified, and of how the public servant ideology attached to teaching has become so difficult to dislodge. Treating teachers and what they do with a form of contempt, by regarding them as invisible, serves to increase feelings of isolation and alienation. While paralysis of action is never universal or complete in schemes like this, it nevertheless conveys an unambiguous message as to who 'knows best' about teaching, and what kind of importance to attach to what teachers say is significant about their work. In other words, teacher evaluation (contrary to conventional wisdom) is not a neutral, objective, value-free activity; it is imbued with a very deliberate political agenda.

Chapters 4, 5, 6 and 7 are about the rationale and some evidence relating to two alternative teacher evaluation strategies that we have worked with that depart radically from the ensconced views we have so roundly critiqued in the remainder of this volume. While they differ in substance in important respects in terms of where they have come from and how they are worked through in practice, horizontal evaluation and a 'critical' version of clinical supervision both share a common ideal in that they aim to provide teachers with ways of penetrating the mystique that can surround teaching. All of this represents a significant departure from the processes we have taken issue with.

In writing and piecing together this book, as authors we have sought very hard to emulate the dialogical and communicative model we advocate in the text. We have critiqued and interrogated one another's writing almost to the point of exhaustion, and have involved a community of colleagues and students in our respective education systems and universities in America and Australia. We remain firmly convinced that there is currently no volume that seeks to engage with and unravel the complexities of teacher evaluation in quite the way we have chosen to do here. To that extent, we will be very interested to hear from colleagues and practitioners who take up the challenge to join with us in the struggle to reconstrue what it means to be involved in teacher evaluation in educative ways.

Andrew Gitlin
John Smyth
August 1988

Notes
1 The authors contributed jointly and equally to the writing of this book; the ordering of the names is purely alphabetical.
2 We use the term 'teacher evaluation' to encompass the term 'teacher appraisal' throughout this book.

Part I
Contesting the Dominant Mode

Chapter One

'Educative' versus 'Dominant' Views of Teacher Evaluation

Few issues in education are guaranteed to generate such heat as the evaluation of teachers. Voice the word 'evaluation' within earshot of teachers and there are noticeable signs of apprehension, if not outright agitation (Smyth, 1988). At first blush, this may seem surprising given that issues of worth loom so large in what transpires in schooling. Under greater scrutiny however it becomes clear that what angers teachers about evaluation practices is the attempt to control their behaviour while ignoring the ways they understand schooling. Teachers are not opposed to evaluation but rather the particular form it tends to take (Gitlin and Bullough, 1987). We will argue throughout this book that what we describe as the 'dominant' view is not only oppressive for teachers, but also serves conservative interests by fostering authoritarian notions of pedagogy leaving intact current educational aims and purposes. We argue further that the problematic nature of dominant instrumental approaches can be contested by reconceptualizing teacher evaluation within the framework of an 'educative' model (Fay, 1977, 1987). To begin this rather complex process of reconceptualizing teacher evaluation, this first chapter will detail the nature and importance of an educative model, and show, through a brief focus on the history of teacher evaluation in three cultural contexts, why dominant forms of evaluation have come to be narrowly conceived.

An Educative Model

One of the primary commitments underpinning an educative model is that 'changing people's basic understanding of themselves and their world is a first step in their radically altering the self-destructive patterns of interacting that characterize their social relations' (Fay, 1977, p. 204). As opposed to instrumental models that concentrate only on identified behaviours which are attached to a set of supposedly agreed upon aims, an educative model considers how behaviour and understanding are intimately linked. Teachers are given an opportunity to 'decide for [themselves], on the basis of lucid, critical self-awareness, the manner in which [they] wish to live' (Fay, 1977, p. 207). Focusing on the relation between understanding and behaviour does not mean that teachers are simply asked how they feel, for such enquiries ignore the way school structure is both sustained by and textures teacher understandings and beliefs. Instead, the educative model must take a critical approach which challenges teachers' taken-for-granted notions of schooling. By doing so, teacher evaluation has the potential to be a catalyst that sparks participants to change the way they live and react to others (Fay, 1977, p. 206).

One process particularly well suited to this type of change is embodied in the notion of dialogical relations. A dialogical relation is not established by having actors simply talk to one another, but rather involves a true conversation which, as Bernstein (1983) notes, 'is not to be confused with idle chatter or a violent babble of competing voices – [but] is an extended and open dialogue which presupposes a . . . tacit sense of relevance' (p. 2). Dialogue of this sort does not pit one actor against the other to determine who can win the argument, but rather enables the participants to work together to understand the subject discussed:

> When one enters into dialogue with another person and then is carried away by the dialogue, it is no longer the will of the individual person, holding back or exposing itself, that is determinative. Rather, the law of the subject matter is at issue in the dialogue and elicits statement and counterstatement and in the end plays into each other. (p. 66)

When the dialogical relation is successful, 'The person with understanding does not know and judge as one who stands apart unaffected, but as one united by the specific bond with the other, (s/he) thinks with the other and undergoes the situation with him (her)' (Gadamer, 1975, p. 288). To speak of dialogical relations is not, therefore, to assume equality of perception or judgment between actors, but to enable participants to work together to understand the topic under discussion. Neither does gaining an understanding require that all prejudices or prejudgments are removed, for this is clearly impossible (Pierce, 1931–5); the aim of the dialogue is to make prejudices or prejudgments apparent and to 'test them critically in the course of inquiry' (Bernstein, 1983, p. 128). It is the critical testing of prejudgments that empowers the actor to challenge the taken-for-granted notions that influence the way they see the world and judge their practice.

While dialogical relations may free individual teachers from 'self destructive patterns of interaction', fundamentally altering the nature of schooling requires more. Specifically, attempts must be made to extend the dialogue beyond those initially participating in the process. This is so for several reasons. At the classroom level, particular individuals may have the same 'blindspots' and therefore leave unexamined issues which constrain what it is they do. Extending the dialogue by allowing others to participate in critically assessing teaching and schooling practices makes it more likely that these blindspots will be identified and contested, thereby opening up new possibilities at the level of classroom practice. This is to acknowledge that there is more to school change than merely altering what teachers do. It is the structures and relations which support constrained notions of teaching and learning that need to be contested. Unfortunately, individual teachers on their own are unlikely to have the power to alter these oppressive features of schooling. Extending the dialogical process, therefore, also allows teachers and other members of the educational community to act collectively based on an alternative view of the way schools might be. It is collective action of this sort that is most likely to challenge the structures and relations that define schooling in narrow ways.

In sum, teacher evaluation approaches that fit within the framework of an educative model would take into account the relationship between teacher ideology and practice; encourage participants to form dialogical relations which critically assess this relation; and make attempts to shift the dialogue beyond individual teachers so that as many members of the community as possible become actively involved in assessing educational aims and practices.

The difficulties of putting into place an educative model of teacher evaluation are formidable. Teacher isolation, the reward structure of most schools, and the lack of opportunity to make links with non-teachers inside and outside schools are just a few of the problems. It seems worthwhile to ask, therefore, what is to be gained by embracing such a model of teacher evaluation.

Dialogical relations confront traditional forms of authority and replace them with the power of argument and persuasion. Traditional forms of authority are based on status and position in the hierarchy. For example, a school principal might be assumed to have the right to evaluate teachers. This authority is derived from the principal's position relative to teachers in the school hierarchy and has little to do with his or her insights about schooling. Teachers, on the other hand, lack this authority given their position on the lower rungs of the school hierarchy. They are not, therefore, asked to be involved in the choice of an evaluator or to enter into discussions about the constructs used to evaluate their work. By replacing this form of authority with the power of reason, argument and persuasion, teachers are able to begin to challenge the view that evaluation is something done to them, while at the same time confronting the school hierarchy which has come to constrain their role in such dramatic ways (see Gitlin, 1983; Smyth, 1987a; Apple, 1982, about the proletarianization of work). In doing this, teachers do not merely change places with others in the school hierarchy, but they actually begin to take steps to replace that hierarchy with a more egalitarian order. As Arendt argues:

> Authority . . . is incompatible with persuasion, which presupposes equality and works through a process of argumentation. Where arguments are used authority is left in abeyance. Against the egalitarian order of persuasion stands the authoritarian order which is always hierarchical. (Bernstein, 1983, p. 93)

The educative model, therefore, attempts to further egalitarian and democratic ideals through a process of empowerment. Not only does this entail attempts to 'flatten hierarchies' which constrain those on the lower rungs, but teachers who have traditionally been silenced may begin to make their own history and 'separate themselves from manipulation and . . . the routine flow of time' (Shor, 1980, p. 48).

Empowerment of this sort has dramatic implications for the education offered students because, once in this position, teachers are able to identify problems that were previously hidden. Teacher problems, according to Carr and Kemmis (1986), are generated out of the experiences of practitioners and only emerge when the ways in which these experiences are usually organised are found to be inadequate. Because most teachers do not have the opportunity to reflect critically on practice with others, the inadequacy to those practices often remains hidden, and analysis remains fixated at the level of attending to technical problems. Moral, ethical and political issues that may be cause for alarm often remain invisible or impenetrable to the teacher. Educative models of teacher evaluation encourage teachers to assess critically such concerns and enable them to 'recognise the intolerable and act against it' (Pagano, 1987, p. 121). While this result can never be assured, it is more likely to occur when teachers argue about the rightness of practices with others, rather than submit to habit or remain subservient to the views of those in positions of authority.

Finally, educative models of teacher evaluation provide the means for teachers to be involved in the same kinds of processes many of them desire for their students. The Boston Women's Teachers' Group made this point when they questioned whether we can 'expect schools to educate, encourage and expand the horizons of our children if these same institutions serve to restrict and retard the growth of teachers?' (Freedman, Jackson and Boles, 1983, p. 3). Currently, there are few and diminishing opportunities for teachers to enter into educative relationships with one another. In-service classes often do not speak to teacher problems, and when they do teachers rarely have an opportunity to debate the issues, try them out in practice or modify the recommendations to fit their particular context. University and college courses, on the other hand, are often equally unhelpful because the burden of making links with practice rests totally on the shoulders of teachers. Educative methods of teacher evaluation, therefore, seek to make it possible for all those who work and live in schools to be involved in a learning process that, as Shor notes, 'contradicts hierarchical society' (Shor, 1980, p. 95).

The Dominant View

In contrast to an educative model of teacher evaluation the dominant form usually involves some kind of classroom visitation by an administrator, on an isolated and episodic basis, with no real sense of the teacher's psychological and physical workspace. These forays into the teacher's world are justified on the alleged grounds of accountability, so that the public can be convinced that educational dollars are not being wasted, and at a more practical level so that information can be gleaned on which to make decisions about retention, tenure and promotion. As Gitlin and Goldstein (1987) note:

> These abrupt observation visits are initiated with little sense of the classroom's history and upon completion are not integrated into its ongoing history. In making these judgments, the administrator is usually armed with a summative rating scale which lists any number of desirable teaching outcomes . . . The evaluator acts as an expert who knows the script and score and has in mind how it can be best realised. The teacher satisfies or does not satisfy the expert in varying degrees. If the teacher is fortunate, she will learn the reasons for her evaluator's assessment and ways to modify what needs improvement. The activity is essentially monologic, essentially a process of communiques, of one way declarations about the state of things: the goal is to change practice to be more congruent with the expert's standards of how classrooms should be controlled and ventilated, or how to introduce the Pythagorean Theorem. (p. 17)

Our argument is that processes like this, far from generating excellence in teaching and learning as alleged, actually serve to entrench further already existing hierarchical and submissive relations:

> What stands out as a major characteristic of this procedure is that it is hierarchical. Those who are thought to be experts impose standards concerning desirable teaching outcomes on those who supposedly need the feedback. The problem is that even if the feedback changes the teacher's behaviour in acceptable ways, the hierarchical relation between the expert and the teacher is reinforced. And if change occurs, it will not be based on joint enquiry into the rightness of particular teaching outcomes, but rather will be based on standards that are imposed solely through a group's position in the hierarchy. This type of strategic action which characterises most evaluative procedures, makes it likely that the expert/teacher relation will be one of domination and that the teaching ends will not be critically assessed. (p. 17)

7

To understand adequately and appreciate the nature and intent behind current teacher evaluation practices, what they purport to do, and why, it is necessary first to have some sense of the history of teacher evaluation. As Simon (1984) argues, in order to engage in 'transformative change', whether that be teaching or evaluation, we must first figure out 'why things are the way they are, how they got that way, and what set of conditions are supporting the processes that maintain them' (p. 380). This is to acknowledge the C. Wright Mills (1959) point about the importance of personal biography and collective professional history in the understanding of current practices. His claim is that unless we are able to locate our experiences and practices in their historical context, then we are at a loss to explain how they came about or what it is that continues to maintain them. By looking at history we can see how things have come to be deliberately constructed. Teacher evaluation has an important legacy in this regard, that must be addressed.

In the section that follows, while we do not present anything like a 'history' of teacher evaluation, we draw upon some salient examples from the USA, UK and Australia as a way of illustrating our central point about the socially constructed nature of teacher evaluation in western education. These locations were chosen because of the way they typify how evaluation systems have been developed within western industrial societies. There is certainly uniqueness in each of the situations we have chosen to describe, but as we will show, there are as well some uncanny resemblances.

How Teacher Evaluation Came to Be: Glimpses from the Past

What we want to argue in this section is that with practices like teacher evaluation, we have to work out the 'political algebra'. Put another way, we have to ascertain why it is that historically certain things managed to 'get shoved off the agenda'. According to Landry *et al.* (1985), unless we find ways of re-writing that agenda, then the 'same flawed perspectives will continue to dominate the politics of the present' (p. 9). Not understanding past failures will inevitably lock us into a cycle that amounts to a replaying of those shortcomings.

We can obtain an entree into this reconstruction through language. Because of the way language is closely aligned with dominant practices, it is important that we look to history to see how language itself has changed. If the language and the practices of education are to be open to discussion and not remain trapped within a particular world view, then the prevailing metaphors within that language will also have to be continually struggled over. As Lakoff and Johnson (1980) have shown, the metaphors we use in social discourse to a large extent frame our thinking, our language and our social action.

When we consider the related terms of 'pedagogy' and 'evaluation', and look at what has happened to these two ideas, we can see the interplay of language and practices. Pedagogy, for example, had an original meaning quite different from its excessively narrow present-day one of 'instructional science'. As Kohl (1983) has noted, pedagogy comes from two Greek roots: padio-, meaning boy or child; and -agogos, meaning leader:

> Paidagogos originally meant 'child leading' and referred to the ancient Greek practice of a slave leading a child to school. This original meaning, which had nothing to do with teaching or learning, eventually became expanded to refer to work done in the service of the growth and development of the child. Service is the key word. Pedagogy takes as its focus the child to be taught and refers to the way in which adults think through the task of working to serve. (p. 28)

In a similar way, the meaning and intentions of evaluation have somehow become twisted and distorted, making it inappropriate for doing other than supporting the status quo. From its Latin origin meaning 'to strengthen' or to empower (Handford and Herberg, 1966), the term evaluation has come to take on a quite different complexion that refers to the process of 'ascertaining the amount of or finding a numerical expression for' something (*Concise Oxford Dictionary*, 1976, p. 357). Evaluation as measurement, therefore, becomes an 'end' rather than a 'means' to ascribing worth to some valued social purpose. When language is transformed in this way, it reflects a constricted view of the way evaluation is commonly practised. What tends to happen in these circumstances is that the act of measurement often becomes more important than strengthening teacher practice.

Window on the USA

If we are interested in focusing upon and bringing into question the problematic values behind the dominant mode of teacher evaluation, then in the USA we have to turn to something of the history of supervision. While the term supervision may be open to varied interpretations, the general intent is for those outside classrooms to influence the actions of teachers in particular ways. Although there may be some subtle differences between supervision and teacher evaluation, we will regard them as interchangeable for the purposes of discussion here. Certainly the aim of supervision in US schools since the nineteenth century has been to change teacher behaviour in the direction deemed desirable by experts (Button, 1961). Furthermore, this has been accompanied by a well-entrenched view that schools should be run according to the business management canons of efficiency, effectiveness, inspection and quality control (Smyth, 1984a). The interconnectedness of these two facts is not inconsequential.

If we look at the history of education, it is clear that the intention of the Common Schools in nineteenth-century America was to change the nature of society, and that those who wore the label of 'supervisors' were the front-line evangelists in this process. Blumberg (1984) has drawn upon data from the *Annual Report of the Superintendent of Common Schools in the State of New York (1845)*, as evidence of this particular type of social reconstruction. Summarizing the sentiment of these superintendents, Blumberg put it as follows:

> The future of this country and its republican form of government, as [the supervisors] saw it, was intimately connected with the schools. It would only be through [the] success and popularization [of schools] that the country would have an educated populace capable of making informed decisions and learning the skills necessary for productive adult life . . . Failing to develop a viable widespread school system would result . . . in the replication in this country of the condition of the South American republics which 'have fallen into revolutionary decrepitude and generated into military despotisms . . .' (p. 3)

> Without a good system of public schools, the thinking went, the great experiment in republican government that was America, where each person had the opportunity to be what he or she could be, would degenerate. Wealth would be concentrated in the hands of a few and such concentration of wealth 'enables its possessor to monopolize intellectual attainment, and robs the mass of motive power to effort' [citation from the superintendents' reports]. Public schools were the antidote to this possibility. (p. 5)

It is interesting to note in passing that this vision has proved largely unattainable with somewhere around 1 per cent of the population in the USA holding around 35 per cent of the wealth. The experiment of the Common Schools has clearly failed, and we shall argue that this is not unrelated to the same set of structural conditions that have produced the dominant form of teacher evaluation.

The same zeal that characterized these early reports on education was projected by the supervisors in their granting and withdrawing of teacher certification. They operated intuitively as to what they regarded as 'effective' teaching and sought to enforce their own standards and beliefs about teaching. Doyle (1978), for example, has argued that it was the rush by superintendents to gain autonomy for themselves, and hence control over schools, that led directly to the search for scientific justifications (and hence the quest for indicators of 'teacher effectiveness') to support the exercise of power and control. In schools the right to control teaching was, therefore, fought out at the supervisory level, where the rigour of science was seen as being preferable to the imposition of idiosyncratic views of what constituted improved teaching. But this brought with it its own mystification of teaching, and its unacknowledged political agenda.

Bagley (1907) was an early proponent of efficiency in US education. His argument was that teacher incompetence could be eliminated if teachers were actually prevented from establishing the ends towards which they worked (a view strongly endorsed by latter-day converts like Rosenshine, 1981). What was needed was 'unquestioned obedience' by teachers to the goals prescribed for them by wiser authorities than themselves outside classrooms (Bullough and Gitlin, 1984). Indeed, the need to tolerate any freedom *at all* for teachers was considered necessary only as long as it would solve the technical problem of fully prescribing what teachers should do. It was here that supervision came to the fore. There was a widespread belief that in science lay the legitimation that enabled superintendents to wrest control of teaching from local boards, and hence separate teaching from the influence of patronage. Cubberley (1922), for instance, saw in testing the opportunity for the supervisor to change 'school supervision from guesswork to scientific accuracy, and [to] . . . establish . . . standards of work by which he may defend what he is doing' (Buros, 1977, p. 10). The intent was to shift the status of supervisors from being at the whim of local political influence and personal favours, 'to a scientific service capable of self-defence in terms of acceptable standards and units of accomplishment' (Cubberley, cited in Jonich, 1968, p. 227). The evaluation of the work of teachers through the promulgation and enforcement of 'standards' in the name of value-free 'science' was to be the means for establishing an oligarchy over what was to count as knowledge about teaching. By seeking to legitimate teaching by removing it from the realm of the mystical, it was possible for those who laid claim to possess definitive pedagogical knowledge effectively to control and direct teaching. Through the use of indicators of efficiency and effectiveness the actions of supervisors could therefore:

> . . . be linked directly with outcomes of schooling. Effectiveness indicators would thus have substantial symbolic value in establishing the technical qualifications of administrators to manage the affairs of education. Of equal importance were the immediate practical consequences of control over entry into the classroom. Possession of a scientifically-derived set of teacher qualities related systematically to effectiveness would enable superintendents to decide on disinterested, rational grounds who would be appointed to teaching positions. In this manner, the profession would gain a powerful weapon in the fight against the political patronage system. Who could reasonably question a decision not to hire the ward boss' niece when she did not meet 'scientific' criteria of effectiveness? (Doyle, 1978, p. 145)

Preoccupation with order, control and social efficiency was deeply embedded in the notions of scientific management and contrary to what is often thought, schools were not so much victims of business influence and pressure as they were exponents of it (Karier, 1982, p. 8). It is worth reminding ourselves what it was that Frederick Taylor (1911), as the major spokesperson for scientific management, actually stood for. His words speak eloquently.

> One of the first requirements for a man who is fit to handle pig iron is that he shall be so stupid and so phlegmatic that he more nearly resembles the ox than any other type . . . [He] must consequently be trained by a man more intelligent than himself. (p. 59)

Despite the passage of more than a half-century, we still seem not to have been able to sever the connection between teacher evaluation and the industrial/managerial model with which it has been so closely affiliated. As one commentator put it:

> The terms have changed but the ethos is the same. The language has the appearance of being objective, rational, scientific and value-free. It is, of course, nothing of the kind. Each statement is intertwined with values related to efficiency, productivity and what some people regard as politically and administratively important. It is easy to forget that basically what we are talking about is one group of people which uses technology and knowledge to do things at, and to, another group of people in a systematic and manipulative way. (Baker, 1977)

Something of the UK Experience[1]

The English experience is informative as well. What is especially interesting about the beginnings of teacher evaluation in Britain in the nineteenth century was the social agenda behind what was being attempted: the evaluation of teachers was an instrument for limiting social class mobility. This situation may have existed in the USA and Australia too, but it has certainly been exposed to a greater extent by British writers.

In describing the nineteenth-century origins of teacher evaluation in Britain, Grace (1985) shows how British schooling had a longstanding concern about teacher quality and competence, especially insofar as teachers of urban working class pupils were concerned. He claims that the question of what constituted a 'trusty' teacher was inextricably bound-up with a particular view of the religious and moral character of the teacher ' . . . "goodness" was much to be preferred to "cleverness" for the teachers of the people' (Grace, 1985, p. 5). Just as important was the teacher's part in the transformation to an industrial society. Schools were seen as places in which to ' . . . raise a new race of working-class people—respectful, cheerful, hardworking, loyal, pacific and religious' (Johnson, 1970, p. 119). In this context, Grace (1985) claims that:

> ... the good teacher was pre-eminently at this time one whose character and general ideological stance was acceptable to the authorities and one who could be relied upon to act as an agent of social control and social cohesion ... (p. 6)

While careful screening of those about to enter teaching was one way of ensuring the achievement of these social objectives, ideological reliability was measured according to teachers' ability to exercise management, maintain discipline and achieve order in their classrooms. Grace (1985) claims that it was no coincidence that the needs of industry for docile subservient workers occurred at a time in which teacher competence was judged in terms of the ability of the teacher to dominate and subjugate pupils through obedience, hierarchy and the establishment of respect.

Given the tenor of the times, it seemed that the intent behind the forms of teacher evaluation that existed in Britain was dictated largely by the demands to impose an extensive network of controls over teachers. In describing what existed at the time, Johnson (1970) argues that educational historians have tended to miss the significance of the political sociology behind the measures in which ' ... control over the teaching profession was achieved by three phases of teacher-training and by extended financial support' (p. 117). He describes the intricate system of supervision that existed to induct teachers, and to ensure their continuing compliance.

The first phase was a system of apprenticeship in which the school itself was inspected and assessed as to its suitability in terms of its management, instruction, curriculum and finances. The intent was to ascertain the 'teacher's ability to act "as a guide and an example in the formation of the character of the apprentice" ' (Johnson, 1970, p. 118). Once satisfactory apprenticeship arrangements had been made and the necessary moral allegiances extracted from both student and 'teacher', the apprentice became 'a paid dependent of the Department' (p. 118). Annual inspections ensured that the necessary levels of diligence by teacher and trainee were observed. There was also the continual threat of withdrawal of financial aid to the teacher and the possible blacklisting of both school and teacher. In the second stage the trainee teacher was required to pass a competitive public examination, the outcome of which determined whether he/she was able to undertake a two year course at an 'inspected training college' (p. 118). The award of a Certificate of Merit at the conclusion was linked to starting salary, and future financial rewards conditional upon inspected performance. In the final stage, even retirement and the attainment of a pension were determined by inspection and conditional upon a teacher having 'taught at an inspected school for at least seven years' (p. 119), as well as being deemed to be a worthy character in an efficient school. The consequence, according to Johnson (1970), was that:

> Taken together, these regulations comprised . . . a system of control
> of great rigour . . . The intensity of control . . . was all the more
> striking, since it rested not on statutory sanction but on departmental
> discretions . . . The apparatus of teacher training, with its
> conditional offers of stipends, a degree of security, openings in the
> public service, a modest house and pension, amounted, in effect,
> to a system of guided, limited social mobility . . . [Teachers] were
> to form, in short, an army of highly-trained, highly-motivated
> mercenaries. (p. 119)

Grace (1985) makes this same point by arguing that British teachers deemed
to be 'good' at their job were *not only* engaged in a process of achieving
strict classroom order, but they were unwittingly caught up in a process
of wider structural significance. They were 'crucially engaged in the
production of the conditions for socio-political order' (p. 7) in which teacher
evaluation served *two* purposes. On the one hand, it ensured a form of
technical control consistent with a particular ordered view of teaching. At
the same time, teacher evaluation was also ensuring that the kind of students
emerging from schools would be 'acceptable' to the new emerging forms
of industrialization.

Teachers did not simply accept these purposes; they acted against them.
As Giddens (1979) notes, power relations are never one-way—there is always
another side to them:

> . . . all social actors, no matter how lowly, have some degree of
> penetration of the social forms that oppress them . . . (p. 72). Power
> relations . . . are always two-way, even if the power of one actor
> or party in a social relation is minimal compared to another. Power
> relations are relations of autonomy and dependence, but even the
> most autonomous agent is in some degree dependent, and the most
> dependent actor or party in a relationship retains some autonomy
> . . . (p. 93)

In the British scene, even in the most apparently oppressive of circumstances,
oppositional forces were at work. Grace (1985), for example, claims that
within the tight control exercised through the inspectorate, there was not
a total hegemony: 'There were spaces, there were contradictions and there
were resistances' (p. 7). The paradox was that, even with the screening
devices and the surveillance apparatus that existed, schooling in Britain had
somehow ' . . . developed its own dynamic which had resulted in forms
of curriculum development, forms of teacher initiative and forms of
cultivation of intelligence which had never been intended for working class
schooling' (p. 7). There were real and justified fears at the time that working
class schooling, ostensibly established to create factory labour, had begun
to get out of control. There was a concern that public schooling for the
masses might actually surpass the quality of that provided by middle class
private schools, and bring about an inversion of the social order. Grace

(1985) claims that it was teachers themselves who were largely responsible for this. Not only were they being provided with a college education, but they ' . . . had become interested in the novel and the unusual and were neglecting the basics of instruction' (p. 7).

British teachers at this time were struggling to be evaluated as 'professionals and not as pedagogic technicians' (Grace, 1985, p. 8). Teachers were beginning to claim the right to have their teaching evaluated on the basis of ' . . . intelligent and humane teaching as well as mechanical teaching' (p. 8). What is surprising, and somewhat paradoxical, is the acquiescence of the state in this new thrust by teachers for autonomy. It can only be explained, according to Grace (1985), by reference to complex political factors, at the core of which was the fear of socialism. It was deemed more prudent to allow teachers to pursue their notions of 'detached professionalism' than for them to continue to remain aggrieved and perhaps form dangerous political alliances. Implicit in this ploy was a carefully contrived agenda by the authorities:

> It was in these circumstances that the principle of school and teacher autonomy was effectively born. *The political produced the ideology of the non-political*—the non-political school, the non-political curriculum and the non-political teacher. (Grace, 1985, p. 11)

By legitimating the notion of teacher professionalism along non-political lines, what the authorities were doing was establishing a new form of leverage over teachers. What we see occurring here is an interesting paradox. On the one hand, schools had been created to produce a docile and subservient workforce, with teachers being evaluated according to their capacity to establish and maintain order and control in their classrooms. On the other hand, the struggles by teachers for autonomy and the threat that an otherwise docile workforce might form socialist alliances resulted in the state capitulating. In a quite unexpected way, teachers had their contradictory roles as workers and as professionals resolved. They had been bought off, but at the cost of being silenced by their own claims and aspirations for professional status. The tragedy is, as DeYoung (1986) argues, such claims to professionalism by teachers may have little substance to them:

> Describing classroom teachers . . . as professional educators may serve certain rhetorical interests but [it] has no conceptual validity. Teaching isn't a profession, never has been, and never will be . . . (p. 78)

Times have indeed changed; a decade or so ago schools were in a situation of healthy growth; now in the UK (as elsewhere), schools are in a situation of rapid decline. This reversal of the numbers game has had an especially dramatic effect on the rise of forms of managerialism in schools, exemplified by the situation in the UK. According to Walsh (1987), the view over the past few years that schools are failing society and the economy (at least in that part of the world) is 'based more in prejudice than in evidence' (p. 150). She cites the creation of the British Assessment of Performance Unit as evidence of the centralist thrust by conservative governments towards mechanisms that pursue the value-for-money philosophy related to schools. This is not the place to rehearse the complex political manoeuvring surrounding the teacher appraisal issue in the United Kingdom (see Walsh for a detailed account of that), however, it is clear that there has been a decided move away from the 1970s' notion of schools having a good deal of power over monitoring their own performance, to a situation in the 1980s in which the focus of responsibility has been squarely shifted onto individual teachers (Suffolk Education Department, 1985). The Education Act of 1980 made provision for the introduction of 'a national system of appraisal should the LEAs (local education authorities) fail to deliver satisfactory schemes' (Walsh, 1987, p. 147). To outsiders, the British system of teacher appraisal seems to be a complex mix of power in the hands of the central Department of Education and Science (and the government generally), LEAs and teachers, with neither side having total control: 'Employers have not simply been able to impose their preferred form of appraisal. But nor have teachers been able to fully assert professional independence and peer control' (Walsh, 1987, p. 149). In this controversy over teacher appraisal, Elliott (1987) claims that allowing the battle lines to be drawn exclusively between teachers and the government is to miss a more fundamental point. It is too simplistic to portray it as a naked grab for power by the government. As he says:

> Power strategies are constructed in complex social networks of organizational groups, which operate at a variety of levels and locations in the social order. Central government is perhaps best viewed as a facilitator of power strategies already operating within our society (p. 11)

Allowing the introduction of a national system of teacher appraisal to be used as a way by which teacher unions can brand the government 'the enemy', is to deny the ways in which 'the foundations of formal appraisal are being laid in the subtle transformations of power relations taking place day by day in their own classroom[s] and school[s]' (p. 11). At the same time, it is important to realize that the thinking that lies behind hierarchical forms of teacher appraisal is alive and thriving in the UK. This can be seen as recently as 1983 in the Secretary of State for Education Joseph's Report on *Teacher Quality*:

> The government welcome recent moves towards self-assessment by schools and teachers, and believe these should help to improve school standards and curricula. But employers can manage their teaching force effectively only if they have accurate knowledge of each teacher's performance. The government believe that for this

> purpose formal assessment of teacher performance is necessary and
> should be based on classroom visiting by the teacher's head or head
> of department . . . (cited in Elliott, 1987, p. 12)

Implicit in this, as Elliott (1987) argues, is a reputedly objectivist view that allows the work of teachers to be separated from the personal qualities and experiences each teacher brings to the task of teaching. The slippage occurs when 'competence' is construed in terms of 'observable performance', and the latter becomes the basis of claims to standardize what constitutes teaching. Even reports of a 'softening' of the rhetoric by the Secretary of State, in that 'a measure of peer review and reciprocity should be involved' (Elliott, 1987, p. 14) in classroom observation and that this might extend beyond the head to incorporate 'senior colleagues', should be taken with a grain of salt. While collegial and collaborative opportunities exist, hierarchical and oppressive forms of evaluation are gaining in popularity and importance.

Beginnings of Teacher Evaluation in Australia²

In Australia, the beginnings of teacher evaluation were inextricably associated with the struggle over who had the right to establish and maintain schools—Church or State? This battle was fought out in terms of the capacity of each to control and standardize the work of teachers, and hence remove it from those considered ill-suited to educate the young. As Smart (1977) has noted, early Australian teachers were ' . . . with very rare exceptions, vulgar, illiterate, sottish adventurers; the refuse and insolvent outcasts of some trade or mechanical occupation' (p. 7). While it was the Church and the clergy who established schools in Australia, close supervision and control were deemed necessary because teachers were ' . . . persons of the most worthless character who had formerly been convicts and who were notorious drunkards' (p. 7). The subsequent development of centralized government systems of education meant that there was a substitution of one form of control over teachers, by another (Smyth, 1984a, p. 428).

In the quest for efficiency, inspectors filled an important role as economic watch-dogs in nineteenth century Australian schooling. Teacher evaluation in Australia at that time is an example of scientific management and bureaucratic control at its autocratic best. The drive for efficiency was attributable, in part, to the attempt by the State to legitimate its right to be the 'proper' provider of education in the face of continuing hostility by the Church to maintain what it saw as its traditional prerogative.

William Wilkins, a key government educational figure in the nineteenth century, was instrumental in the attempt to standardize all teaching procedures. By laying down ' . . . methods of instruction, methods of inspection, classification of teachers, classification of pupils . . . with a single document (the Table of Minimum Attainments) he dispensed with the teacher's individual judgment' (Austin, 1965, p. 114). Tronc and Harris (1985) are convinced that the role of inspectors in the evaluation of teachers was indisputably that of judgment (and judgment of a particular kind):

> The quest for efficiency grew to dominate all other educational concerns. Inspectors of schools were set the task of testing school children's proficiency and recording the numbers of pupils who reached the standard laid down in the Table of Minimum Attainments. On this basis, the efficiency of teachers was then judged. (p. 45)

In the state of Victoria, the purpose of inspectors was even more clearly articulated: it was to regulate and police the system of 'payment by results'. In the form in which that system had been introduced from England into Victoria in the mid-nineteenth century (and later into South Australia and Western Australia), teachers were paid a basic salary plus additional emoluments for the performance of their students on standard examinations, on the regularity of school attendance (which was regarded as an index of effective teaching), and general teaching and administrative competence. As the parliamentary debates of 1867 indicate, teachers were paid an additional eight shillings for each child who passed the examination in basic literacy and numeracy and an extra four shillings for each who passed in grammar and geography (Dear, 1975, p. 89).

Even though inspectors were counselled to give the appearance of enlightenment and humanity, in practical terms it often proved impossible for them to veneer over the paternalistic and dominant social relationships that existed. The Board of Education's advice to inspectors in Victoria in the latter part of the nineteenth century was as follows:

> In your intercourse with teachers you are to treat them with the utmost kindness and respect, counselling them privately on whatever you may deem defective or faulty, but by no means addressing them authoratively or animadverting on their conduct in the hearing of pupils. To the pupils, also, you are to exhibit a considerate and affectionate manner, carefully guarding against peevishness, harshness or abruptness in your communications with them. (quoted in Dear, 1975, p. 81)

On other occasions, however, even these superficial pleasantries were discarded, and the power relationship could be seen in fairly blatant ways:

> He comes into a school without bidding the teacher good day or good morning and as for shaking hands, he would not defile his aristocratic paws by bringing them into contact with the digits of a school master. (Bland, 1975, 92)

The literature of the nineteenth century (and even later) indicates that it was difficult for many inspectors to avoid a ruthless, capricious and arbitrary performance of their duties. Their 'head hunter' image was widespread and acknowledged (Jones, 1973). According to Tronc and Harris (1985):

> . . . they were saddled with an image of fault-finding examiner, conservative keeper of standards and preserver of the status quo. For the early inspector, discipline and order were the supreme virtues. The inspection became an almost unbearable authoritarian inquisition, with teachers sacrificed on the altar of efficiency . . . In many ways, the school inspectors of the past earned much of the opprobrium which was heaped upon their name. (p. 45)

Yet there was more to teacher evaluation at this time than just the image of the inspector. What is disturbing in Tronic and Harris' (1985) portrayal of Australian school inspectors as the victims of history is the impression given that methods of teacher evaluation by inspectors can be simply written-off as the result of the personalities and attitudes of individuals taking advantage of an authoritarian system. Missing from this view is the understanding that authoritarianism of this kind was socially and structurally created. It was not a disembodied accident that can be separated (Paton, 1973, p. 19) from what was seen to be the 'proper' role of teachers, namely, enforcing social control over students. As Grace (1978) argues, the problem of authoritarianism is one of '. . . role and structure not "personality" and "attitudes" . . .'(p. 90). Under the guise of economic efficiency, the state established and maintained the right to determine and control the nature and content of schooling bureaucratically. This meant that the 'ends' of schooling were regarded as impersonal, indisputable and unproblematic. All that needed to be done was to find more efficient technical ways of ensuring that the work of teachers measured-up to pre-determined goals. But schooling was not, and is not, like this!

   An unfortunate aspect of those Australian discussions of the early history of teacher evaluation (Jones, 1973; Moore and Neal, 1969; Thomas, 1972) is that they have tended to focus only on the person of the inspector and the 'ogre-like' or the 'messiah-like' personal qualities of the individuals. Such discussions end up mythologizing the act of teacher evaluation and, in so doing, obscure the exploitative and dehumanizing set of bureaucratic relationships that adhere to the system of inspection. Trivializing the work of inspectors in terms of 'humourless endeavours and hilarious consequences', as Tronc (1987) does, is to turn attention away from serious enquiry into the macabre social circumstances that led to the creation of such processes in the first place. The more interesting issue lies in the social forces that enabled inspectors to become the unquestioned definers and arbiters of 'pedagogic excellence', and how these were resisted. As with any imposed 'system' there were cracks and crevices to be exploited through forms of resistance. While it was true that inspectors found it difficult to escape their fault-finding role, teachers had ways of subverting these forms of domination, as Austin (1961) has noted with regard to the payment-by-results scheme:

> Attendance rolls could be falsified, children's ages misreported, talented pupils with infectious diseases kept at school, backward children discouraged from attending and copies of inspector's questions passed quickly ahead from school to school. The teacher was fighting for his livelihood, and could only hate the man who had the power, on a brief annual visit, to take part of it from him.
> (p. 251)

More recently, moves by the government of New South Wales to re-arm the inspectorate (Nay, 1985), as part of a push for 'teacher efficiency' in 1985, were met by such vigorous resistance from the teacher unions that eventually the government had to admit its misreading of the situation and withdraw the proposals. The punitive measures designed to eliminate 'inefficient teachers' were widely acknowledged to be educationally unsound in that they sought to destroy good existing relationships at the school level; were seen as nothing more than a cynical attempt to reconstruct hierarchies; were viewed as trying to shift onto individuals responsibility for problems that were those of the education system; and were regarded as being destined seriously to undermine the credibility and status of teachers. The alternative, some kind of in-service programme, seems not to have gone ahead because of a lack of funds (Preston, 1987).

For the moment, the role of the inspector in teacher evaluation has diminished (but not disappeared) in Australia. There is still a limited role for promotional purposes, and the prospect always exists for the revival of their economic watchdog function. New South Wales, for example, has procedures to determine annually the 'fitness' of teachers to teach; probationary teachers are assessed by the principal, teachers who are candidates for promotion are reported upon by inspectors, with all other teachers being ranked by the principals as 'efficient' (on a Teacher Assessment Review Schedule) or 'unsatisfactory' (in which case a further assessment is made by an inspector). There have been no 'inspections' in Victorian secondary schools since 1970, largely because of a dismantling of that system by an extensive programme of militant action by teachers in the late 1960s. Reviews on a cyclical basis are conducted in primary schools, with assessment for permanency (usually at the end of the first year of teaching) being made by the principal. Evaluation for promotional purposes takes the form in Victoria of teachers presenting a case (through interview and based on the presentation of documentary evidence) to locally constituted panels comprising teachers, parents, teacher unionists, principals and representatives of the Education Department. Separate procedures exist for principals to use in cases of incompetence or improper conduct. The external inspectorial role has also disappeared from South Australia, with evaluation procedures remaining the responsibility of the principal, and with the Director General of Education having the power to order an evaluation of an entire school if necessary. Recent moves in that state are, however, in the direction of re-arming superintendents as 'quality controllers' to conduct 'educational audits' and establish 'quality assurance schemes' based upon individually developed 'school achievement plans' (Cox, 1987).

By way of summarizing the contemporary scene in Australia, the fashionable rhetoric being used as a smokescreen for the extensive reintroduction of hierarchical forms of teacher evaluation goes under the rubric of 'monitoring school performance' (State Board of Education, 1987). In the guise of a benign form of managerialism aimed at serving the corporate interests of the educational bureaucracy, schools and the community are being sold the idea that 'comprehensive performance indicator frameworks' (p. 18), against which there can be a 'close tracking of costs, and the routine association of data on inputs, processes and outputs' (p. 18), is the way to ensure efficiency and effectiveness in schools. Authorities in Victoria and other states favour a naive process of re-arming an allegedly apolitical inspectorate (in what is a highly charged political environment) in a move that is supposedly designed to 'inspire public confidence' in schools (State Board of Education, 1987, p 19), while winning over teachers because it will be 'close to practice' (p. 19). Behind all of this is a not so subtle corporate budgetting process, borrowed directly from industry and used unashamedly as a way of checking-up on the efficiency and effectiveness of schools and teachers. To believe that it is possible through this means simultaneously to disseminate 'good [educational] practices' (Ashenden, 1987, p. 7) reflects the level of unreality that has begun to permeate official educational thinking in at least some quarters in Australia. It amounts to a poorly disguised attempt to reintroduce via back-door means (after a decade of more enlightened alternatives—see Deakin University, 1982; Boomer, 1982; Smyth, 1984b) dominant forms of teacher evaluation that have patently failed to produce anything meaningful in the past.

Shaping the Dominant Form

It is clear that within and across each of these brief historical portrayals are some interesting parallels or themes. Present in all three settings, for example, is the notion that teacher evaluation can be used as a potent instrument for shaping and achieving wider social agendas. The social agenda is not an educative one that has to do with the development of informed or liberating pedagogy, so much as it has to do with ways of controlling teachers and through them the socialization and learning of students. A second theme running through the historical material is the epistemological assumption that we know and acquire knowledge about teaching through technocratic rationality. Within this framework questions about the rightness of particular goals are obscured, allowing an exclusive focus on teacher behaviour and practice. Alternative epistemologies such as 'reflection-in-action' which link theory and practice so that actors can remake and if necessary reorder the world in which they live (Schön, 1984, p. 42) are ignored. Finally, these historical overviews suggest that dominant forms of evaluation both reflect and reinforce constrained notions of pedagogy. Specifically, teaching is understood to be a kind of commodity made up of a number of technical behaviours which supposedly allow teachers to fill the 'empty' heads of students with appropriate knowledge. Authoritarian and technical aspects are strengthened, while a more relational view that sees teachers and students working together to understand and debate moral, political and ethical issues is denied. Authoritarian relationships are, therefore, totally dependent on systems of surveillance to control behaviour, for it is only by devising techniques for observing that behaviour and reporting upon it that 'remedial' action can be decided upon (Elliott, 1987). In the section that follows we discuss these themes in more detail so as to understand how and why dominant forms of teacher evaluation are defined in particular ways.

Social Control

The dominant form of teacher evaluation did not come about by historical accident—it was deliberately constructed to shape schools, teachers and teaching in ways which reflected 'national interest'. In the US, for example, the launching of Sputnik in 1957 marked something of a watershed as endeavours were systematically mounted to harness schools to the national interest which was seen to lie in the restoration of military supremacy. The catchcry was for 'rigorous' and 'systematic' evaluation methodologies aimed at restoring the US to its rightful place in the arms race. As commentators of the times indicated (Worthen and Sanders, 1973; Guba and Lincoln, 1982), there was a virtual flurry of papers that rehearsed what was lacking (and leaking) in current evaluation strategies. The 'problem' with evaluation at this time and the impetus for reform was that current forms did not do enough to shape schools in the national interest. By framing the problem in this way, the appropriateness of the supposed national goals or the interests served were never debated. Instead, there was the misguided belief that it was actually possible to separate 'goals' from 'practice', so that evaluation became nothing more than a technical process. Teachers, however, do not lead their institutional lives in such neatly ordered and detached ways; they have their own goals which may be grossly at variance with those officially prescribed. As Popkewitz (1984) says:

> Ideally, practice emerges from the interrelation of purpose with situated actions. To separate the two is to deny that interrelationship and the interplay of thought and action. (p. 167)

Evaluation reform actually prevented teachers and students from engaging in judgments about the relationship between goals and practices. The consequence is 'fake' reforms that smother critical thinking and produce docility. It seems that the plethora of supposed reforms that has been visited upon schools is not about creating participatory institutions, characterized by an informed and active citizenry, so much as being about a 'hidden curriculum of passivity' (Boyer-Carnegie, 1983).

It is important to note, however, that teachers and students did not collapse under the strain of these reforms: rather, they resisted, often in small ways, the political interests embedded in these reforms. Besides the types of teacher resistance alluded to in the historical sketches, students also resist oppressive aspects of schooling. As Apple and Beyer (1983) note, not only do certain categories of students actively reject the school's covert curriculum of '. . . punctuality, individual achievement, and authority relations', but in a more positive fashion such students work at beating the system by refusing to do school work and thus legitimating their own rights to '. . . control their own space and time. . . [and thus] learning skills that will give them informal control at their workplaces later' (p. 433).

While control is never complete, dominant forms of teacher evaluation become associated with, and continue to be limited to, the identification of technical aspects of teaching. Again and again this limited form is justified on the grounds that teachers should facilitate identified goals, not debate them. The assumption that evaluation should be tied to issues of social control defines in no small way the limited nature of the dominant approaches.

Technocratic Rationality

There is more at stake, however, than one group (supervisors) having and exercising authority over another (teachers)—the problem lies in the notion of 'technocratic rationality' (Schön, 1983). Emerging as it does from the historical process of bringing narrow views of science and technology to bear in purging thought and action from the grip of mysticism, superstition and meta-physics in the physical world, technocratic rationality has come to be applied to social, moral and political issues as well. When applied in this way, the determination of 'value' becomes decidedly utilitarian, requiring only the assessment of the extent to which programmes and practices actually meet pre-established goals. In other words, the technocratic approach can only be maintained within a social setting if it is assumed that goals are agreed upon. Furthermore, this epistemology is based on a narrow view of science, what Harris (1979) refers to as 'scientism', which results in a 'structured misrepresentation of reality'. The distortion that occurs can be clearly seen in the form that teacher evaluation tends to take in schools. There is an unstated but deeply felt presumption, for example, that there are 'experts' in teaching (administrators, supervisors and researchers), and also the 'inexperts' (teachers and students). But these categorical distinctions have no rational basis. Teachers as a group are no less nor more 'expert' than administrators; rather, it depends on the individual case. In this way, hierarchical arrangements actually misrepresent reality and become the linchpin for narrow views of teacher evaluation which diagnose and portray the deficiencies of teachers according to some arbitrarily determined standards of what constitutes 'effective' teaching (Bridges, 1986). Unfortunately, much of the debate and discussion about teacher evaluation in the educational literature (Darling-Hammond *et al.,* 1983) has been concerned with refining, elaborating upon and perpetuating more effective means for directing and controlling the work of teachers (Millman, 1981; Borich, 1977). What is problematic about subjecting the work of teachers to such allegedly rational forms of bureaucratic scrutiny is that the evaluative practices themselves leave unexamined the highly contestable purposes to which teaching and schooling are directed.

The inability of technocratic rationality successfully to resolve entrenched social issues has resulted in what Habermas refers to as a 'legitimation crisis' (Habermas, 1976a). By way of illustrating what Habermas (1976a) meant more generally, Pateman (1981) put it thus: 'Not only have grandiose National plans had to be abandoned, but even more limited, expert formulated wage and price policies have been ditched in favour of ad hoc coercion, political bargains, compromises and understandings' (pp. 386–7). And even if these plans could be picked up off the cutting room floor, their implementation would create another set of problems. As Pateman (1981) notes in commenting on British attempts to implement accountability measures in schools, 'the effect of the political and administrative measures being proposed may only be to increase conflict at the classroom chalkface; and to deepen the antagonism between teachers, government and parents and within the teaching profession itself' (p. 387).

What has been lost in this total reliance on technocratic rationality is consideration of alternative notions of school change. Where technocratic rationality strengthens the view that change occurs by controlling what teachers do, emerging paradigms, such as reflection-in-action, emphasize forms of knowing that empower actors to remake and reorder their world. As Schön (1984) notes, reflection-in-action takes the form of 'on-the-spot surfacing, criticizing, restructuring, and testing of intuitive understandings of experienced phenomena . . . to empower us to remake, and if necessary reorder, the world in which we live' (p. 42). Although this emergent form of rationality is not without problems, the form that teacher evaluation takes should at least consider its potential to address social issues in a less utilitarian way.

Authoritarian Notions of Pedagogy

Notions of evaluation are shaped by and reflect views of teaching and pedagogy. Embedded within the dominant form of teacher evaluation is the assumption that teaching is a commodified product in which expert teachers deposit the 'right' information into the heads of students. From this authoritarian, 'banking' notion it follows that school 'problems' can be corrected by changing what teachers do. However, unlike other forms of work, teaching is not an individual act—it is a social, relational and an interactive process that depends for its success on notions of sharing and community. The denial of this relational view of teaching, and the continued reliance on an authoritarian conception of pedagogy, is no historical coincidence. As Broadfoot (1981) notes, the shift from a collective and communal notion of social responsibility within traditional society, to one of individual interdependence in modern societies, occurred at a time when the capitalist system was demanding that the 'individual—not the family or community...take the responsibility for a particular unit of production...'(p. 203). In education, this individualistic rationality took expression in the form of an emphasis on '...personal needs, personal responsibility and personal rewards' (p. 104). Within this framework educational discussions invariably degenerate into a 'blaming the victim' rhetoric in which teachers are portrayed as being derelict because they have disciplinary problems in class, because they have imperfect mastery of subject matter, or because they are incapable of imparting all the content from a certain subject area to students (Bridges, 1986, p. 5). The solution, so the argument goes, is to have better systems of monitoring, detecting and evaluating what it is that teachers do so as to remove the offensive behaviour from the classroom. Evaluative solutions of this sort however amount to a further entrenchment of an 'authoritarian pedagogy' (Beyer, 1985) through a general tightening-up of discipline in schools, calls for enhanced academic standards, and even more measurement-oriented outcomes geared to forms of teaching and learning.

By linking evaluation with this authoritarian, commodified view of teaching there is a 'wrenching apart of the co-operative project' (Hextall and Sarup, 1977, p. 157) as the social act of teaching is progressively dismembered so that value can be placed on artificially created teacher behaviours. Unless forms of teacher evaluation explicitly challenge this notion of pedagogy, then teachers will continue to be blamed for problems that more accurately reflect the priorities and failings of our economic system. In addition, the continuation of current dominant teacher evaluation practices will help to sustain hierarchical, authoritarian arrangements within schools which silence students.

In sum, the most common forms of teacher evaluation have been shaped by assumptions about purpose—the need for social control, the reliance on technocratic rationality, and restricted notions of teaching—all of which depend upon narrow, authoritarian views. These assumptions both reflect and serve conservative interests by allowing questions about the rightness of educational aims to be obscured, while giving legitimacy to the forms themselves by relying on the often unquestioned faith in science, narrowly understood. Teachers are not only silenced in this quest to have schools correct problems, which often reflect economic failings, but are also blamed for these problems in the process. Authoritarian views of teaching attempt to silence students in much the same way that the evaluation approaches try to silence teachers. Rethinking teacher evaluation, therefore, to a large degree means challenging current taken-for-granted views about the conservative relation between schools and their cultural economic context.

Notes

1 and 2 Portions of these sections are reproduced with permission of Deakin University Press from Smyth, J., *A 'Critical' Pedagogy of Teacher Evaluation,* Geelong, Australia: Deakin University Press, 1988, pp. 9–16.

Chapter 2

Towards Educative Forms of Teacher Evaluation

With the plethora of recent reports aimed at reforming schools in the USA, Australia and England it is not surprising that issues of teacher evaluation have come to the fore and are being hotly contested. What is unfortunate, however, is that so much of this recent work on teacher evaluation rests upon unquestioned assumptions that derive from the dominant tradition: that school change is fostered by attempting to control what teachers do; that educational goals are not part of the evaluative process; and that pedagogy is narrowly understood as a one-way process of depositing fragments of knowledge into the heads of students. To understand the interests served by this traditon it is necessary to look at the assumptions that have come to inform those practices, namely, the way teacher evaluation separates knowing from doing within teaching; the supposed neutrality of the process of teacher evaluation; the one-way or monological communication between evaluator and teacher; and the entrenched notion of individualism that lies behind this view of evaluation. Once we can see more clearly the guiding assumptions that frame the dominant tradition of evaluation we will be better positioned to outline and argue for alternative practices that serve more educative interests.

The Separation of Knowing from Doing

In the most fundamental sense, the dominant paradigm of teacher evaluation is one that is predicated on an indefensible dichotomy. There are a number of different ways of expressing this separation. Lundgren (1983), for example, speaks of a distinction between two educational contexts—the contexts of 'formulation' and 'realisation'. In less elegant terms this means a distinction between 'knowing what' and 'knowing how', or a separation between theory and practice. In Braverman's (1975) language, this amounts to a separation of 'conception' from 'execution'; that is to say, a situation in which there is a temporal separation between those who actually do the work of teaching, as distinct from those who lay claim to planning and designing teaching. Whichever way we choose to describe it, what is at issue is a distinction which has its origins in power relationships that are legitimated on the grounds of a technologization of reason (Kemmis, 1984). In this scheme, the distribution of educational tasks is based solely on the sequencing of functions along bureaucratic or superordinate lines, which are 'scientifically' determined, and which are allegedly based on information and techniques that are 'objectively' verifiable and quantitatively validated.

Squeezed out of this objectified and stratified scheme of things is the notion that teachers could possibly have anything significant or worthwhile to say about teaching; their knowledge is treated as being incidental and is largely relegated to the realm of folklore, which is not altogether surprising given what we know about the gendered nature of the teaching force. What we are talking about, then, is a struggle that has to do with an enforced division of labour between those outside the classrooms who lay claim to know good teaching on the basis of 'scientific research', and those inside classrooms who lay claim to know what constitutes teaching by virtue of their doing the teaching. In many ways, these two exist in the tense atmosphere of a private cold war (Blumberg, 1980).

It is not surprising in this context that teachers have no say in determining the categories within which evaluation might occur, nor that they are not consulted for their understandings of what observed classroom events might signify; instead, the emphasis is upon measuring for the existence of a number of pre-determined behaviours. This limited involvement of teachers is justified on the grounds of a functional specialization of labour whose origins lie in the scientific management movement of the early 1900s. Even though the specialization inherent in this kind of division of labour may appear to have an innocent and plausible ring to it, as Kliebard (1975) has noted, it also has a darker side to it when we consider the social function of keeping teachers in their ascribed places. We would do well to remember the legacy of such a division of labour. As Frederick Taylor (1911) put it:

> One of the first requirements for a man who is fit to handle pig iron . . . is that he shall be so stupid and phlegmatic that he more nearly resembles an ox than any other type . . . He must consequently be trained by a man more intelligent than himself. (p. 59)

We need, therefore, to understand the nature of the interests embedded in the division of labour between teachers and evaluators. It is a separation that reinforces and maintains a constrained view of the teacher's role, in which teachers generally are prevented from developing their 'knowing' and are denied the opportunity of critically assessing the forms of teaching imposed upon them by others. While this separation can never be complete, and teachers always retain some control over the conceptualization of their work, it nevertheless reinforces an anti-educational approach to teaching that promotes a self-fulfilling prophecy in which teachers are denied opportunities to assess critically the ends towards which they work. This role further limits teachers' abilities to mediate and contest the hierarchical interests embedded in dominant approaches to the evaluation of teaching, and deflects them from uncovering the contradictions and unwarranted effects these structures can have in their teaching. In this way, the division of labour between teachers and evaluators contributes to an alienating situation where teachers have less and less control over their work, while at the same time being required to accept and shoulder more of the blame for the economic and social failure.

Not only is there a kind of intellectual imperialism inherent in the view that there are some groups who are equipped through intelligence and training to articulate what another group should do and think, but teachers are denied an opportunity to look closely and critically at the relation between educational conceptualizations and their effects upon the learning of students. While teachers are criticized for being mindless (Silberman, 1970), dominant approaches to the evaluation of teaching paralyze them in terms of entering into the type of educational relationships where reason and argument inform their practice. Without reason, practice is likely to fall prey to the dictates of habit or acquiescence to authoritarian procedures. In either case, the interests served are conservative and maintain the status quo.

Part of the problem here is that dominant forms of teacher evaluation rely heavily on the assumption that 'science' can be harnessed to produce objective accounts of good teaching, which dispense with the necessity to dialogue with teachers about what they know and understand of classroom life. Because these scientific generalizations are supposedly context free, they ignore historical factors about the way teachers, schools and the practices of the teaching profession have been shaped and continue to be influenced. We need, therefore, to question the assumption that science can produce objective accounts of good teaching, as well as how this assumption encourages evaluative approaches that take an ahistorical view of teaching— focusing only on teacher behaviour and ignoring the social, cultural and political conditions that surround it.

Using 'Science' in Support of Evaluation

Those who endorse the dominant tradition of teacher evaluation assume that procedures originating in the physical sciences can be easily exported and applied to social contexts like teaching. Applying to social settings procedures that have their origins in the study of inert substances is to regard such a translation as unproblematic. But what this narrow view of science as applied to the evaluation of teaching does, is hide the political interests that are served by portraying teaching in particular ways.

Knowledge acquired by using the methods of the physical sciences presupposes several things. Firstly, there is the presumption that the enquirer can and does take a disinterested view of the proceedings so as to produce findings that are unbiased. Such an observer, so the claim goes, is able to remain uninvolved and thus is able to measure the effects of different 'treatments' on groups and individuals, in much the same way as the effect of fertilizers can be measured on crop yields. We would want to question both the desirability and the efficacy of this in classroom situations. Secondly, such procedures are claimed consistently to predict a particular outcome, and it is via this means that theories come to have the power of predictive generalization. For example, the fact that water always freezes at 0 degrees centigrade and boils at 100 degrees centigrade is part of a general theory which explains the relationship of gases, liquids and solids. Principles with such constancy and predictive validity become difficult to acquire, and almost impossible to employ in social situations like those applying in classrooms.

Overlooked in this attempt to find scientific generalizations is that in the analysis of a relational process like teaching, unless there is an exchange and a mutuality of intent about what is occurring, there are real risks that an incorrect agenda may be imputed or imposed. As Habermas (Bernstein, 1983) put it:

> It is an illusion to think that we can assume the position of disinterested observers by bracketing all our understandings when it comes to studying other forms of life ... [We] can only ... [understand other forms of life] by adopting the performative attitude of one who participates in a process of *mutual understanding*. [our emphasis] (p. 182)

The practical consequences of not participating in a process of mutual understanding can be seen in the following scenario. If a teacher begins a lesson without giving clear directions to the students as to what they are expected to be doing, then an evaluator watching might respond by pointing out that 'scientific' research suggests that if students stay on-task and, if the teacher starts the lesson with clear and unambiguous instructions, the students will achieve better test results. What is missing in this example is any kind of consensus about what teacher and evaluator respectively see as being important about teaching. We can impute that the evaluator holds high regard for test results, but without any dialogue between the teacher and evaluator it is impossible to determine what the teacher holds to be important. Rather than being negligent, it is possible that the teacher may have been trying to make students more self-reliant by leaving them to their own devices.

Where the teacher's intentions are not able to be considered and given an equal chance of legitimacy alongside those of the outsider, evaluation practices effectively silence the teacher. The use of narrow forms of science to bolster and legitimate particular views of what constitutes 'good' teaching reinforces oppressive hierarchies which prevent discussion of moral questions about what should be the aims of schooling. When this occurs, dominant forms of evaluation preserve the status quo by strengthening those school relations which structure classroom practices. Ironically, the quest for 'objective' knowledge about teaching which ignores context, and which purports instead to produce universals of some sort, ends up supporting the existing state of affairs by denying teachers an opportunity critically to construct accounts of their own practice.

Evaluation as Technique

As we have suggested above, where the primary concern in teacher evaluation is allowed to remain at the level of a pre-occupation with better ways of refining and perfecting the techniques of teaching, then broader questions to do with the moral and educational worth of teaching go unasked. Those who support the dominant paradigm in teacher evaluation are thus able to claim that the techniques they use, such as rating scales and observational instruments, do not serve any particular interests; they simply produce raw data. Harris (1985) is one such person who regards rating schedules in the hands of evaluators as a way of gaining 'analytical procedures that reduce and simplify raw data for interpretation' (p. 177). Harris holds to the misguided view that because a rating schedule is reputed to have been devised on the basis of scientific research it is inviolable, neutral and value-free. Such schedules are, of course, nothing of the kind! Trying to make them more inclusive, like the Florida Performance Management System (1985) with its 121 separate teacher behaviours that an evaluator has to search for the presence or absence of, is equally fanciful. Missing from the fragmented accounts of teaching constructed in this technicist way is the most important ingredient of all—whether such stories about schooling are in the final analysis credible and believable by those whose lives they purport to portray, namely, teachers and students. Almost without exception, such technicist approaches to teacher evaluation fail this ultimate test because teachers and students do not live their lives in the fragmented and dislocated ways suggested in the observation schedules. In the USA this enchantment with technique (based on the view that 'research says . . .') has been carried to the extreme whereby the courts have legislatively mandated the Florida Performance Management System (FPMS) as a valid and reliable method of teacher evaluation. In practical terms, as the recent case of *Sweeney v Turlington* demonstrates (Hazi and Garman, 1988), observers involved in implementing this system have been:

... disenfranchised from judging the teaching act ... Observers
turn their coded FPMS forms over to a machine that calculates the
teacher's score. Thus, a computer—not the observer—
mathematically renders judgment about the teacher's lesson and
identifies who is a superior teacher. (p. 7)

Ignored in focusing exclusively on the technical aspect of teacher evaluation
is the set of social relations embodied in the process itself. By this we mean
that when teachers are subjected to traditional processes of evaluation, there
is an inescapable set of relationships put in place. As Apple (1986) points
out, going into a room and turning the light on not only amounts to using
an object, it also involves 'an anonymous social relationship with a miner
who worked to dig the coal burned to produce the electricity' (pp. 82–3).
In the same way that lightbulbs reflect a relationship between miners and
management, processes of evaluation embody cultural commodities that
reflect the social relations of those who partake in the evaluation process.
Specifically, embedded in most evaluation methods is a hierarchical relation
in which the expert, or evaluator, sets the agenda and determines what is
meant by successful teaching. The practitioner, on the other hand, is
excluded from discussions about goals, what is an educational 'problem',
or how the evaluation is to proceed. In much the same way, students' points
of view, interests or intentions are not considered. On the basis of this we
would claim that far from being value-free, traditional notions of teacher
evaluation serve conservative interests by reinforcing school relations which
are not only hierarchical and authoritarian, but ultimately run counter to
the idea of an active, informed citizenry.

The claim that evaluation methods are neutral and do not reflect political
interests is problematic in several ways. While particular forms of science
may be appropriate for controlling the physical world, they have severe
limitations when it comes to the social world of teaching. Buchmann (1984)
summed it up nicely when she said:

... the public accepts scientific findings not because it shares the
scientific conception of reality but because of the social authority
of science. Scientific knowledge and judgment are opaque and
indisputable for most people. (p. 431)

What occurs is an attempt to portray teacher evaluation as a neutral process
of ascertaining the extent to which teachers 'measure-up' to common-sense
standards. Broadfoot (1981) claims that this permits apparently objectivist
notions of science to masquerade within a bureaucratic style of
administration that twists and distorts the intent:

In practice, this means that issues which are, in reality, questions
of alternative values are perceived as technical problems to which

a 'right answer—an 'optimum solution' exists, waiting only to be discovered. (p. 206)

Arguments about competing and contending values within teaching thus become hidden behind reputedly neutral technologies that claim to be measuring value-free aspects of teaching and learning according to behavioural norms. As the examples above indicate, there is an undisclosed assumption that consensus exists on what teaching goals are desirable. What is not addressed in all of this is the 'conflict and political debate important to goal setting' (Popkewitz, 1984, p. 167). Regarding evaluation as a political process that serves a set of interests, as opposed to a neutral technique, has significant consequences for the nature of evaluation. An evaluator can no longer rely on the 'authority' of science to determine what a teacher should and should not be doing. Teachers must be given the opportunity to take an active role in uncovering hidden interests, thereby replacing hierarchical and authoritarian relations with more dialogical and democratic ones.

The Ahistorical Nature of Knowing

In its conventional form, teacher evaluation attempts to dissociate teaching from the various aspects of its context. As long as teachers are prevented from seeing clearly where educational ideas come from, then they are cut off from the philosophy implicit in those ideas. Practices can thus be disguised in all sorts of ways, to appear to be other than what they really are. In broad terms, it is possible to construe teaching as a series of non-problematic and mechanical actions to be implemented in a designated way, or it can be regarded as a form of cultural politics (Simon, 1988) in which the give and take of ideas and the way they are negotiated continually shape and re-define what is meant by teaching. Schön (1987) captured this paradox nicely when he said:

> In the varied topography of professional practice, there is a high hard ground overlooking a swamp. On the high ground, manageable problems lend themselves to solution through the application of research-based theory and technique. In the swampy lowland, messy, confusing problems defy technical solution. The irony of this situation is that the problems of the high ground tend to be relatively unimportant to individuals or society at large, however great their technical interest may be, while in the swamp lie the problems of greatest human concern. (p. 3)

This is a very apt description of teaching, and it holds important implications for the way we proceed with teacher evaluation. If we hold to the former view of teaching, then debates about what constitutes 'good' teaching become unnecessary and reforms are imposed and enforced through technical approaches to teacher evaluation. Contexts of teaching, whether they be physical, social or historical, are considered irrelevant in this scheme. If on the other hand, we are inclined to the latter view of teaching as described by Schön (1987), then discovering why individuals act in particular ways requires an analysis that 'reveals the historical and social causes of actions' (Carr and Kemmis, 1986, p. 95).

A good example of this can be seen in the collaborative enquiry in Australia by Boomer (1984) in which he found that because teachers are unaccustomed to being exposed to the theory behind their practices, they tend to 'remain spellbound by habit'. His claim is that having developed the habit of not looking closely at what they do (which is no indictment of them personally), teachers are inclined unwittingly to act in contradictory ways. As Boomer (1984) found in his study of one teacher:

> ... she negotiates tasks with students, hands over planning responsibilities, employs group work, uses oral productions as an alternative basis of assessment, and permits movement within established rules ... Alert as this teacher is, and articulate in her personal counter-theories of education, she is likely from moment to moment to drop into practices which belong to the set of educational constructs that she is trying to overthrow.

What this signifies is that teachers are trapped to varying degrees within their personal as well as their professional histories and that dominant practices of evaluation do not require them to question these pedagogical assumptions—indeed, they reinforce them.

'Individually prescribed instruction' provides another example. Most teachers would be shocked to learn that it had its origins in attempts within industry in the early 1900s to standardize industrial production. The intent was to ensure a predictable output in which the 'worker's movements are made so elementary and routine that the product inevitably emerges independent of will or conscious desire of the worker' (Kliebard, 1975, p. 65). What might appear on the surface to be a humanistic process of catering for the individual needs of students is really a process that was designed to subjugate workers into submissiveness by removing any discretionary control they might have had over the work process. As Kliebard (1975) has shown, the US railroad industry was at the forefront of this process of standardization, using ideas that came originally from the military.

The point being made here is that when teachers are cut off, deliberately or otherwise, from the history of the ideas that infiltrate schools, then by adopting particular pedagogical practices they can unwittingly be supporting a philosophy that is quite opposed to their intentions. The way in which dominant forms of teacher evaluation regard knowing in ahistorical terms minimizes the opportunity teachers have for questioning educational views, and their origins. Treating teachers as objects not as subjects means that teachers' consciousness or 'range of vision' about what they do in classrooms is severely limited. The effect is to limit further the understanding of what teachers consider worthy of investigation and how they go about investigating it. As Gadamer (1975) notes, historical consciousness is 'already operative in the choice of the right question to ask' (Bernstein, 1983, p. 142). The vision which teachers have of classroom practices can only be fully understood and critically confronted if the tradition to which the teaching belongs itself becomes part of the evaluative process.

What remains undisclosed in conservative teacher evaluation proposal, is that the measures themselves serve to ' . . . increase the dependence on authority, social apathy, [and] passive involvement . . .' (Beyer, 1985, p. 51) and fail to open-up for consideration the alternative sources of these problems which lie in the dominant value system of the wider social order. They rehearse an 'encapsulated' (Sarason, 1982) view of schools as institutions in which schools and teachers are somehow seen as 'causing social problems but not mirroring them' (Beyer, 1985, p. 47). Hence, the comforting but unrealistic calls for simple solutions to the economic and social ills of western democracies, that emphasize a return to standards, efficiency, accountability and productivity. What this emphasis fails to unmask is that prescribing more rigorous forms of authoritarianism, and strengthening hierarchical relations between evaluators and teachers, will not make in-roads into the ' . . . subtle ways in which inequality, oppression and domination infiltrate our commonsense practices and meanings' (Beyer, 1985, p. 51). If anything, such endeavours will serve only to cloud the real issues which have to do with creating the self-reflexive conditions in schools that can lead to the struggle for more just, liberating and humane forms of teaching and learning.

Searching out the historical roots of teaching practices is one way of beginning to counter these debilitating tendencies.

Evaluation as Monologue

For teachers who have been the subject of dominant forms of evaluation, there can be little doubt that the process involves a one-way communication from the evaluator to the teacher. While on some occasions teachers can comment on what the evaluator has to say, they can neither determine the categories by which they are judged, nor set the agenda for any evaluative conference that might occur. What happens in teacher evaluation encounters is that the teacher is 'informed' after the event of the outcome. This one-way, or monological, process is justified on the grounds that the purpose of teacher evaluation is that of correcting and controlling teacher behaviour in specified ways. To involve teachers by giving them a say in determining the focus of the evaluation, or allowing them to help with the interpretation would be to undermine the very basis of evaluation. Part of the intent is to portray the teacher as being in need, and the expert as identifying the problems and tendering solutions. As well as running counter to democratic and egalitarian ideals, such a monologue entrenches the expert-inexpert distinction and endorses forms of knowledge about teaching that are unrelated to the teacher's world. While teachers may be able to repeat desired behaviours for the benefit of outside evaluators, they may neither understand nor agree with the recommendations. This lack of understanding and agreement encourages teachers to accept the advice of experts by becoming docile. Equally, they may become totally pre-occupied with finding ways of getting around the recommendations, losing altogether the opportunity to gain a greater understanding of their practices and alternative approaches they might try. The consequence is either that hierarchy is strengthened, in which case teachers lose their voice in shaping the nature of educational experiences, leaving teaching unchanged, or they find ways of temporarily escaping the dominating effects of hierarchy. In both cases, the one-way nature of evaluation encourages a type of learning which legitimates authority while subjugating reason. Authority cannot be contested and replaced by reason when communication is one-way. Pronouncements on the way teaching *must be* stifle debate about the rightness of the underlying aims of teaching and how best to achieve them. Authority is attached instead to the evaluator, simply because of status.

Even those recent attempts that appear designed to soften the approach with peer evaluation schemes leave the basic power relationship undisturbed. On closer inspection, we find that one group deemed to be more skilled (i.e., master teachers), still exists to diagnose and recommend how the defects of another group (i.e., ordinary teachers) might be corrected. It is still a deficit model. Many peer evaluation approaches replace an administrator, such as a principal, with a teacher. These amount to a teacher using a rating schedule developed by an evaluation expert, to give a colleague 'the treatment'. As we shall see in Chapter 6, these kinds of relationships can have detrimental consequences. In some parts of the USA, such peer evaluation is coming to be linked with an economic incentive process that pits one group of teachers against another in an ungainly scramble for career advancement. The interaction in such schemes is monological, not only in the way it excludes the teacher whose pedagogy is being observed, but frequently such efforts degenerate into fault-finding missions with all the defensiveness and bitter recriminations that follow (Gitlin and Bullough, 1987).

In silencing one of the parties, these types of peer evaluation fall into precisely the same trap of the schemes they are slowly replacing—namely, they fail to open-up for question the desirability of educational goals. Unless such reconceptualized peer schemes do that, then they are unlikely to confront the one-way communication and asymmetrical power relations that lie at the root of the problem. Any such radical reconceptualization of teacher evaluation along dialogical lines will have to live with the difficulties of overcoming a history of schools having operated along monological lines. Ideas about evaluation have been nurtured and textured by a long history of using certain methods. As Fay (1977) says, 'ideas are a function of social conditions [that] . . . in turn play a causal role in creating and sustaining particular social structures' (p. 205). When teachers embark on more dialogical methods, we should not be too surprised if they still find it easy to slip into traditional roles of 'expert' and 'inexpert'. What this means is that school people have come to see as inevitable vertical rather than horizontal or lateral forms of accountability. This is something that needs to be worked against, and we shall have more to say about that in Chapters 4 and 6.

Fostering Individualism in Schools

Processes of evaluation, like other school structures, actually serve to foster particular types of relations among members of the educational community. In the case of the dominant approach to teacher evaluation, the relations are individualistic in that evaluative norms are established without considering the views of teachers and students. By creating competitive relations among teachers that minimize dialogue, institutional hierarchies are strengthened and reinforced, thus separating teachers, students and administrators.

The lack of consideration about the norms that underpin teacher evaluation is not something to be brushed aside lightly. By emphasizing the supremacy of technique in any discussions about evaluation, commentators like Worthen and Sanders (1973) fall into the trap of claiming that there is, therefore, no requirement to examine the worth of the objectives being pursued in the particular evaluation. In doing this, they not only ignore the raging debates within the scientific community itself about the efficacy of such procedures, but they obscure the nature of the social vision implicit in the procedures themselves. As Popkewitz (1984) put it, by not considering the social visions associated with the use of evaluation procedures, these supposed experts 'remove scientific procedures from their self-correcting communities' (p. 166). Over time, this kind of non-disclosure and absence of critical debate means that the values embedded in evaluation take on the appearance of being natural. In particular, the individualistic nature of dominant forms of teacher evaluation supports relations which allow normative issues associated with evaluative procedures and notions of good teaching to go uncontested by those most intimately involved in the process of education, namely, teachers and students.

The constraints on the establishment of an educational community, however, go much further. At the core of dominant forms of teacher evaluation are hierarchical separations which obscure common interests among the groups working in schools. Where evaluation means something that is 'done' to a teacher, the evaluator becomes the object of contempt, with teachers understandably seeking to conceal what is really going on in the classroom. Such antagonistic relations mean a climate is created in which teachers and their adversaries spend a great deal of time wrestling with each other, and fail as a result to take up the opportunities to debate questions that are of common concern. This lack of dialogue can only result in 'reforms' being imposed on teachers, resulting in various forms of resistance.

Students, of course, are not unaffected by the dominant relationships that exist in teacher evaluation. Where teachers are treated as commodities to be shaped, there is an expectation that students will similarly be moulded. While it is true in the reality of classrooms that students do not constitute pliant raw material to be shaped to fit some pre-specified standards of achievement, there is a strong presumption among those who hold to dominant views of teacher evaluation that this is so. The effect is to insert an antagonistic relationship into the way teachers interact with those they teach. Demanding, for example, that teachers strive for increasing levels of time on-task with their student, means that fragmentary relationships are elevated in importance above ones that are more communicative, discursive and democratic. The self-fulfilling prophecy becomes one in which students are urged to work in ways that fracture their relationships with fellow students (by working on individual activities), in much the same ways that these alienating and authoritarian pedagogies are imposed on teachers. That students do effectively resist these oppressive structures is well documented (Willis, 1977; Everhart, 1983; Steedman, 1982; McLaren, 1985). However, these resistances often only penetrate, as opposed to transform, the oppressive teacher/student relations, fostered by dominant forms of evaluation.

Dominant forms of evaluation also separate teachers from one another, for example, by ranking them. Evaluation of this sort does not encourage teachers to develop shared communicative structures in which knowledge about teaching is debated; rather, it encourages them to compete with each other, so as to look better on some evaluation criteria. What this does is limit the sharing of ideas and the identification of common interests that enable teachers to act collectively. In this way dominant forms of evaluation constrain educative relations among teachers by promoting the virtues of isolation over communication and by under-emphasizing the merits of teacher discourse. What makes this even more insidious is that teachers, as a subordinated category, have come to accept (Freedman, Jackson and Boles, 1986) as natural the notion that their work should be subjected to the scrutiny of externally legitimated experts—even when this is clearly not in their own best interests.

By way of summarizing the arguments we have presented so far in this chapter, it can be seen that dominant forms of evaluation as technique, separating knowing and doing, fostering a one-way or monological communication between the evaluator and those evaluated, and bolstering hierarchies and encouraging competitive relations of the worst kind, detach students and teachers from their language, experiences and histories. What is deposited in their place are managerial forms of discourse about the nature of schooling that are alien to the cultural lives of people in schools (Smyth, 1987b). We should not underestimate the pedagogic dislocation caused as teachers and students become confused about the relative legitimacy and potency of their lived practical experiences. The 'management pedagogies' (Giroux, 1985a) that lie behind dominant modes of evaluation become: the reduction and standardization of knowledge; the measurement of attainment against arbitrarily determined objectives and standards; and the allocation of teaching resources so as to maximize output. These management pedagogies, to use Bourdieu's (1977) terminology, represents a form of 'symbolic violence' which militates against teachers' own intuitive understandings about how children learn and what works in classrooms. There is a progressive devaluation and disconfirmation of teachers' own knowledge in a context that actively endorses reputedly neutral views of what constitutes 'good' and 'effective' teaching.

Not only is there a travesty of justice in the sense that the teacher is unable effectively to locate his/her actions in some broader view of education, but reductionist evaluations of the kind indicated actively ignore the overwhelming importance that teachers' personal and professional histories play in the construction of meaning about classroom events. We may well ask whether the submissive rule-following actions implicit in procedures like this, between teachers and their superiors, are the same kinds of relationships we want to foster and engender between teachers and their pupils. As one teacher put it, if we treat teachers as if they are 'hired hands' (Levy, 1985) without any real stake in the educational enterprise, we should not be too surprised if they react like hired hands (Sizer, 1984). When teachers are excluded from and treated as if they are invisible in the cultural debate about schooling, then the practices of education become '. . . . a fact of nature to be managed scientifically' (Pagano, 1987, p. 119). Practice becomes confused with technique, and practical reason becomes confused with instrumental reason (Lasch, 1984). The educative and moral imperatives that are so central to the act of teaching are somehow lost as teaching comes to be seen as some kind of neutral activity capable of being disembodied from the social, cultural and political lives of the people involved. None of this is to suggest that locating, describing, analyzing and attaching worth to aspects of teaching is in any sense undesirable. As we shall show later, it is a desirable, laudable and indeed indispensable process in understanding and changing teaching. What is far from satisfactory within the bureaucratic scheme of things is the view that the existing power relationships are right and proper—the view that one person, because of status, is 'in' authority and has the unquestioned right to impose knowledge about teaching upon another.

Rethinking Teacher Evaluation

The basic assumptions behind the dominant view of teacher evaluation, as we have sketched them here, must be confronted and contested if evaluation is to support other than conservative interests. Because teacher evaluation in whatever form expresses a particular view of social relationships in schools, a step in the direction of pursuing more educative (and we might even argue more 'empowering') interests is to expose and acknowledge the nature of these relationships. Acknowledging whose interests are being served is crucial in moving away from alienating and oppressive hierarchical relations based on authority towards educative and democratic ones that are based on reason. This amounts to putting educational goals or ends back into the evaluation process. The relentless quest for certainty about what is appropriate teaching has led those who claim to be evaluators to rely heavily on procedures from science that disavow any disagreement about the goals or ends to which teaching is directed. The problem comes to be seen as one of diagnosing, inserting and policing the correct procedure.

On the other hand, educative and democratic relations require that teachers and the views they hold about teaching become a central part of the evaluation process. Leaving the teacher out of the process (except as an 'object') amounts to regarding the teacher as a commodity to be shaped and manipulated. It also leaves unattended and unquestioned the underlying orientation that guides teachers' practices. Taking teachers fully into the process of evaluation not only allows knowing to be a mutual process but, more significantly, it makes dialogue and reasoned debate a possibility. It is through involvement of this kind that teachers come to consider and challenge taken-for-granted views about their pedagogy, and see how particular actions contribute to or confront deeply entrenched relations found in society. Confronting belief structures means that the personal and professional history that teachers bring with them to teaching also becomes an important part of the evaluation process. If we are to be serious about giving teachers an opportunity to understand how their educational histories influence their 'range of vision', then it is important that evaluation be able to reflect upon how those practices came into being.

Under the kind of conditions we have sketched here in our critique of the dominant mode of evaluation, it is no longer appropriate to think in terms of one participant as 'the evaluator'. What we have instead is two participants who work together to understand teaching critically, and through that to transform it. Shifting the centre of gravity of evaluation in this way confronts the oppressive division of labour which leaves teachers either totally alone without any collegial interaction, or dependent on 'expert' advice which they are expected to accept and follow unquestioningly. Once commenced among teachers, the communicative and educative notion of evaluation canvassed here can be extended to include other teachers, as well as members of the wider educational community.

Moving involvement in teacher evaluation beyond individual teachers means that the evaluation of teaching can be shifted from one of blaming the teacher for educational problems to a circumstance in which the wider community begins to accept its legitimate responsibility and role in setting, debating and monitoring the agenda, norms and goals of schools.

Chapter 3

The Politics of Educative Evaluation

Introduction

As we have seen in previous chapters, the issue of teacher evaluation and appraisal is guaranteed to raise temperatures. The struggle is between two paradigms—on the one hand, a process of control and surveillance exercised through hierarchical and bureaucratic means, and on the other, a process of creating educative relationships in which teachers, students and parents can develop the space within which to create self-knowledge. Among other things, the contrast is between the managerial relations of inspection, domination and quality control, versus the educative relations of collegiality, reflection and empowerment.

The politics of how domination and resistance are played out in schools was captured by Elliott (1987) when he said:

> Relations of domination need a system of surveillance covering as many aspects of the lives to be dominated as possible. Such a system is necessary to exert the kind of control over every detail of individual behaviour which domination requires. (p. 6)

He goes on to point out that what is at stake in teaching is the 'craft tradition' which relies on tacit knowledge and which is not amenable to bureaucratic control and standardization. It is worth quoting him further on this point:

> In the craft tradition of teaching disciplinary power operates through the authority teachers possess by virtue of tacit knowledge they acquire through experience . . .
> The resistance to bureaucratic standardisation, which the possession of craft knowledge generates in teachers, can only be overcome by eliminating the conditions under which this knowledge is

constructed and transmitted i.e., professional privacy and freedom from external regulation. Any forms of teacher appraisal which change these conditions by establishing a system of hierarchical surveillance and control over teachers' activities constitutes a strategy for eliminating the craft culture. (p. 8)

Now, while discussion about eliminating the craft tradition of teaching may sound quaint to American readers on the grounds that they have become increasingly accustomed to bureaucratic intrusions into their classrooms, this has not been the standard fare (until recently) in England, Australia and in some parts of Europe. Our point is that such intrusions are by no means natural or inevitable.

What we want to do in this chapter is to consider a number of factors which make the dominant mode look as if it is natural and commonsensical, when in reality claims as to its rightfulness are far from being settled. We commence by outlining the manner in which textbooks have come not only to frame and structure the content of teaching, but actually to give teaching an undeniable technical orientation. It flows from this that as a curriculum form, the textbook has also come powerfully to shape the kind of evaluative practices that occur, especially in the USA. Compliance is bolstered, we claim, through the reward structures in teaching that elevate individualism, while downgrading the importance of the communicative and the dialogical. We show that where corporatist images of schooling (derived from business and industry) prevail, then schools become void of any kind of overt political agenda. Teachers take on a kind of public servant ideology in a system where they are required progressively to purge themselves of actions that serve their own and their students' interests. As the technical act becomes supreme, the result is a kind of hardening of the educational arteries. Centrally-driven processes that purport to 'rationalize' what should be taught actually have the effect of intensifying and trivializing the nature of teachers' work, and make dialogue about that work seem not only impossible, but also pointless. Lack of time to confer about educational purposes is symptomatic of a much greater malaise that has come to grip schools—the imperative of the smoothly running classroom.

Radically changing the practices of teacher evaluation requires correspondingly fundamental changes in the structural and ideological forces that shape and constrain education. New models, no matter how powerful, have few long-term effects if they are not accompanied by strategies that confront traditional educational practices and school relations. In what follows we describe some of the limits, and suggest changes in thinking necessary to allow more educative conceptions to have an impact at the level of practice. Where earlier we saw that educative notions of teacher evaluation place teachers at the centre of the evaluation process, here we want to propose that these schemes help teachers go beyond the technical and see the political and ethical consequences of their work as well. When teachers act in ways that enable them to reflect on their taken-for-granted understanding of schooling, they come to create rather than just appropriate knowledge. In James McDonald's (1988) words: 'They must be constantly encouraged to shift from the "How?" to the "What?" and the "Why?"' (p. 165).

Technical Nature of Teachers' Work

Textbooks have come to be the centrepiece of the school curriculum. Reports suggest (Apple, 1986) that in the USA as much as 90 per cent of teaching relies on textbooks. At first glance, this common school structure may seem benign, even helpful or essential, However, on closer inspection it becomes clear that texts, in concert with other school structures, serve to focus teachers' attention on how best to transfer information to students and not on what is educationally important.

One particular expression of this has come in the form of the 'core' or 'common' curriculum. While the notion of core curriculum means widely different things in various parts of the world, in the USA it has come to be closely associated with a sequential set of objectives prescribed by mandate for all teachers of a subject at a grade level in a local or state-wide system of schools. In a situation where knowledge is regarded as a commodity to be packaged and disseminated through schools, this obviously has a significant impact on textbooks. The knowledge domain is construed as a set of 'standards', each with a subset of 'objectives'. For example, in one US city a grade six science standard states that 'the students will classify the groups of anthropods, describe metamorphosis and explain the proliferation of insects' (Utah State Board of Education, 1987, p. 32). So that there can be no confusion, and to facilitate total standardization, the objective is labelled standard number 3060–30. Computers are used to record and monitor the extent to which students attain these standards. What this kind of cultural mindset does is prevent teachers from exercising control over knowledge by locking them into texts based on non-negotiable mandated standards.

In the grouping, labelling and tracking of students associated with schooling of this kind, the evaluative dimension is made to seem a necessary adjunct to reaching goals. In reality, of course, it amounts to 'the epitome of domination . . .' (McDonald, 1988. p. 171). As McDonald puts it, practices of this kind are nothing short of 'a tyranny of cognitive knowledge and skills in our schools' (p. 172). Among other things, what goes undetected in this unreflective mode of teaching is that men dominate the senior positions of publishing firms and make gender-blind decisions about what knowledge is included in texts, together with a form of 'cultural capital' (Bourdieu and Passeron, 1977) that endorses middle class rules and perspectives. Textbooks not only fail to challenge the dominant attitudes, values, morals and perspectives (that support certain social and economic structures), but they also fail to encourage and enable teachers to begin the process of reshaping in critical ways the moral, ethical and political worth of schooling.

Coupled with the use of textbooks in this way are strong ideological forces working to ensure that 'proper standards' of teaching are maintained and indeed enhanced. In Britain, for example, reform proposals have already been put forward that would create national testing standards for children aged 7, 11 and 14 (with proposals to do likewise in some parts of Australia). The undeclared agenda in both countries is not only to ensure allegedly uniform outcomes of schooling but to expose and eliminate deviant teachers. Publishing 'league tables' in newspapers based on student performance on national tests, as has been proposed in Britain, is designed not only to inform the public on how schools are performing but to homogenize what is taught. Penultimate public examinations at the end of secondary schools are still seen in Australia as a way of maintaining what some would regard as uniform standards, while allaying public fears that the public is getting value for their educational dollars.

What tends to occur in such circumstances are varying degrees of rationalization within the curriculum, with the most extreme forms having highly specific behavioural objectives, accompanied by pre- and post-mastery tests for each objective. The attempt, is to focus teacher decision-making on narrow 'how to' questions that have to do with static processes of transmitting knowledge. This form, which first gained popularity in the 1960s, was thought to make the curriculum 'teacher proof'. One of the most prominent examples from the USA is Individually Guided Education in which:

> . . . the children's day is spent doing paper and pencil tasks from a worksheet or workbook. The teacher explains the assignments, and the students complete them at their desks . . . When students finish, they either hand their papers in and quietly line up at the teacher's desk for correction, or meet with the teacher as a group for correction. The general pattern is one of teachers explaining how to do assignments and correcting completed work while students do their assignments . . . Almost every teacher sits, head bent over the desk, correcting papers. (Bullough, Goldstein and Holt, 1984, p. 44)

This means that teachers who use a rationalized curriculum are occupied with aspects of teaching such as marking, recording and regrouping students for a good part of the school day. Because the objectives are predetermined and linked to mastery tests, it is difficult if not impossible for the teachers to modify, add to, or delete objectives. As was true of texts, teachers have little or no control over what is taught.

For example, in a sixth grade social studies class in the US, a teacher was following teacher materials that contained an objective intended to enable students 'to discover that the period of industrialization was a time of rapid and great change in the production of goods'. She had one group of students pursuing a task individually, and another group using an assembly line technique. The point of the technique was to show that the latter was more cost-efficient in terms of time. What proved problematic about the exercise was that it was structured in such a way as to endorse the reputed advantages of mass production, while concealing the manifest drawbacks. By becoming enamoured with the pre-programmed technicalities of the teaching materials, and accepting the testing that came with it, the teacher was prevented from seeing that there were other more important issues that *could* and *should* have been pursued. While this may appear to reflect a personal inadequacy on the part of the teacher in not being more astute, this misses the point. Rather, what it reflects is a manifestation of teacher de-skilling and a serious indictment of the way in which the curriculum form can give teachers a false sense of legitimacy for what they are doing, even when there are quite unacceptable cultural biases built into it.

In Australia the rationalized curriculum has occurred in a somewhat more subtle form. With the gradual disappearance of centrally-prescribed curricula in most states in all but the last year of secondary school a decade ago, it has begun to re-emerge more recently (in South Australia and Victoria) in the form of 'Curriculum Frameworks'. While the instigators of these centrally-driven curricula are at pains to emphasize their non-prescriptive nature, what is well understood is the strength of local community pressure to ensure uniformity of subject content so that students will not ultimately be disadvantaged in pursuing post-secondary studies or in seeking employment. In many ways there might as well be prescription, because conservative community thinking in difficult economic times produces the same result. Textbook publishers, with an ear always closely tuned to the potential for profit, have been quick to act. Like their predecessors, the 'curriculum materials products' of the 1960s, these materials can be guaranteed to have extensive adoption in Australian schools. As Hannan (1986) put it:

> While it is strictly true that no textbook or reading kit is actually prescribed by someone in head office, it is observable that certain books and kits might as well be prescribed because thousands of classrooms use them. Obviously, even if there is little or no demand for prescription, there is a big demand for materials that give the backbone of a course. And teachers actually seem to prefer using the same materials as other teachers. (p. 16)

In Britain the quest for objective-driven forms of evaluation has been given a quite frightening twist in a proposal emanating from the Treasury, a move allegedly designed to enhance accountability. A Department of Education and Science document outlines how performance indicators might be used to engineer socially acceptable standards of dress, punctuality, discipline and demeanour in schools. It is claimed that basing school performance solely on student test results is too narrow and should be extended to incorporate aspects of social behaviour. The document points out that:

> An attendance objective might specify that 'each class should have an average attendance throughout the winter and spring terms of 85 per cent or better ...' Within the general objective for attendance, unauthorized absence would need to be monitored systematically against standards set by period of the day and year of the course ... Objectives would need to be ... based upon nationally set standards and conventions ...

> A disciplinary objective might aim at keeping the number of recorded disciplinary sanctions below a certain percentage of pupil numbers. The approach and the objective would be based on internally set procedures. 'It will be for consideration whether an externally moderated objective by using, say, police records, would also be appropriate. Close liasion with the local public authorities would be required to obtain suitable comparable statistics'.

> A second disciplinary objective might be to 'keep the proportion of pupils found guilty of indictable offences below the average level for the age group within the locality ...'

> A demeanour objective might specify that 'pupils' appearance to be public on arrival and departure from school should be classified as satisfactory or better by at least [90 per cent] of those approached in a sample survey'. Senior pupils could carry out the interviewing. (Surkes, 1987, p. 5)

As one commentator said, 'it would be tempting to write off' (*Times Educational Supplement*, 28.8.87) this discussion paper as a ludicrous attempt rigidly to quantify diverse factors relating to teacher performance, if it were not for the recent history in England. With nation-wide testing, benchmark standards and teacher appraisal schemes, such pseudo-scientific endeavours do not seem at all far fetched and must be taken seriously.

Discussion so far of the influence of textbooks, core curriculum and rationalized curriculum indicates that school structures encourage teachers to behave in technical ways. These structures are likely to limit development and implementation of educative forms of evaluation because of the difficulty of teachers adopting a critical posture. None of this is to suggest a situation of hopelessness, or that teachers and students is somehow incapable of resisting or contesting the structures within which they live and work in schools. Clearly, there are a variety of ways in which teachers actively and passively resist management pedagogies (Giroux, 1985a) that aim to remove the planning and conception of teaching from them and into the hands of policy-makers and others outside of schools. What needs to be more carefully explored are systematic ways in which teachers and others can develop a style of discourse that runs counter to the

> new efficiency-smart and conservative-minded discourse [that] encourages schools to define themselves as service institutions charged with the task of providing students with the requisite technical expertise to enable them to find a place in the corporate hierarchy. (McLaren, 1987, p. 59)

For the moment we need to acknowledge that this can occur through students and teachers becoming active agents in resisting the kind of structures spoken about above. As a first step, this means coming to see how their own acquiescence to dominant curriculum forms really amounts to a collusion in the construction of a reality that is palpably oppressive.

The questions that need to inform and frame this counter-discourse, and which are in part the subject of Chapters 4–7, include the following:

> What are the moral variants against which we shall construct ourselves? How can problems related to class, race, gender and power be ideologically folded back into questions of educational quality and excellence? How can we reposition ourselves as educators against the dominant discourse in order to reconstitute our own subjectivity and that of our students? How can educators construct a political project that legitimates a radical form of intellectual practice? . . . (McLaren, 1987, p. 61)

Taking on such a radical but necessary posture will obviously entail uncovering the sedimented layers surrounding the role that teachers have come to play in adopting an uncritical stance towards their curriculum and pedagogy. Whatever else happens, it must also be recognized that educative forms of evaluation are never easy, and that such new forms, as well as being time-consuming, are difficult in the sense that they involve a degree of discomfort in having to reconsider what has become commonplace and habitual.

It is a sad but true reflection on the state of teaching that neither are such actions rewarded. Based on his own early teaching, Thomas (1985) illustrates this by referring to one of the first lessons he ever taught in which he sought to bring some wonder and perplexity into the classroom. In dealing with the puritan writer Jonathan Edwards, he wanted to do something quite different. He drew the blinds, asked the students to raise their desk tops in simulation of puritan pews, and setting the lectern on top of his desk, delivered in muted Edwardian tones the fire and brimstone of *Sinners in the Hands of an Angry God*. Thomas recalls feeling happy with the lesson because 'the students sat gaping and transfixed in their pews'. The outside evaluator who was present was less than impressed: 'What had been the objective of the lesson? What had the students learned? How did the teacher propose measuring this learning objectively? What skills had the students employed and what had been the strategy for reinforcing them?' (p. 221). Clearly, there were no rewards for the creative part of the lesson. What really counted for Thomas, but not for his evaluator, was his ability to see the impact of this lesson on his students:

> I see now that in many years it was the kind of lesson that only a young teacher might try, valour seeming the better part of discretion, and theatrics the lessor part of precision. Today, it would not occur to me to leap upon the desk, and more's the pity, for in the impulse lay a certain logic that I have come to appreciate. (p. 221)

Schools are not structured, by and large, in ways that encourage this kind of self-analysis, and certainly the official reward structures do not encourage the laudatory spontaneity displayed here. The point being made is that the ways in which teachers are rewarded, through forms of supervision, powerfully shape and legitimate what is regarded as acceptable teaching.

The Public Servant Ideology

While the structural influences bearing upon curriculum-making are considerable indeed, it came as a surprise to us not to find more examples of alternative practices of teachers who have challenged their narrow technical role. That this has not happened extensively or uniformly in the USA, England or Australia testifies to the 'public service' ideal that has come to characterize the teaching force. As long as teachers view teaching as being supposedly apolitical, neutral and value-free, they effectively bargain away their political power to challenge and supplant those interests bent on making teaching the way it is.

The origins of the public service ideal date back to the time of Plato when service to the public was defined in terms of the desirable behaviour of the guardian class. In the *Republic* he suggests how this class should eat, sleep, accumulate possessions, find happiness and live (Bullough, Gitlin, Goldstein, 1984, pp. 416–21). Specifically, public servants must abandon or suppress individuality in every aspect of life, living in Spartan rigour, materially poor, but spiritually rich in their selfless identification with the State's welfare (pp. 412–21). In Hegel's writings, civil servants were also seen as 'a class having no political interests beyond their efficient administration of the state' (p. 344). The ideal of a public servant is explicit in much early twentieth century discussion of teaching. Bagley (1911), for example, argued that in the USA there was a grave danger in allowing teachers the power to establish the ends towards which they worked because to do so as quoted in Bagley 'multiplies . . . [their] chances of failure, not by two, as one might assume at first thought, but almost by infinity' (p. 44). Bagley went on to argue that the first rule of efficient service is that it should be masked by humanistic or democratic language. This goes a long way towards explaining why it is that much of the current day lexicon of management applied to schools is couched in what appear to be benign forms of language.

Those who endorse tight behavioural objectives, as championed in such forms as Individually Guided Education (Klausmeir, 1976), argue that these programmes allow students to progress at their own rates (a humanistic goal), while implying that teachers should be limited to conveying information to students (a public service orientation). Rationalized programmes of this kind are predicated on the view that it is experts who determine what is the common good, and it is teachers, as public servants, who facilitate those ends.

Studies of teacher ideology and change (Bullough and Gitlin, 1985, 1986) suggest that a long history of working within structures that reflect public service values encourages teachers to internalize these values. There are teachers, for example, who willingly sacrifice their own well-being for the good of others, the teaching team and, especially, for children. This absence of self-seeking was nicely summed-up by the teacher who said: 'Most of the time I'll put their needs ahead of mine and just say I'll catch up later, that's where my priorities are'. What attitudes like this do is reinforce the view that the real 'experts' are not teachers, but others who are higher up the educational hierarchy.

The public servant orientation, where it holds, has several implications for educative forms of evaluation. For example, it makes teachers more accepting of the narrow limits within which they are encouraged to act. The presumption is that teachers should not be involved in the difficult business of determining the values students should hold, but rather be limited to involvement in effectively communicating knowledge to students. What the public service ideology does is reinforce a technical view of teaching that makes it less likely that teachers will seek out opportunities to question curriculum ends and the means being used to achieve them. This same ideal makes it less likely, as well, that teachers will autonomously argue for educative forms of evaluation that involve collaboratively assessing and analyzing each other's work. Dialogical processes of this kind runs counter to the public service notions of subservience, disinterest and deference, and is not at all consistent with notions of expertise that are rooted in contestation, debate and persuasion.

The technical nature of teachers' work, combined with the publicservice ideology, present some problems for implementing an educative approach to teacher evaluation. However, neither school structures nor ideology are monolithic. Teachers are at times angered by their constrained part in schooling. 'I feel down on the rock bottom with the kids, and [those who design programmes] are sitting on their thrones making . . . decisions' (Bullough and Gitlin, 1986, p. 29), was the way one teacher put it. Not all teachers, of course, totally accept public servant values; neither do structures determine behaviour in absolute ways. Extending, establishing and consolidating educative forms of evaluation may mean commencing in areas in which teachers have demonstrable leeway in curriculum-making, and where the public servant ideology is less dominant. It makes sense, at least initially, to work with teachers who value their peers, who feel they have something to contribute to the assessment of teaching and who see themselves as having at least a modicum of autonomy. Besides, it is contrary to the intent of educative evaluation to impose it upon teachers, for to do so would be to replace one form of oppression with another. A more likely scenario is to identify the interstices that already exist in schools, that represent pockets of resistance to the values of dominant styles of evaluation, and to use these as a basis for expanding support for educative approaches. Groups of teachers, like those described by Freedman, Jackson and Boles (1983) and McDonald (1986), who network and share experiences with one another, are continually working at building up collaborative relationships within which to scrutinize teaching. Groups that are able to develop their own momentum, as it were from the 'inside', are less dependent and vulnerable to the withdrawal of 'outside' support that can so easily cause ventures of this kind to wither. Sympathetic facilitators still have an important role in all of this, but it is of a different kind from being 'at the frontline'. Where outsiders act as 'critical friends', they provide an important sounding-board for helping groups to take stock of their progress (or lack of it), rather than being evangelists directing, manipulating and stage-managing the way educative evaluation should unfold. The role of the 'critical friend' is quite a different function from that normally ascribed to outside experts, and one that has to be very tolerant of insiders making their own mistakes and discoveries, and developing their own forms of ownership of the process.

Intensification of Work

One of the stumbling blocks to furthering educative approaches to evaluation is the growing intensification of teachers' work. According to Apple (1986), this can range 'from being allowed no time at all to go to the bathroom, have a cup of coffee or relax, to having a total absence of time to keep up with one's field' (p. 41). Rationalized forms of curriculum intensify teacher work by using the theory of scientific management to break the entire teaching process into a series of definable concrete parts, to lay objectives out sequentially, and to set the number of those objectives to be covered in the particular course or over the year of study. Having teachers spend up to 80 per cent of class time marking post-tests, grading papers and moving students from objective to objective, means that the pace of work does not lend itself to careful reflective thought about what is occurring, or why. As one teacher involved in this characteristically American form of teaching put it:

> I would like to be more creative and innovative but you are so hung up with correcting papers, reading papers, giving out tests . . . that by the time that you even think about something else you're too tired.

Another teacher put it this way:

> That's the machine that we get going, simply plug the kids in where they pass on the placement tests and then move them forward according to what they are able to handle . . . If the pace was such where there were breaks anywhere in the day where I could focus more on curriculum things or just more individual things with the kids, it would make a lot of difference in the way I feel about teaching. (Bullough and Gitlin, 1985, pp. 229–30)

We can expect intensification to be heightened as computers come to take on more and more of the checking-up on what teachers do, and as those who program those computers become yet another level of expertise that sets teachers further apart from their work.

However, as with the technical nature of teachers' work, these structural arrangements alone do not determine what it is that teachers do. Teacher ideology plays a role in reinforcing or mediating the influence of structure. The notion of professionalism, for instance, has been used to define teachers' work. As Apple (1986) argues, '[teachers] feel that since they constantly make decisions based on the outcomes of these multiple pre- and post-tests, the longer hours are evidence of their enlarged professional status' (p. 45). The irony of this view of professionalism is that decision-making is not only limited, but freedom to make such decisions is seen to be part of a professional obligation to accept longer hours and a more rapid pace of work. Professionalism, as understood by some teachers, acts as a self-fulfilling prophecy to strengthen the school structures that intensify work. For the teacher who remarked, 'I didn't have a very good year, only twenty-three students reached objective sixty-two [in the mathematics curriculum]' (Gitlin, 1980, p. 190), working harder and faster meant being a better teacher.

The intensification of teachers' work has important implications for educative forms of evaluation because of the demands this approach makes on teachers' time. Educative forms of evaluation, no matter how helpful, will not be accepted by teachers or used properly if they are simply added onto an already unbearable work schedule. In school situations where time is a disputed, even contested, form of currency, it is clear that control over the way teachers and students spend their time is a potent way of shaping what happens in school. An absence of time among teachers critically to reflect upon the nature of their work and to ask questions that allow them to locate their teaching within broader social and economic structures is similar in many ways to the problem of illiteracy. As Freire (1985) argues, illiteracy itself is not a *real* obstacle—it is a consequence of some other hindrance that generates the obstacle. People do not choose to be illiterate— they become illiterate because of lack of power and domination. Both the illiterate, and the teacher confronted with an intensification of work can only understand the significance of their respective forms of deprivation by first recognizing its problematic nature. For teachers, this means adopting a 'resisting' rather than an 'accommodating' posture to the way their work is determined by forces outside schools. While it would be seductive to proffer a range of 'how-to-do-it' solutions that teachers might act upon in reclaiming the time necessary to reflect on their work, this would not only be too simplistic but it would be to misinterpret the nature of the problem. What teachers need to see is that the way time is allocated in schools and the way it impacts on the pace of their work do not come about by accident. In specific historical situations and contexts, they need to see how their pedagogy is orchestrated from outside classrooms through rationalized curricula and pre-packaged forms designed for optimum learning efficiency. They also need to see that the real agenda is one of ensuring that what occurs within schools conforms to certain values. Fragmenting the work of teachers and trivializing what it is that students do are part of a wider process of appropriating the cultural capital (Bourdieu, 1977) of the dominant culture. This can be most readily seen in the way the curriculum forms described above actually fit with practices like insisting on homework, punctuality to class, tidy dress, speaking politely and working quietly—all of which are part of a view that subjugates rather than liberates students. As McLaren (1988) put it, schools on close analysis turn out to be 'strange and disturbing institutions that not only *teach* subjects but also *produce* unreflective human subjects who, in their day-to-day activities, play out the ideologies of the dominant culture' (p. 2). Lichtman (1982) put a somewhat finer point on this when he argued that schools:

> . . . must distribute enough literacy to make a contemporary industrial system possible, but not in such a way that reason becomes a technique commonly employed to dissect and challenge the system of power. (p. 247)

The intensification of teachers' work in the terms we have described above is fundamentally about the imposition of dominant values. Questions about the pace of work are really questions about who has the right to determine the values to be communicated through schooling—ones that have to do with unquestioning respect for authority, or ones that have to do with unmasking and demystifying the social relations of power. Questions about who controls the pace of teachers' work, why and whose interests are served are therefore fundamental if those in schools are to gain control over the way they live their work lives.

Teacher Invisibility

The way schools are structured along lock-step batch-processing lines, with individual teachers attending to age-related cohorts of students in single classrooms, is essentially anti-dialogical. As Jackson (1968) has demonstrated, while schools are crowded and noisy places with high levels of interactions between teachers and students, they are at the same time intensely insular and lonely places. One of the factors that tends to give isolation a sense of quasi-legitimacy in schools is the false presumption that consensus exists among all interested parties about the mission of schools. The sleight of hand by which this is achieved is through official top-down proclamations (i.e. reforms) of the way teaching ought to be, in which the only discussion possible is of a reactive kind limited to the technical processes of teaching. There is a resounding silence about questions like: 'What am I doing?'; 'What are my reasons?'; and 'What effect do my actions have on my students?' (Smyth, 1985, p. 1) that open-up for discussion the injustices and inequalities that pervade classrooms and society.

Both Sarason (1982) and Lortie (1975) testify to the way in which the cellular organization of schools with layers of separation between classrooms actually mitigates any kind of dialogue about the ends or social purposes towards which teaching is directed. While this particular design feature of schools has long been applauded because of the way it has permitted an expansion and contraction of schools and facilitated the turnover of personalities in teaching positions, there is another more spectacular but less publicized aspect too. It is the division of labour between those who are empowered and charged to administer and co-ordinate these cellular structures, and the inhabitants (teachers and students) who are required to conform to whatever administrative conveniences are foisted upon them. The cost is obvious enough: the discouragement of co-operation, enquiry, collegiality and participation in fashioning of a school-wide culture (Lortie, 1975, p. 56). This is compounded, as Sarason (1982) argues, by teachers adaptation to being left along (p. 106). Teachers come to associate this kind of isolation with autonomy. As one teacher put it, 'I don't like the isolation, but I like the independence that I'm in my own classroom and can do whatever I want' (Bullough and Gitlin, 1986, pp. 30–1).

The twisted view of professionalism that equates with teachers being left alone, silent and isolated, has a downside to it that is pernicious. As McDonald (1986) put it, isolation can amount to a 'protective response to subordination' (p. 358), so that closing one's door can seem like a rational response to incoherence. The short term benefits of this kind of isolation can appear quite attractive at a time when it is almost impossible to meet ever increasing demands put on teachers'. As one teacher remarked, 'Trying to . . . meet everybody's needs leads to failure and the . . . feeling you're a piece of shit' (Bullough and Gitlin, 1986, p. 31). It is easier to close one's door than it is to open it to a barrage of criticism. Such a view can also lull teachers into believing that they are more powerful than they actually are, with the consequence that they feel 'responsible alone . . . [for] correct[ing] complex societal and institutional dilemmas' (Freedman, Jackson and Boles, 1983, p. 291). By taking the blame individually and accepting help in shoring up their coping skills, teachers become isolated in a way that obscures the institutional and societal sources of their problems. Because of these structural and ideological factors, when teachers converse with one another it is invariably over matters designed to ensure that classrooms and schools continue to run smoothly—student discipline, lunch money, time-tabling, field-trips, parent-teacher conferences and the like. What this reflects, rather than any individual deficiencies in teachers, is that the dominant discourse of schooling is organized to prevent teachers from having an active voice in determining what passes as knowledge in schools (Smyth, 1987b).

Breaking down the structured silences that have come to characterize teachers' lives is no easy task. McDonald (1986) found that when teachers begin talking with one another, their first reaction is to engage in 'collegiality for collegiality's sake' (p. 357). As a member of a group of high school teachers who met as a support group over an extended period of time outside school hours, McDonald (1986) found that initially the group became even more morose, insular and self-absorbed:

> Initially, we had thought it wonderful just to know others who felt the same joys and frustrations in their work that we felt, and to share those joys and vent those frustrations together. But after a few months of sharing and venting, the wonder wore off, and it seemed that we ought to do something more. In fact, after some meetings, we felt worse about our work rather than better, as if complaining about this or that working condition, we had recognized our own bitterness and sealed ourselves in it. (p. 356)

The paralysis of action that McDonald (1986) and others speak about among teachers has its source in deep-seated feelings of uncertainty among teachers themselves about the nature of teaching. It is closely related to the way in which knowledge confers power. As we have seen elsewhere in this book, the prevailing view is that the experts in teaching are not teachers but scientifically-trained technocrats. Although teachers might know a great deal about teaching, the system of hierarchical subordination conveys a clear message that in matters of complexity, ambiguity and value conflict (Schön, 1983), intuition and tentative knowledge rate low in the scheme of things. Provisional knowledge of the kind that teachers have is discounted and has little chance of competing with that which is scientifically legitimated.

Under such conditions teachers are neither prepared for the type of interactions required by educative forms of evaluation, nor are they likely to see the long-term benefits of such interactions. Overcoming this constraint requires more than restructuring the school day so that teachers can find the time to get together to visit one another's classrooms: it requires developing a perspective in which the entire enterprise of teaching is construed much more collaboratively and dialogically. Discussion groups of the kind described by the Boston Women's Teachers' Group (Freedman, Jackson and Boles, 1983) can have intended as well as unintended effects. In the words of one teacher: 'It has helped me identify some of the concerns of my profession and helped me clarify my position on some of these issues'. A member of another teaching group 'found [support group meetings] depressing and enlightening. I find myself re-examining what I do and what goes on in my school and the community as a whole' (Nicastro, 1986, p. 66).

Clearly what is required is that teachers jettison the view that 'being a "good" professional [means] facing the issues alone' (Freedman, Jackson and Boles, 1983, p. 298). They must recognize that the way forward lies in the collective analysis of how educational and social structures deeply affect school relationships. As in the case described by McDonald (1986), breaking the silence of teachers amounts to taking a voice in policy matters. This means no longer being prepared to be passive recipients, but to develop informed views about policy issues to do with teaching, and to be vocal and articulate about these in a context of searching to link-up with sympathetic parent, union and community groups.

Moving towards Educative Alternatives

Educative forms of evaluation are only a small part of a much larger project of establishing a dialogical community that must affect not only teachers, but other members of the educational community as well. Certain hierarchical relations which obstruct dialogical relations must be confronted. One such relation is the artificial division of labour between those who are reputed to hold educational 'theories' and those who engage in the 'practice' of teaching—all education practitioners hold such theories which guide and inform what it is they do, not just those people who are labelled researchers, policy analysts or educational reformers.

Educative forms of evaluation cannot be understood in isolation from school structure and the perspectives which teachers and others bring with them to schools. What this chapter has tried to show is that ideology and structure act to encourage a narrow view of schooling which limits educative possibilities for school change. Specifically, teachers need a say in what and how they teach. While it is understandable that some form of accountability is necessary, this does not mean that its form has to be impositional. We need practices that highlight the tensions, contradictions and distortions in schooling and that permit alternatives to be debated and adopted. Accountability of this kind means that teachers not only acquire a voice in the determination of educational aims, but that they do so on the basis of a joint assessment of the political, ethical and moral implications of schooling.

While educative forms of teacher evaluation can begin such a reconstruction, they are likely to have few long-term effects if the structures and ideologies which support a limited technical role continue to shape teacher behaviour. The aim of such a reconstruction is not to have teachers trade place with others in the educational hierarchy, but rather to contest the hierarchies which obstruct dialogical relations. We have argued that to do so teachers should be given a say in determining curriculum aims and purposes, have time to engage in substantive critical dialogue with others and be rewarded for furthering educative relations.

Part II
Two Possibilities

Chapter 4

A Dialogical Approach to Understanding: Horizontal Evaluation *

Introduction

Our focus in this chapter is upon a relatively new approach to evaluation, horizontal evaluation (Gitlin and Goldstein, 1987), which we feel can begin to restructure schools in educative ways.[1] Horizontal evaluation's potential to do this results from a somewhat dramatic rethinking of evaluation. Where dominant approaches, as we have argued, try to reform schooling by getting teachers to behave in specified ways, horizontal evaluation attempts to foster school change by enabling teachers to base practice on a critical accounting of the moral, ethical and political consequences of schooling. Change, where it does occur, is an outgrowth of dialogue that attends to questions about the nature of schooling. Furthermore, where dominant approaches are characterized by a one-way communication from evaluator to practitioner, horizontal evaluation utilizes a dialogical orientation. This orientation transforms the role of the evaluator from that of 'fault finder' to one who works with the teacher to understand schooling in ways which enable them to escape habit and challenge taken-for-granted views. Finally, where dominant approaches to evaluation silence teachers, horizontal evaluation strengthens their ability to contribute to discourse on educational means and ends. In explaining further what horizontal evaluation is, we will (1) discuss its purpose: understanding, (2) present a cursory overview of the method, and (3) describe the method in detail while illuminating its underlying theoretical framework.

*An original draft of this paper appeared in *Educational Theory* 37,1, 1987 and was co-authored with Stanley Goldstein.

Understanding as the Aim of Evaluation

As opposed to most evaluation schemes that aim to change teacher behaviour, horizontal evaluation attempts to change people's basic understanding of themselves and their teaching world. But what is it about understanding that gives it the central place in this process of evaluation? Why is a concern for improved performance not enough? What do we mean when we assert that understanding, not just improved performance, is the proper aim of teacher evaluation?[2]

According to Habermas (1976b), understanding occurs at different levels. In a minimal sense, participants can gain understanding by coming to an agreement on the meanings or values embedded in a linguistic expression. Its maximal meaning takes the process a step further and encourages participants to rethink those values in relation to an agreed upon and debated normative framework.

> In its minimal meaning it indicates that two subjects understand a linguistic expression in the same way; its maximal meaning is that between the two there exists an accord concerning the rightness of an utterance in relation to a mutually recognized normative background. In addition, two participants in communication can come to an understanding about something in the world, and they can make their intentions understandable to one another. (p. 3)

Because the purpose of horizontal evaluation is to enable teachers to see the world differently and tranform what are often destructive patterns, it is the maximal meaning of understanding that this process focuses on.

Understanding has this transformative potential because actors are 'capable of entertaining the result of their action even before initiating the action' (Freire, 1985, p. 70). In other words, they are beings who can project toward an identified goal. Freire (1985) makes this clear when he notes that:

> A bee puts to shame many an architect in the construction of her cells. But what distinguishes the worst architect from the best of the bees is this, that the architect raises his structure in imagination before he erects it in reality. (p. 70)

This ability to project makes it possible for actors to question the type of 'structure they want to construct'. And this questioning can begin when actors work together to understand the appropriateness of educational goals and their relation to practice. Given the large number of studies that show the role of schools in reproducing inequalities based on gender, race and class (Apple, 1987; Weis, 1985; Everhart, 1983; McRobbie, 1981; and Willis, 1977), is important that teachers engage in dialogue which questions the type of 'structures' they help construct.

Understanding also enables participants to express their 'humanness'. What distinguishes humans from animals, according to Freire (1985), is their ability to be *in* the world and *with* the world. While animals are always guided by habit (in the world), humans have the potential to step back from reality and remake it, based on their visions of what is desirable (with the world). When teachers consider how reality has become constructed in particular ways and how it might be reconstructed, for example, they utilize their human potential. The focus on understanding therefore is very much tied to overthrowing the alienating and dehumanized condition which dominant forms of evaluation inflict on teachers by denying them an opportunity to reflect on their world and remake it based on a sense of what schooling should be about.

The Horizontal Model: An Overview

If horizontal evaluation is to help participants achieve an understanding of schooling, there are certain general conditions which can facilitate this process. First, the conversation should be seen by both participants as an opportunity to comprehend what occurred; no participant has a monopoly on the 'correct' interpretation. Second, the participants should accept that their view of what happened is always partial, sometimes wrong, and that they can capture more completely and accurately what happened through dialogue. While the use of horizontal evaluation can help those involved to move in this direction, where participants enter the process holding these values, evaluation is more likely to be dialogical and enhance understanding. However, no matter how truly dialogical the process is, there will always be 'blindspots' and distortions. An outsider or 'critical friend' therefore can play an important part in the evaluation process by helping participants reflect on the discourse. If the discourse, for example, ignores the way historical traditions shape current teaching practice, the critical friend can initiate dialogue with the participants on this topic. It is not as if the view of history presented by the critical friend is the correct one but rather that historical concerns can further understanding for all the participants. Emphatically, the critical friend must enter the dialogue under the same set of conditions as is recommended for the participants.

To begin the horizontal evaluation process participants are encouraged to analyze the relationship between teacher intention and practice. This type of relational analysis is of central importance to the approach because it allows the value inherent in all teaching practices to be examined. It also enables participants critically to view both practice and intentions by pointing to 'living contradictions' (Whitehead and Lomax, 1987), the gap between what we choose to do and what we desire to do. And even where there is congruence between intention and practice, teachers are urged to think through the question of why it is desirable to achieve the identified ends as opposed to assuming that this matching of means and ends is beneficial *prima facie*.

To clarify this relation, intentions can be stated in advance or emerge from the dialogue. If they are stated in advance, they should not be viewed as reified concepts that are set in store, for this leads to a mechanical view of teaching. Rather, the emphasis should be on an examination of the values embedded in what the teacher intends to achieve. A teacher, for example, might state that her intention is to get all students to obey the rule 'raise hands before speaking'. Instead of simply accepting this aim, and determining the degree to which practice reflects this teaching end, the observer should dialogue with the teacher about why this rule is important. Once the values embedded in this typically taken-for-granted intention are clarified, their desirability can be examined in relation to an articulated and debated normative framework. It is at this time that more pragmatic considerations can be raised about the relation of intention and practice.

A teacher might also be unsure about her intentions and therefore be unable to state them in advance. In this case intentions can emerge out of dialogue about practice. If a teacher is using a question/answer strategy where the teacher asks all the questions and students search for answers, the discourse can illuminate what intention [s] this strategy satisfies. Once these are identified, the dialogue can proceed as before by clarifying these educational ends and considering their desirability.

Figure 1

To enable teachers to examine the political, moral and ethical nature of teaching practices and ends, horizontal evaluation draws primarily on the work of Gadamer and Habermas. While Gadamer (1975) has written little on public education, he is keenly aware of the limitations of deferring to experts, so common in dominant approaches to evaluation:

> The problem of our society is that the longing of a citizenry for an orientation and normative patterns invests the expert with an exaggerated authority. Modern society expects him to provide a substitute for past moral and political orientations. (p. 312)

The exaggerated authority of experts, he goes on to say, is related to the destruction of a craft orientation and the dominance of technologically organized work:

> Not only has craftsmanship been replaced by industrial work; [but] many forms of our daily life are technologically organized so that they no longer require personal decision. (pp. 313–14)

Because teachers' work appears to have taken a similar turn, Gadamer's concerns about industrial society are relevant to the constrained position teachers find themselves in today. His emphasis on 'decision-making according to one's own responsibility—instead of conceding that task to the expert' (in Bernstein, 1985, p. 159), echoes horizontal evaluation's attempt to overcome school structures which silence teachers by enabling them to make decisions which reflect thorough consideration of educational means and ends.

While horizontal evaluation owes much to Gadamer in this regard, Habermas' (1976b) work in universal pragmatics is also informative because he shows that even though communication is distorted in most instances, the structure for communication based on reason is still embedded in our speech acts:

> Communicative reason is anticipated and presupposed in the general structures of possible communication. [And although this potential] is silenced again and again, it nevertheless develops a stubbornly transcending power. (p. 191)

What this suggests is that even though teacher dialogue may reflect distorted types of communication that assume the legitimacy of particular positions and meanings, the analysis of the dialogue itself can free participants from these distortions and enable them to make decisions based on reason. Because horizontal evaluation attempts to encourage this type of communication between teachers, Habermas' ideas are an essential part of this attempt to reconceptualize evaluation.

Specifically, Gadamer's and Habermas' ideas have resulted in two methods with which to analyze the relationship between educational means and ends—what we call communication analysis and historical perspective. Participants are not required to employ these methods and others associated with horizontal evaluation in all circumstances, but rather are encouraged to utilize them whenever possible because of their power to enhance understanding. As is true of all aspects of horizontal evaluation, these methods can be initiated by the observer or observed teacher.

Communication Analysis

Where teachers often chat with each other about students, organizational matters and tricks of the trade, these conversations rarely free teachers from habit or enable them to see the world in different ways. Communication analysis provides a structure where participants can examine the way in which the prejudgments they hold helps to form a particular view of teaching. If a participant mentions that the reason for the chaotic student behaviour was the 'low' nature of the group, the other participant could ask, 'What do you mean by the "low group"?' This question allows what are often taken-for-granted values to be made explicit and reconsidered by the participants. And the reconsideration of these values can tranform the way teachers make and remake school reality on a daily basis. For example, if the teachers realize that the labelling is inappropriate because it is based on the socio-economic status of the students, then classroom structures and pedagogy can be reorganized to reflect a more egalitarian view of students that does not act as a self-fulfilling prophecy.

Historical Perspective

Historical perspective allows apparently commonsense notions and actions to be seen as choices which are part of an evolving historical tradition that serves a set of interests. If a participant notes that a banking view of pedagogy is being used, historical perspective can encourage discourse on how priorities of the capitalist system within which education is embedded have historically helped sculpt certain commonsense ways to teach. Once these factors are considered the interests embedded within teaching can be more fully analyzed.

Alternatives

In addition to these two approaches, horizontal evaluation asks participants to link the insights gained through discourse to the realization of alternative teaching practices. The alternative is not an end point, an unalterable part of the teachers' repertoire, but rather a turning point for further discourse on the relation of intentions to practice. In other words, while the dialogue may end with a suggested alternative, this alternative then becomes part of a new set of practices which are examined by the participants.

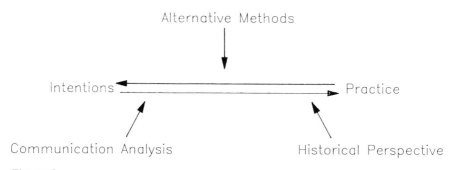

Figure 2

Challenge Statements

In addition to the above mentioned methods, horizontal evaluation suggests using a series of challenge statements. The purpose of challenge statements

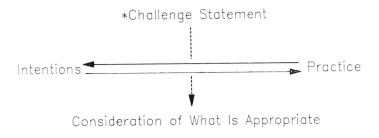

*Challenges may be raised by the observer or observed.

Figure 3

is to push dialogue along in those circumstances in which it has stalled and cannot go beyond clarifying values and prejudgments. If a participant notes that students should obey her classroom rules in all circumstances, questions can be raised about student and teacher rights and adult authority. The challenge issued in this case concerns the type of teacher/student relations that is desirable in the classroom. The resulting conversation might probe the legitimacy of adult authority and the implications of this position, especially for the education of students in a democracy.

The participants might also raise challenges about the evaluation process. One possible line of enquiry is the relationship between the participants. Specifically, challenges might be raised about the one-way nature of the communication or the emphasis on 'tricks of the trade' which actually excludes discourse on the moral, political or ethical underpinnings of such techniques.

In the sections that follow we provide a more complete account of the horizontal method, while considering its relation to our stated intention, to further understanding. By so doing we use the horizontal method to structure our discussion of the model itself.

The Horizontal Method and Understanding

Intention and Practice

Basic to our aim of understanding is the consideration of intention and practice. All practice involves choices 'of deciding for something or against something else' (Gadamer, 1984, p. 81). But often when teachers make choices, the implications are clouded or not considered because (1) with the reliance on experts, the teacher's role is limited to finding effective ways to meet established ends rather than considering the legitimacy of those ends

(Gitlin, 1983); and (2) in a technological society how much is 'produced' in terms of student achievement scores or success on 'O' and 'A' level exams is assumed to be the primary aim of education, making reflection on the hidden implications of practice appear less important; (3) within this limited role, a 'good teacher' is primarily involved with finding ways to satisfy experts and the demands of society, and is not necessarily concerned with fostering educative relations which empower students to transform oppressive relations and further democratic ends.

To confront this limiting role, horizontal evaluation encourages teachers to make intentions explicit and relate them to practice. And, where possible, teachers should communicate their understanding with other teachers if not other members of the educational community. This is an important part of the evaluative process because it allows teachers to examine their view of classroom reality in relation to other perspectives. In the ideal, expanding the dialogue in this way allows all members of the educational community with a legitimate interest in the education of students to take part in debates which focus on the question of educational aims and practices. If a pair of teachers, for example, comes to realize through dialogue that their multi-cultural curriculum does nothing to illuminate the oppressive conditions some of these groups experience, by sharing these insights the educative process started between the participants can spread to other teachers. Not only do the original participants gain 'critical friends' but other teachers have an opportunity to rethink their intentions and practices in the area of multi-cultural education. Teachers as a group therefore can replace habit with an educative process that challenges taken-for-granted aims and practices. Further, by extending the discourse to the community level, parents who are usually left out of debates about the school experiences children and young adults encounter (Connell, 1982) can play an active role in contributing to these important decisions. A more democratic orientation to schooling is thus established where the strongest arguments, not the status or power of particular groups, determine the school's normative framework and practices. As Gadamer (1984) notes:

> The more what is desirable is displayed for all in a way that is convincing to all, the more those involved discover themselves in this common reality; and to the extent human beings possess freedom in a positive sense, they have their true identity in that common reality. (p. 108)

What follows illustrates how analyzing the relation between intention and practice can confront a constrained teacher role and open possibilities for a more educative school community.

Given the dominance of technocratic rationality (Bullough, Goldstein and Holt, 1984), teachers often do not think about their work in terms of intentions, but rather focus on the means to achieve taken-for-granted ends. If teachers do identify intentions, they often rely on those stated in a text or pre-packaged curriculum. To help clarify and rethink teachers' understanding of educational purposes the participants using horizontal evaluation can begin by questioning a stated intention. If a participant states that her intention is to cover all the math units in the text, the values underlying this intention can be disclosed by asking, 'Why this objective?' If a teacher replies that the aim is to supply students with the knowledge of math necessary to 'function' in present society, the participants can use communication analysis to clarify words like function. They can then consider what should be the relation between school and community needs by asking whose interests are served by a 'functional' relation. The interests served become particularly complicated if it is noted that several students are falling behind in the teacher's attempt to get through all the units. By investigating the values and interests served within a particular intention and relating intention and practice, the teacher is able to see how individual interests, such as those of the two students who are falling behind, can conflict with the need to function in society and therefore can begin to re-evaluate the appropriateness of particular choices.

For other taken-for-granted intentions, such as developing students' 'potential', participants might explore how the use of the term 'potential' actually serves particular interests, while often being used as an apolitical catch-all phrase. If observations indicate, for example, that the teacher gives the physically difficult tasks to boys and asks the girls primarily to do secretarial-type favours, these observations can start reflection on how choices about teaching practice reflect a sense of 'potential' based on the docility and compliance of female students. The resulting conversations should consider the desirability of seeing 'potential' in this way, as well as exploring alternative practices which serve more egalitarian interests. Again the possibilities for rethinking educational means and ends are rich.

Communication Analysis

Embedded in the words used and the sentences formed in trying to capture the meaning of teaching are pre-understandings and distortions. By analyzing these words and sentences, the participants can work free of some distortions and thus understand more completely the meaning of what occurred.

Let us consider once again our example of the teacher who attributed certain student behaviours to the supposed fact that a class was the 'low group'. The label has explanatory power for the teacher. The purpose of communication analysis is to explicate that utterance 'low group' in order for the teacher to be clearer about the claims and values implicit in her explanation. In this context, a relevant notion for guiding analysis of speech acts is Habermas' (1976) 'Universal Pragmatics'. Habermas has identified four validity claims present in every speech act: comprehensibility, truth, sincerity and appropriateness (pp. 1–8). These four claims help clarify the underlying prejudgments and values inherent in speech act and their appropriateness. All four claims are always present, explicitly or implicitly, in any communication acts and can be raised for each sentence or utterance being analyzed. It is often sufficient to work with one claim, while being aware of the others. In practice the direction of the discussion will suggest which claims need to be raised.

As applied to the horizontal evaluation model, the first claim, comprehensibility, would consider whether the teacher's statement is understandable. Because language is ambiguous or confusing, questioning what is meant by a particular phrase provides the basis for a critical enquiry into the values inherent in a particular speech act. 'Did you say that you thought the students' behaviour was determined by the fact that they are in the low group?'

Applying the truth claim to a statement such as 'The students behaved as they did because they are the low group' is a more complex undertaking. The underlying issue is whether, or in what ways, the sentence can be a true description of those involved and of what happened. To clarify this issue, questions can be raised about the accuracy of describing this group as low. Beyond this is a series of questions about the link between being in a low group and behaving in a particular way and, further, about whether the behaviour is caused by being a member of the group or because of other factors. Careful consideration of what can be agreed upon as the facts of the situation actually serves to clarify whether the views we hold are justifiable and supportable.

Statements which appear obvious must be discussed to explicate their meaning; this highlights the importance of Habermas' sincerity-validity claim. If the observer and the teacher are to come to an understanding, then sincerity is essential. Both participants must ask themselves and be willing to be questioned by the other about whether they are making clear comments which reflect their perceptions and feelings or being strategic and trying to please the speaker. One necessary step in this process of clarification is to grasp how interests and values colour views of reality. We are influenced by more than just our feelings; of concern are the taken-for-granted values that we have acquired from living in a society. Categorizing groups of students as high or low ability may well occur because the significance of such labels is never considered; they are simply accepted as having obvious meanings. Habermas' formulation emphasizes what we intuitively know, that our prejudices and values influence what we see happening in teaching. Thus, what I sincerely utter indicates both my understanding and that which I accept without reflection. A way of getting at this is by examining the feelings about and categorizations of the social world which we reveal in sincere comments. Potentially, then, discourse of this sort may disclose tensions or discrepancies between feelings and understandings, and how we communicate them. Through this type of communication teachers can lay hold of the systematic distortions built into their utterances.

With consideration of the comprehensiveness, truth and sincerity of the statement, the final validity claim—Is the labelling justifiable, right?—helps in separating what is from what ought to be. This claim poses at least two related sets of questions: is the labelling in accordance with the purposes and norms of the institution, and can these norms be supported by reasons which we mutually agree are right? Using the example of the 'low' group, this validity claim can be examined by relating the values underlying the label to the normative values and then critically assessing these norms. Inherent in this claim is the belief that teaching is a moral activity about which moral judgments are made. The concerns of the teacher can no longer be merely technical—Did I reach my objectives?—but must also concern the rightness of the values inherent in both intentions and the means used to realize them. If a participant notes that a teacher responded almost exclusively to the verbal students, and the verbal students tended to be boys, the discussion might focus on the moral implications of this occurrence. 'I think all students, boys and girls, deserve the same treatment'. Through dialogue, both participants would use the rightness-validity claim critically to examine the values underlying this statement. If there is general agreement, the teachers could then explore possible alternative practices that would better fit this agreed upon aim.

To make the point about communication analysis in a somewhat different way, we can argue that through conversation about teaching, statements are made that require a more careful consideration of their validity if mutual understanding is to occur. Thus, the sentences formed indicate the view of the social world we currently see and the assessment of those statements allows this world view to be re-examined. The hope is that through this type of discourse teachers can transcend taken-for-granted views and habits that are thought of as social compulsion. Habermas' identification of the validity claims possible in speech acts empowers teachers to be clearer about and reconsider the choices they make, which matches the purpose of horizontal evaluation.

Historical Perspective

To gain understanding, horizontal evaluation encourages participants to see current practice in relation to past events. In the context of horizontal evaluation we refer to this as the historical perspective method. While communication analysis can explicate the normative values that inform teaching practice, the use of historical perspective clarifies how these normative values are established in the context of tradition. 'For tradition mirrors on a large scale the lifelong socialization of individuals in their language' (Habermas, 1977, p. 340). Historical perspective complements communication analysis by allowing linguistic meanings, and hence the way teachers act, to be seen as part of a tradition they step into and help remake on a daily basis. This perspective pushes the discourse beyond the context of a particular classroom and gives participants an opportunity to see how evolving world views shape classroom life and serve particular sets of interests. We can concretize this notion of historical perspective by considering what it would mean for a discussion of the open classroom concept of education.

A teacher taking a job in an open classroom is stepping into an organizational framework that reflects some basic assumptions about educating students, assumptions rooted in a tradition. To help understand them, a participant might start by asking the significance of the word 'open'. Specifically, they might explore the 'external reality of what is supposed to be an existing state of affairs, the internal reality of what a speaker would like to express, and the normative reality of what is generally recognized as a legitimate interpersonal relationship' (Habermas, 1976b, p. 288). Once this type of communication analysis has started, historical perspective can be used to clarify how current realities are part of a tradition which is often constructed by those in power to serve their own interests. Specifically, the original organization of the open classroom, that centred on student choice, could be contrasted with a current version of the 'open' classroom that allows students to progress at their own rate but through a standardized set of objectives. The discussion might try to understand how this term has come to be distorted by examining the social forces that influenced such wide sweeping reforms and the interests served when individualized instruction of this type becomes associated with the open classroom concept. If the conversation is successful, the teacher would see the current open classroom as part of a history which reflects societal influences and the teacher's unique response to these influences.

The use of a historical perspective is not limited to tracing the roots of educational philosophies; personal histories of teachers and students can provide a focus for this type of analysis. If a teacher decides to make the students stay in during recess because they have not finished their work, this decision can be understood as part of a tradition that has historical roots. The teacher's decision is related to a set of historical factors including past student behaviour and the teacher's response to the behaviour. Unfortunately, much of this classroom history is lost when teachers are trying to keep up with the current realities of schooling. To overcome this form of presentism, dialogue can expose the general themes that over time can help mould classroom life. Once these themes are revealed, the teachers can use communication analysis or challenge statements to reconsider goals and means.

Schools also have histories which influence student and teacher roles. In certain schools the students are seen by teachers as unruly and out of control, while the teachers are viewed by students as insensitive and authoritarian. Although many factors can contribute to this perception, the discussion of pertinent historical events and policy decisions such as frequent changes in administration, the degree of community support for curricular innovations, teacher workload, and even the particular recreational programmes offered students, may allow teachers to see role boundaries as changing sets of characteristics that can be reinforced or remade as current practice becomes part of the school's history. The discussion should neither glorify the past nor reject current interpretations of role but instead elucidate the trends that help account for role boundaries.

If dialogue incorporates historical perspective on a regular basis, teachers will begin to see events in a new way, such that 'one learns to see beyond the near and the all-too-near not in order to overlook it but in order better to see it in a large whole and with a more accurate sense of its proportions' (Gadamer, 1975, p. 288). Historical perspective in essence provides a translation between past and present interpretations of events in which there is a confrontation of one's own values with what is foreign. This rupture can lead to revisions in practice and, as Giroux (1983) states, 'minimize the effects on our students of those parts of our "sedimented" histories that reproduce dominant interest and values' (p. 241).

Challenge Statements

Teachers often seek a definitive interpretation of practice and focus on means that will effectively confront a known reality. In this situation questions about whose interests are served and the implications of teaching techniques are concealed and often forgotten. The purpose of the challenge statement is to create enough doubt so that it 'becomes more important to trace the interests guiding us with respect to a given subject matter than simply to interpret the evident content of a statement' (Gadamer, 1984, p. 106). Once interests are exposed teachers can reflect on the desirability or rightness of particular choices. It is the consideration of rightness that links challenge statements to the process of communication analysis. The power of challenge statements to clarify the interests served and encourage teachers to reconsider intentions and practice can be illustrated by the following reconstruction of a conversation between a teacher and observer.

In an observed lesson the teacher had students make a dessert treat, 's'mores', using an assembly-line method to show how this organization could speed up production. The students enjoyed the activity, and almost all connected assembly line to efficiency on the matching part of the post-test. After the lesson the observed teacher commented that she thought the lesson went well because the students scored high on the post-test. For this teacher, post-test results appear to provide the standard against which the quality of the lesson is to be judged. In response to this statement the observer posed a challenge by asking whether tests can capture what students learn, what the teacher would not know about students if only the test were considered, and who benefits most by judging lessons according to test results. The conversation that followed shed light on the limits of testing and the problematic nature of seeing schools as meritocratic institutions. The teachers were now in a position to reconsider what criteria, including testing, might be proper in judging the quality of a lesson.

If, on the other hand, the teacher had responded that the lesson went well because the students understood that technological improvements make life better, challenges could be raised about the values underlying this statement by asking how the assembly line affects workers' lives. By exposing another set of interests, that of the workers, the teacher may feel less sure about the activity and make future modifications based on a better understanding of the lesson's implications.

Other possible foci for these challenges are the values embedded in the observer's statements. If the observer notes that the lesson 'failed because the teacher didn't keep the kids on task', the other participant could challenge the view that keeping students on task is the equivalent of a good classroom. Challenges could also be posed about the observer's interpretation of teaching practice. If the observer states that 'I don't allow talking in my class', the teacher could challenge this practice by noting that it encourages an authoritarian pedagogy and denies students the opportunity to talk to each other about the issues discussed. The relationship of the observed teacher and the observer can also be an important topic for discussion. The teacher might focus on the observer's questions; are they an attempt to understand teaching or control the agenda and silence meaningful responses? Challenges of this kind are an important part of the horizontal evaluation model because they keep the process from being a one-way line of enquiry that falls prey to the pitfalls of the dominant approach.

In sum, challenge statements provide a way of examining what are often unquestioned values. By questioning the taken-for-granted, the teacher begins to see more fully the implications of practice and can take these into consideration when deciding what to do in the classroom.

Conclusion

To conclude, we will summarize the main values of horizontal evaluation for teachers. In a sense our outlook is nicely caught by something Clifford Geertz (1973), the distinguished anthropologist, said about his (hermeneutical) orientation to anthropology: 'The whole point of a semiotic approach to culture is, as I have said, to aid us gaining access to the conceptual world in which our subjects live so that we can, in some extended sense of the term, converse with them' (p. 24). The idea that teachers, students and the community can converse 'in some extended sense of the term' about educational intentions, aims and means is really the heart of the matter. Our analysis has tried to show just what an extended conversation, horizontally conceived, will involve when mutual understanding—'gaining access to the conceptual world' of others—is paramount.

The most fundamental change for education that would come with the emphasis on understanding concerns the role of the teacher.[3] When teachers attempt to consider the desirability of choices and the implications of their aims and means, they challenge the view that they are simply functionaries, technicians, or merely glorified clerks managing materials for others' ends. With respect to a manipulated society, the technocracy we in fact inhabit, the implication of such a changed relationship is far-reaching. It promises fresh vitality for democratic processes (Gadamer, 1984) by challenging educational hierarchies and the division of labour between thinkers and doers that silences teachers, empowering teachers to base decisions on reason not habit, and helping establish a strong sense of community where all those with a legitimate interest in the type of schooling afforded students have access to educational discourse.

If we look at horizontal evaluation in its narrowest context, at the teaching level, the outcomes are also desirable, as they make for less alienated teacher work. The dialogic endeavour that marks horizontal evaluation means that the teachers so involved will have a much greater part in determining what is taught how it is taught, and when it is taught than is the case at present. The process requires that those who do the teaching also significantly participate in determining the value, meaning and character of what and how they teach. As this is necessarily a less estranging, more humanizing work context, there is, on this count alone, good reason for its widespread practice.

The ideal of teacher dialogue aimed at understanding holds significant meanings as well for institutions that train teachers. Traditionally the issue in teacher education has been how we can shape teachers by giving them the competencies they need to facilitate established educational goals. An expanded teacher role suggests that the question in teacher education should rather be: "*How can we encourage the conditions necessary for teachers to enter into a dialogue aimed at understanding?*" With this question as the central problematic, the idea of a good teacher is redefined. Now a good teacher is not one who simply demonstrates an ability to restrain classroom chaos and produce high academic results, but one who thoughtfully and consistently engages in a dialogical process of trying to understand what links choices among various means, purposes and aims in teaching. The importance of seeing good teaching this way is that it points to the teacher's part in making history. For, as Gadamer (1984) says, 'Understanding also and above all is a happening and makes history' (p. 41). And we want to be very careful about the kind of educational history we are making.

Notes

1 What we mean by 'educative' is extensively discussed in Chapters 1 and 2.
2 Improved performance does have its place. However, changes in behaviour often leave hierarchical relationships between educators, such as administrators and teachers, in place. As a result, although there is an appearance of change, the constraints and opportunities inherent in one's place in the educational hierarchy remain the same and inhibit communicative action (see Habermas, *Communication and the Evolution of Society*) and school change.
3 It should be noted that horizontal evaluation is unlikely to change all teacher roles. Teachers who have, for example, long-standing racist views may resist discussions of anything other than the techniques. However, if one participant does not share these racist attitudes, challenge statements and communication analysis (the rightness-validity claim) can be used to soften or modify these views. Horizontal evaluation never guarantees a particular result; indeed, our claim is that it opens up possibilities to evaluate and reconsider aims and means.

Chapter 5

'Lived Experiences' in Horizontal Evaluation

Introduction

If we are to take seriously the claim that educative models of evaluation can alter the nature of schooling by enabling teachers to examine educational means and ends, then it is important that we look closely at what influence these alternative approaches have on their 'lived experiences'. In this chapter we do so by analyzing how one such approach, horizontal evaluation, affects teachers' understanding of educational issues and what they do in the classroom.

To gather such data twenty teachers volunteered to use the horizontal evaluation model. For the most part these teachers were quite typical of elementary school teachers in the United States; they represented all grade levels, held a wide range of political beliefs and came from varied socio-economic backgrounds.[1] At the beginning of the 1986–1987 academic year this diverse group of teachers was introduced to the horizontal evaluation model in a workshop. Following the workshop, they broke up into groups of two or three of their own choosing and audiotaped trial runs with the model. At a second group meeting, the transcripts were read and discussed to identify and clear up any problems or uncertainties concerning the use of the model. After the second meeting the teachers began using horizontal evaluation approximately once a month for the eight months remaining in the school year. Thus, each teacher was observed by a peer and acted as the observer eight times over the course of the study. After each observation a post-conference was held and audiotaped by the teachers. Finally, at the year's end, all the teachers were interviewed to obtain their reflections on the evaluation process itself.[2] These interviews were also audiotaped, transcribed and analyzed along with the post-conference transcripts. From the analysis of the evaluative dialogue and teachers' reflections on the process three strong themes emerged: teachers altered their views about evaluation; they challenged both on an ideological level and in practice the prevailing rationality that guides many school practices; and they took some modest steps toward creating a dialogical community. Discussion of these three themes follows.

Changing Views of Teacher Evaluation

Evaluation as Something Done to Teachers

One of the most powerful assumptions held by teachers is that evaluation is something done to them, an assumption justified by common evaluation practices such as the following:

> When he [my principal] does his evaluation, he comes in, he watches me, we sit down and he tells me what I did. I don't have to tell him anything. I don't have to explain why. I don't ever have to say anything to him.

If teachers retain this view when educative forms of evaluation are implemented, they are likely to put on a show for the evaluator and avoid serious discourse. 'New' dialogical approaches will quickly be transformed into hierarchical game-like exercises that resemble the dominant form, unless fundamental assumptions about the nature of evaluation are reconsidered. A review of the transcripts indicates that over time most of the twenty teachers did indeed begin to rethink evaluation. Specifically, they abandoned the notion that evaluation is something done to them and began to see it as an enabling process. The following is typical of their views:

> I think it gives me a new perspective on what I'm doing. I'm more able through talking with someone else to see what I'm doing instead of just doing it. It's something I can almost not explain because you think you know what you're doing but there's so much that is taken-for-granted. But when you sit down and someone asks you why are you doing that, what was your intention, why is it important to you, you really have to think about it. Is that something I've done because it is easier or because I've done it before?

As the teachers changed their views on evaluation, other behaviours which seemed 'natural' within the confines of the dominant approach started to disappear. Specifically, the teachers were more willing to let the observer see commonplace everyday teacher practices.

> With the principal [during evaluation observations] I made sure that my lesson fit the model we were supposed to follow. I'd get my

anticipatory set [the Hunter design for lesson plans] and everything laid out. With horizontal evaluation I wanted it to be more natural in the way I usually do things. Inside I didn't want to be that perfect model like when the principal came in. I wanted to look at myself so I could be evaluating myself.

Teachers' willingness to open their classrooms suggests that they are more likely to resist a socialization pattern that encourages them to put on a show when an evaluator enters the classroom, if evaluative procedures are enabling. This openness also challenges the commonly voiced complaint that teachers do not want to be evaluated. They do want others to examine what they do when the evaluative process is an integral part of teaching, not something imposed on them.

While this openness makes it possible for teachers to have serious discourse on schooling, teachers also have to be willing to push each other and ask hard critical questions if educative approaches are to challenge taken-for-granted notions of schooling. By the end of the study most of the teachers started to see through the public servant tradition (Bullough and Gitlin, 1985) that encourages them to be overly accepting and docile and learned how to raise difficult, critical concerns.

I think one of the things I thought as I listened to the first tape [of a post-conference] was I was very accepting of everything. I just went through and said this is nice, J. I never really got below the surface. From the last tape I felt I was beginning to be able to ask questions better. I learned how to ask the questions that were important that would push her.

By opening their classrooms and asking difficult questions, these teachers were able to rethink prejudgments that act behind their backs to shape what they do. These changes in evaluative behaviour suggest that educative forms of evaluation will only be empowering if teachers see the process as an integral part of their teaching.

Evaluator as Fault-Finder

The dominant tradition in teacher evaluation also assumes that the evaluator is the fault-finder and the observed teacher is the needy recipient. As long as these roles are taken-for-granted evaluation will be monological, hierarchical and ultimately oppressive to teachers. Furthermore, the process will do little or nothing to enhance teachers' self-understanding or understanding of schooling. An encouraging aspect of this study is that teachers over time saw through these oft-times taken-for-granted roles and acted in ways to develop a more reciprocal arrangement where both participants questioned one another about teaching. What is most striking about the examples that follow is that teachers confronted unforeseen hierarchical tendencies in the horizontal evaluation approach to alter these role boundaries.

When dialogue is based on the observation of only one participant, there is a tendency to have the observer ask all the questions while the other tries to respond. This focus on the observed teacher makes it more likely that the evaluator will act as the grand inquisitor or fault-finder. To overcome this problematic aspect of the horizontal evaluation process, teachers on their own accord decided to combine two post-conferences. By doing so, the post-conference dialogue reflected the observations of both participants, and neither teacher felt obligated to ask the bulk of the questions.

> [toward the end of the experience], we would dialogue without the boundaries of I will interview you and you respond to my questions. All of a sudden those boundaries disappeared and we just started talking about things in common . . . justifying why we did those kinds of things. Or not justifying but saying maybe we shouldn't be doing those kinds of things. Why do we fill our time with this? Is it really teaching that we're doing when we are doing that?

Another indication that the teachers had started to rethink the traditional evaluator/observed teacher role was the establishment of common topics for discussion at the end of a post-conference for the next session. What follows is a brief example of this sort of joint agenda setting.

> [*Observer*] Is there anything you want to think about in terms of next time so this has some continuity?

> [*Teacher*] It would be helpful if we could figure out a way to not check students verbally on whether they listen.

> [*Observer*] Or another possibility is the thing about wait time. Maybe you could record me giving instructions.

In the following post-conference the teachers focused on both giving instructions and checking students in non-verbal ways.

These actions suggest that the teachers were no longer content to accept the traditional role of the evaluator and the observed teacher. They took steps, as a consequence, to correct what were hierarchical tendencies in the model. The teachers were not prisoners to an approach but rather transformed the approach where necessary, to further educative interests.

In sum, the teachers started to rethink what is evaluation. They did so by putting into sharper focus the limits of traditional forms of evaluation, seeing value in educative forms, and casting aside patterns of interaction that constrain the potential empowering effects of such approaches. Clearly, teachers' resistance to traditional forms of evaluation is not simply an attempt to close their doors and be left alone. Teachers want to examine critically what they do and why they do it. And if given the opportunity to do so, they can begin to challenge taken-for-granted views and practices hidden within the fabric of classroom life. What follows are examples of how teachers initiated such a process of educative school change.

Challenging Technocratic Mindedness

Teachers' actions are often constrained by the powerful influence of taken-for-granted forms of rationality. Of particular concern is a form of rationality Bullough, Goldstein and Holt (1984) refer to as technocratic-mindedness, where:

> value issues—those in the realms of the social, the political, the ethical and the educational—get reduced to technical questions. The concern is not what should be done but rather how it can be done. (p. 7)

When this type of mindedness dominates, the teacher role is limited to finding ways to facilitate expert determined ends. In this situation teachers often do not see the political nature of school problems and instead focus on more technical concerns such as how to get information across to students, how to raise test scores, and how to control the classroom so that information can be delivered to students.

This limited teacher role is evident in Willis' (1977) ethnography of a working class school. The teachers in this school focus exclusively on how to keep the 'lads' under their control and therefore cannot see how their actions and those of the lads are part of a reproductive process where working class kids are filtered into working-class jobs. If teachers are to confront injustices of this kind, they must escape the grip of technocratic-mindedness. While doing so will not *assure* particular practices, moving beyond the technical makes it possible for teachers to act on these hidden dimensions of schooling. Put differently, challenging technocratic-mindedness allows teachers to 're-experience the ordinary' and see ways to act where previously there were none (Shor, 1980). They are no longer 'submerged in life with no possibility of emerging from it' (Freire, 1985, p. 68), but can begin to make their own existence.

> Unlike men, animals are simply in the world, incapable of objectifying themselves or the world . . . Men, on the contrary who can sever this adherence and transcend being in the world, add to the life they have the existence which they make. (p. 69)

The 'lived experiences' of the teachers in this study indicate that they moved beyond a technical framework and started to pose problems that examined political, ethical and moral dimensions of schooling.

Posing Problems

For many teachers the issue of classroom management is foremost in their mind. Unfortunately, the assumptions and values underlying the 'problem' are often not addressed and discussion is limited to the instrumental concern of how the teacher can control a class of students. What is ignored in this quest for control are questions about the desirability of this hierarchical teacher/student relation, as well as alternative explanations of student behaviour that consider the ways that seemingly disruptive actions can be a response to alienating school practices. By posing problems that went beyond the technical, the teachers began to assess these taken-for-granted aspects of classroom management.

One group of teachers started such a process by looking closely at an observed practice, the use of a reward system:

> When you planned out the afternoon you decided on a reward system for the [students]. Is that because they have been responding to a reward system?

By asking why the teacher decided to use a reward system, some of the values underlying this decision emerged. It became apparent that the reward system was a compromise between two concerns. On the one hand, the teacher was worried about having enough supervision for the students:

> That's [using the reward system] because I knew there were only two coppers [volunteer parents] there. I was just afraid that there wasn't going to be enough supervision . . . Also the sad truth is that kids respond to external rewards.

On the other hand, she wanted students to complete their work because they enjoyed the activity and wanted to learn:

> I want them to realize internal motivation. Moving from completing work for some kind of reward or recognition to completing work for the sake that it feels good and there is learning.

At first blush, the use of the reward system suggests that internal motivation had been sacrificed to maintain control over students. On closer inspection, however, the teachers came to the conclusion that underlying the concern for internal motivation was the need to have students complete their work. By assessing this assumption, it became clear that the need for completed work was another more subtle way for teachers to control students. And the 'cost' of this subtle form of control was not only internal motivation but the quality of the students' work.

> That's one of my dilemmas. I find myself thinking, now, am I doing this just so kids have something to do. Sometimes I trade off quality for that busy kind of work.

At this point in the discourse the teachers had arrived at a new problematic: the desirability of practices that enable teachers to control what students do. To explore this problem further, the observer used communication analysis, an aspect of the horizontal evaluation process, to clarify what the other participant meant by quality work. Although the participants did not come up with a precise definition, they realized that forms of control often obscure concern for the quality of students' work.

> When I say to students if you do these three things you will get extra recess, the natural consequence is that students will dash to all three tables as fast as they can and get the work done. That must have gone through my head at some point because that is when I said, now, what does it mean to spend quality time at those places?

By going beyond a technical view of classroom management, teachers were able to see how their prejudgments, such as the emphasis on completed work, reinforced a hierarchical teacher/student relation. Teachers also examined the appropriateness of this relation by considering how 'worries' about supervision often stood in the way of having students do quality work and developing internal motivation. This understanding of management empowered teachers to reshape school experiences based on articulated and debated educational ends as opposed to the taken-for-granted assumption that teachers need to have control over students.

Teachers, however, did not always escape the grip of technocratic-mindedness. In several post-conferences, for example, the discourse started with a technical concern. Fortunately, as the participants explored the issue in more depth, this techical orientation often gave way to questions about the desirability and importance of particular educational ends.

In one instance, the observed teacher was interested in seeing 'how *much* cooperative learning I can use in lots of different subject areas'. This issue seemed to express a value commitment on the part of the teacher, however, she admitted that, 'I don't think I've really ever thought about what I was doing'. In other words, the teacher had assumed that cooperative learning was worthwhile and was initially only interested in how to implement such a process. What seemed to be hindering the implementation of cooperative learning for this teacher was the perception on the part of many students that sharing was the same as cheating.

> I've had some problems with cooperative learning in the past because the kids in the sixth grade have not had a chance to work together. I think they see cooperative learning as cheating in a lot of ways. Somehow they think sharing answers is some kind of cheating.

In response to this technical problem the teacher decided to 'have [students] answer these exactly together'. In other words, to counter the notion that you are cheating when you work together, the teacher made 'cheating' a requirement by insisting that students share their views and write down exactly the same words in response to a particular question. Instead of simply analyzing whether this strategy 'works', the participants turned this type of technical question on its head and discussed what intention(s) such a strategy would satisfy.

> One of the questions I had as I was going around, because I noticed your response to several of them was, 'is it exactly word for word'. What was the intention behind that?

By doing so, the dialogue that followed centred on what is cooperative learning and its importance as an educational aim.

> I guess this takes us back to why would you do cooperative learning. Why is it important to do in the first place? I think the important thing is that we are telling kids that they have the responsibility for each other. Sometimes students have to put behind what they want and think of someone else.

This debate enabled teachers to escape an exclusive focus on finding ways to get more cooperative learning into the classroom and pose problems, about the appropriateness of this learning process. By posing such problems the teachers challenged not only technocratic-mindedness but the legitimacy of a teacher role which is limited to making faddish innovations 'work'. Questioning this limited role enabled teachers to act on such schemes and, to refer back to Freire's (1985) words, 'add to the life they have the existence they make' (p. 69).

Going beyond the Classroom Context

Technocratic-mindedness does more than encourage teachers to see problems in terms of how to achieve taken-for-granted ends; it also frames problems within the context of the classroom. When technocratic-mindedness is used as a lens to view schooling, more fundamental issues which cut across classrooms are not addressed. The 'lived experiences' of these teachers indicate that they challenged this narrowing of educational concerns by posing problems about the teacher role and school programmes.

Questions about the teacher role became the focus of discourse when one participant asked if teachers should be role models.

> I never thought about that. Well clearly the kids see me in that way . . . I think they put an importance on that. But when I think of the kids I see just the opposite. They seem like a role model to me. I tell them that . . . More than anything it [being a role model] makes me nervous because there is such diversity. Again it comes back to the question I have of the difference between talking to one human

being and dealing with five groups. I have one kid who is raised in a liberal open household and another in a conservative one. Somehow I have to temper my own feelings in a way that will be understandable to both of those kids.

By raising this issue, the teachers were able to look closely at the teacher role and, importantly, begin to see how their prejudgments help shape that role. In particular, the participants explored the expressed view that a teacher should treat a student who comes from a conservative family differently than a student who comes from a liberal family. Once clarified, this prejudgment is examined further: 'Do you think that the kids on either extreme could not take your honesty about the subjects?' To which the teacher replies:

I think they [students] can but its the parents who can't take it. So I suspect it's not so much the kids. This is really amazing to hear myself say this. I guess I'm more concerned with parents.

Discourse that started with the question of a teacher as a role model brought to the fore two prejudgments: the differing political persuasions of the students' families are thought to require varied responses from the teacher; and parents will not accept the teacher's sincere opinions on a subject. By making these prejudgments problematic, this teacher is no longer submerged in a role but can help form that role by rethinking these taken-for-granted views. As Rizvi (1986) argues in a different context:

We have to begin from where we are, but first we have to determine where that is . . . Self-reflection of this kind is indeed empowering, for it enables us to become ethically aware of the forms and the consequences of our linguistic practices. (p. 161)

The teachers also posed problems that went beyond the classroom context by looking carefully at school programmes. In the past, when 'open classroom' teachers talked about their programme they relied on slogans. In one sense these slogans became a substitute for more substantive discourse. It is not surprising that when the teachers seriously addressed programme issues, they were not sure what an open classroom is:

I'm not really sure if I know exactly what an open classroom should look and feel like. But, maybe together we can come up with something we agree upon which will be valuable in understanding the programme better.

To consider this question, they analyzed and explored in more depth some of the educational slogans they had so easily thrown around in the past. One such slogan is the Deweyan notion that school life and 'outside' life should be related. 'It's really important that they [students] integrate their outside school life at school'. Teachers assessed this programme aim when one responded to a query about the importance of linking school life and outside life by saying:

> So does that mean kids should have control of the situation? Where do they take total responsibility for their learning? You said earlier it was hard for you to let them take the time.

The response to this query reveals what Whitehead and Lomax (1987) refer to as a living contradiction. The teacher wants students to have control over the curriculum, but is reluctant to give them this control because of the large amounts of time needed to have students plan the school day.

> It takes me so long just to get the planning over with. Then they [students] are fidgety and sharing doesn't work well.

Another slogan that often is voiced by open classroom teachers is that their classrooms are child-centred. The teachers assessed this slogan by considering the relation between this taken-for-granted programme aim and classroom practice. When they did so, it became clear that much of what happened in the classroom was teacher directed. In fact, one participant suggested that child-centredness was really a cover up for a programme that in practice was teacher-centred. 'I think underneath [the open classroom] is very teacher directed. I think all of our classrooms are'.

To further this discourse the teachers turned to the question of what a child-centred classroom would look like. While they could not come to a consensus, they did agree that the gap between the programme aim and practice was partially due to the difficulty in defining what is child-centred and the external constraints which shape what teachers do.

> A child-centred classroom, first of all, it is a concept that is not easily defined. Second, I think it's a concept that is difficult to work with in its pure form given that we work in a public school and have these external constraints and limitations that we operate under.

Exposing the way slogans often act to legitimate an array of practices encouraged the participants to consider in what ways, if any, the open classroom differs from more traditional classrooms.

> That's one of my questions about the open classroom. What kind of decisions do we let kids make? What kind of responsibility does that develop? That's all in the name of what end? And how different are we from more traditional classrooms?

Discourse on these educational slogans enabled teachers to consider carefully what is an open classroom programme. Posing these broad problems illuminated 'living contradictions' as well as tensions between programme aims and classroom realities. Once illuminated, teachers as a group could rethink taken-for-granted practices based on an examination of what are desirable programme aims. By posing problems which went beyond the classroom context, these teachers set before them a cluster of previously unexplored problems. These problems are important not only because they challenge the limiting effects of technocratic-mindedness but also because they create a bridge or a common terrain for teachers to discuss valuative issues that go beyond the confines of one or two classrooms. As one teacher noted:

> Questions and issues were raised that I don't think I would have come to on my own. I think it was helpful to talk about issues that are common across the teaching profession, issues that are not just specific to the classroom.

These teachers no longer have to accept uncritically 'expert' determinations about what is a good teacher, or a programme for that matter, for they have generated a kind of practitioner knowledge (Smyth, 1987) which empowers them to dialogue with supposed experts, teachers and others about these common issues. With this practitioner knowledge, teachers can reshape their own classrooms and contribute in important ways to school debates that focus on issues that go beyond the classroom context.

Acting-on-Understanding

To continue our discussion of how teachers challenged technocratic-mindedness, we turn now to the ways teachers acted on their understanding of schooling. By doing so, we present a more complete picture of what might be referred to as the 'cycle of educative change', where teachers reflect on practice, act on those reflections, and then assess once again the new practices. Illuminating the linkage between understanding and action also shows how teachers are able to avoid the trap of verbalism where individuals continuously reflect without ever acting, and activism where individuals act without any sort of reflection (Freire, 1972). Avoiding such traps is an essential part of educative school change because those who reflect without action can not alter schooling, and those who act without reflection are likely to support the status quo by facilitating taken-for-granted educational views and practices.

Unfortunately, teachers often fall into the trap of activism because the fast pace of schooling makes it difficult for teachers to find time to reflect. And when they do find the time, these efforts are rarely rewarded (Gitlin, 1983). Many practices, as a consequence, tend to remain unchanged because the assumptions underlying them are taken-for-granted. One of these commonplace aspects of schooling is the 'banking' approach to teaching. Within this approach students are viewed as a commodity or raw product to be finished. To 'finish' the product the teacher attempts to fill their heads with what is assumed to be appropriate school knowledge.

The 'banking' approach has dramatic consequences for students and teachers alike. For students, the process effectively silences them; teachers need not ask what they think, or enquire whether the deposited information has anything to do with their actual experiences. On the other hand, because the teacher is primarily concerned with finding ways to deposit these seemingly important bits of information, the political aspects of schooling often remain hidden. The 'banking view' sets up the same type of alienating, oppressive relations between teachers and students that we have argued throughout this book characterize the relation between teachers and supposed experts. Students are not only denied access to the educational process, but teachers are locked into a technocratic view that makes it difficult, if not impossible, for them to see inequalities and injustices of all kinds.

By posing problems that went beyond the limits of technocratic-mindedness, teachers in this study were able to 'see through' and act on the 'banking' approach to teaching. Specifically, they challenged common-place student and teacher roles, as well as the structures that support these role boundaries. Before describing these actions it is important to note that what follow are the teachers' impressions of the way their practice changed; it is not an actual accounting of those events by the authors of this text.

The Student Role

A good student, from the perspective of a teacher trying to deposit information, is one who impedes this process as little as possible. Behaviours that give teachers control of the learning process, therefore, tend to be most valued. While we can surely agree that chaos benefits no one, an emphasis on control often conceals the difference between a quiet student and one who is passive; a busy student and one who is learning; and more importantly, an obedient student and one who is involved in an educative process. An emphasis on control also obscures consideration of the more political aspects of schooling. This seems to be the case for the teachers in Weis' (1985) ethnography of a black community college. Because the teachers spent most of their time making sure that students were on time and attending regularly, they did not pay much attention to the way the school curriculum forced blacks to choose between their cultural values and the values of the school. An emphasis on control not only shifted teachers' gaze from the political but limited their ability to act on this important aspect of schooling.

Because the teachers who used horizontal evaluation had an opportunity to reflect on practice, they were able to see beyond the aim of control and act on some assumptions associated with a 'banking view' of teaching. In one case a teacher confronted the notion that a good student is one who is quiet, docile and obedient by viewing this assumption in relation to her stated aim: to develop cooperative learning. After much dialogue the teacher acted on this understanding and introduced activities where students could talk and learn from one another.

> I work well with a quiet classroom. So when I do activities that the children should be able to talk and move around I often don't let them go on long enough. I think I've tried to stretch that a little because I realized that cutting them off I wasn't reaching my intent to develop cooperative learning.

The emphasis on depositing information also encourages teachers to be concerned with keeping students on-task. The more time on-task, the greater the likelihood that the information will be deposited in the heads of students. But the fact that students are on-task says nothing about the desirability of the task itself. By asking questions about the worth of the activity, one teacher could see that her learning centres kept students busy but had little educational import. Over the course of the school year she shifted her focus from developing activities that would keep students busy to developing activities that had more educational value.

> After talking with him [peer observer] I looked at those [learning centres] a little more closely and I remember I changed the content. I developed activities that would accomplish some sort of goal so there wasn't as many time fillers, so that there was a little more educational value.

The 'banking' view is also inherently authoritarian because all educational decisions rest with the teacher. At the beginning of the study many teachers saw students through this authoritarian lens and expected them to obey their directives without question. One teacher expressed this common sentiment this way:

> I assumed that kids ought to listen to me when I say they shouldn't fight because it's not the thing to do, they shouldn't question that.

At the end of the study this same teacher was able to see the limits of this authoritarian relation. Specifically, she noted that silencing students made it difficult for her to understand their actions. And without this understanding she often imposed rules on all students regardless of the particular circumstances.

> There was really a lot of good reason for her to question that [teacher's rule about no fighting] because that's what her family does immediately. I was asking her to do something that was completely alien to her. I had no idea.

With these implications in mind, the teacher decided to establish more dialogical relations with students and allow their explanations to influence decisions about schooling. Educative relations started to replace more authoritarian ones that are so much a part of the 'banking' approach to teaching. The teacher put it like this:

> That's [the experience with this student] happened more than once. Now we [student and teacher] sit down and talk about the 'whys' of what is going on. Not just me saying you will not fight because it is a school rule.

In all these examples teachers confronted taken-for-granted notions of a good student that are defined by a 'banking view' of pedagogy. They no longer designed activities and interacted with students primarily to keep them quiet, docile and on-task but rather provided experiences and responded to them in terms of desired educational ends. While teachers surely could have taken this process further in exploring the political, ethical and moral dimensions of schooling, they did begin to establish more educative relations with students.

The Teacher Role

A 'banking' approach to teaching not only helps define the student role in narrow ways, it also puts limits on the teacher role. Because the teacher needs to deposit these bits of information, a direct teaching approach, where learning is viewed as a one-way process from teacher to student, becomes the preferred way to teach. To do otherwise is to chance that the 'right' content will not be taught and that the concerns of students may impede the efficient flow of information. Through dialogue one teacher was able to assess this taken-for-granted part of the teaching role, see its limitations and act to expand her role boundaries.

> I was a direct teacher. In fact, I was upset with the kids if they got ahead of me. I thought that if they turned the page before I did they would spoil the surprise, as if everything had to be anticipated. Now students help determine what we are learning, what is important. If they get to it before the rest of us then they have the responsibility to explain it to the rest of us so that we are all learning from one another.

Another teacher who for years had only used a direct method of teaching came to a similar conclusion and decided to try activities that were more child-centred.

> I have done some different things this year. More child-centred things than in the past. I took a little more risk and left some of the safer things back. Some of the things I knew that worked I said, 'Okay, I'll let this go and we will try something else and see what happens'.

The importance of these changes is not that child-centred approaches are better in some universal sense but rather that these teachers could see possible ways to act where previously there had been none. These possibilities became apparent because discourse pointed to the limitations of a 'banking' approach for teacher and student roles. Acting on this understanding allowed teachers to contest role boundaries that are often formed when ideological positions, such as those associated with a 'banking view', become taken-for-granted.

School Structures

Unfortunately, challenging a 'banking' approach to teaching requires more than teachers acting on taken-for-granted ideological views such as those associated with the teacher and the student role. Teachers also need to act on those structures that encourage them to adopt a 'banking' approach to teaching.

One structure that deflects attention from questions of what should be taught, while increasing the importance of finding ways to get that information across to students, is the textbook. This structure is especially powerful when the information in textbooks is linked to a standardized test. Under these circumstances many teachers assume that all they can do is follow the text and deposit information in the heads of students. To do otherwise is thought to penalize students, they fear. The evaluative process helped one teacher realize that the structure need not force her into a 'banking' approach to teaching. She could act on this structure and insert activities that reflected concerns about what should be taught without penalizing her students.

> Before, I stuck to the textbook and the curriculum that was available because I thought that was the only way you could do it to get students to pass the test or what ever criteria was being used. Using this method [horizontal evaluation] I realized I could do things I always wanted to do and still get the results. Things that I have been spending nine years worrying about took care of themselves when I let myself do the lessons I always wanted to do and not depend so heavy on the text.

Another structure that encourages teachers to utilize a 'banking' approach to teaching is the rationalized curriculum which lays out a set of sequential objectives and tests students on each. Because the objectives for what to teach are predetermined, teachers are likely to spend most of their time finding ways to get this information across to students. When this structure was assessed as part of the horizontal evaluation process, the teachers became critical of the information they were attempting to deposit in the heads of students. Specifically, they objected to the 'product' orientation and decided to insert activities that were more 'process' oriented. By doing so, they resisted the way this school structure shaped their behaviour.

> I thought I wanted to go through *Art Is Elementary* and do all the lessons . . . I was really concerned with the product rather than the process. Then I thought, maybe it's more important just to have students enjoy art than to get through all the elements. I decided those things were more important than getting through *Art Is Elementary*. After we got to that point [in the post-conferences] I'd have students just draw outlines just looking at the shapes, etc.

School- or district-mandated discipline systems such as assertive discipline (Canter, 1979) also can have a dramatic influence on what teachers do. Based on behaviour modification techniques, assertive discipline instructs the teacher to ignore a student when they misbehave and simply put their name on the board. In advance of this procedure, the teacher makes clear that so many checks will result in particular punishments. Teachers do not have to stop the class to respond to negative behaviour and yet students know they are off-task. This approach furthers the interests of a 'banking' approach to teaching by silencing students, viewing them as a commodity and reinforcing a hierarchical relation between teachers and students. When the implications of this taken-for-granted management system were examined in a post-conference, the seductiveness of teacher control became less appealing and one teacher decided to replace this system with a more 'intrinsic approach'.

> I was using assertiveness discipline. M. [peer observer] came in and just said, 'Why is that important? What does it do?' I just had to explain what it did. I am making these kids work for rewards. I realized they aren't going to work for anything unless I give them a reward. Just talking about it I thought this is crazy. Why am I doing this? On the audiotape I didn't come to a conclusion. But later I kept thinking about it. That's right, they are only doing this for a reward. I've got to stop this right now. So I haven't done it since the conference. I don't have the control that I had but I'm using an approach I believe in. Next year I will start from the beginning with a more intrinsic approach.

Posing problems that challenged technocratic-mindedness and acting on this understanding enabled teachers to confront one of the most deeply entrenched aspects of teaching, the 'banking' view. They did so by contesting taken-for-granted teacher and student roles as well as the structures that reinforced those roles. By the end of the study it became clear to some teachers that this 'banking' approach turned teachers into managers and record keepers. To begin 'teaching' again they had to make decisions on what to teach as well as how to teach.

> Because I was never asking myself or questioning myself about what I was doing I just started doing things that I was told to do. It was like I was losing all my power of decision-making . . . I was

becoming such a record-keeper. Not teaching anymore. I feel like a lot of us are not teaching anymore. I honestly feel like after having done a lot of discussing and looking at teaching I'll throw away the percentage chart [the chart used to show how many students had reached a particular objective within the rationalized curriculum] whether the district thinks that's real important or not.

Toward a Dialogical Community

If educative change is to influence the nature of schooling, not just what happens in a few classrooms, the dialogue started among individual teachers must expand to include all those with a legitimate interest in education. This is so for at least two reasons. First, changes in a few classrooms can be accommodated by most schools without altering in any fundamental way the nature of schooling. Only when teachers act collectively are they likely to influence the powerful ideologies and structures which help define the educational process. Second, individual teachers can trade places with others on the school hierarchy, but they cannot challenge the hierarchy itself. This can only occur when a dialogical community is created; where teachers form alliances with others such that change is based on the strongest reasons for a particular view of education, reasons which take into consideration the moral, ethical and political nature of schooling.

Clearly, using horizontal evaluation did, not establish such a community. It did however, help a few teachers confront ideological barriers that make a dialogical community unlikely. One such barrier is that teachers often view themselves in competition with each other. If teachers are not willing to have discourse with each other, surely the process is not going to spread to other members of the community. Several teachers confronted the ideology of competitiveness and saw the need to develop more collaborative relations.

There's this feeling in teaching that you're stealing my idea or you don't want to share because then you won't be as good or someone will be better than you. We are in the same boat so why not work together instead of worrying so much about being better than someone else or superior or out on your own island so to speak.

Teachers also started to develop more dialogical relations with parents. Teachers often react defensively with parents for the same reasons they do not want other teachers to observe their classrooms; they are unsure about what they do, and get little or no feedback. After assessing each other for a year the teachers were better able to communicate what they were doing to others and more willing to involve parents in dialogue about educational issues.

> In a way it [horizontal evaluation] has made me more able to tell them what my intentions are. I have had more practice saying this is what my intention is. It is important because . . . I have had more experience saying that. I think I can communicate with parents better.

Some teachers also included students in discourse about the type of education offered in schools. For one teacher this even applied to first year students.

> When we start a project or something I'll say: Now why are we doing this? What is it for? How is it going to help us? What kinds of things do you want to learn from it? You'd think first graders are not capable of this, at least I always thought that. But they come up with questions and some ideas that I would never consider.

In other instances teachers actually extended the educative process beyond those in the study. Several teacher leaders, who were required to evaluate other teachers, used the horizontal evaluation process in place of the suggested district check list. They did so because the district form created divisions between the participants which limited discourse on educational ideas. When one teacher switched to the horizontal process, she described the change in her relations with other teachers this way:

> I was on the career ladder but I'd be observing people who are at least as good as me at teaching and who didn't get the opportunity then to come back and evaluate me. So, right away I was in a different position from them. Now I'm more open to all teachers. All their ideas become valuable. I confronted the vertical structure that's set up.

Another teacher leader took this process a step further and actually required that the teachers she observed also observed her. This change in the evaluative procedure allowed both participants to speak their mind and be more straightforward about their impressions.

> I feel like it has helped me as a teacher leader. It put me on the same level of a peer rather than someone coming in there, assigned by the principal, as a superior, to watch what they were doing. There was a genuine comfort level. The teachers could point out things to me. Real good things. I don't think they objected to me making comments to them as a result.

Other teachers played a part in extending the evaluative process by writing for a research grant to pay for substitute teachers and therefore enable more teachers to get out of the classroom and use horizontal evaluation. They summarized their proposal by saying:

We have barely scratched the surface of making effective use of this method. We would like to develop further in this method of peer evaluation. In fact we would like to share some of our experiences with colleagues. For this purpose we are applying for financial assistance and administrative support from XXX district.

In all these cases the teachers began to rethink the legitimacy of the school hierarchy and establish more educative relations where reasoned discourse is the basis for decision-making. While this change in school relations was partial and far from conclusive, the educative relations experienced by the teachers in this study seemed to encourage them to set up similar relations with other members of the school community. What is significant about these changes is that the teachers championed the process without outside incentive or help. The changes, therefore, are likely to avoid faddish comings and goings, and have a more long lasting effect.

The lived experiences of these teachers indicate that educative forms of teacher evaluation made it possible for them to challenge educational practices and views that are often accepted without question and act on this understanding of schooling. Specifically, teachers reconsidered the commonplace notion that evaluation is a monological process where supposed experts try to find fault in what teachers do and instead viewed evaluation as an enabling process. By thinking about evaluation in this way, they opened up their classrooms and asked critical questions of each other which would empower them to act on taken-for-granted aspects of schooling. They also escaped a narrow technocratic view of schooling by posing problems which considered the political, ethical and moral aspects of schooling. Teachers who acted on this understanding reshaped an array of practices which reflect a 'banking' approach to teaching. Finally, by extending the evaluative process beyond those in the study, they took some modest initial steps to confront the school hierarchy and establish a more dialogical community. In sum, reasoned discourse about the aims and means of schooling started a process of educative school change that penetrated deeply entrenched hierarchical and authoritarian school practices.

Notes

1 A background questionnaire indicates that nine participants thought of themselves as conservative, seven liberal, and one a left wing radical. Eight teachers indicated that their family background was working class, while the others described their background as middle class.
2 Post-interview questions include:
Why did you get involved in the peer evaluation project?
If you had an opportunity to continue using the model next year, would you?
Was the experience worthwhile? If so, in what ways?

What about the other side? What were the disadvantages of the process?
In what ways could it be improved?
What effect, if any, did the horizontal evaluation process have on your beliefs about teaching?
What effect, if any, did horizontal evaluation have on your teaching style?
What effect, if any, has horizontal evaluation had on what you do in the classroom?
What effect, if any, has horizontal evaluation had on your relations with teachers, parents, administrators, etc.?
Has the horizontal process changed over the year?
Is there anything else you want to say about the experience?

Chapter 6

'Critical' Perspectives in Clinical Supervision[1]

Introduction

In this chapter our focus is upon the process of clinical supervision (Goldhammer, 1969) which we see as another exemplar of how the educative approach to teacher evaluation canvassed so far in this book might actually work. In the years since it began at Harvard University in the 1960s, clinical supervision has had a chequered history and has taken on a variety of meanings and interpretations, some of them not particularly flattering to teachers. We start with a brief discussion of the legacy of clinical supervision and its ideals. Rather than separating the conceptual features of clinical supervision from its historical development, we have chosen to treat them as being inextricably connected to the key ideas of one of its early and most ardent supporters, Robert Goldhammer. The view of clinical supervision we present is, therefore, one that we believe is a continuation and elaboration of the tradition started with the pioneering work of Goldhammer (1969). We discuss the history and suggest how subsequent attempts have not only lost the intent of the model, but present an overly narrow and technical view of clinical supervision.

We try to recapture the lost tradition by proposing a 'critical' view of what clinical supervision might mean. We are not using the term 'critical' in the sense of being negative, carping or disapproving. What we have in mind is Apple's (1975) view of 'a painful process of radically re-examining our current positions and asking pointed questions about the relationship that exists between these positions and the social structures from which they arise' (p. 127).

In searching for alternatives to dominant forms of teacher evaluation, we elaborate in the second part of this chapter upon how what started out as a process with emancipatory potential became twisted and tarnished, as 'converts' like Hunter (1980a) have appropriated the ideas for narrow instrumental ends (Smyth, 1986a). Discussion is not so much in terms of personalities, for that would be too restrictive—rather, we portray the co-option of clinical supervision as part of a wider deliberate agenda within the so-called 'reform movement' in schooling, to reclaim power from teachers and schools and invest it in the hands of the State. We discuss the awesome nature and extent of the forces that are currently at work reversing the advances some teachers have made over the past couple of decades in regaining control over their work. In the final section of this chapter, we argue that processes like clinical supervision (in the revisited form we suggest here) can help re-build fractured and demoralized school communities by enabling teachers to develop schools into informed and critical communities. We believe that this can best occur when a systematic and sequential process of enquiry (similar in many respects to the phased model of pre-observation conference, observation, analysis, post-observation conference and post-conference analysis of Goldhammer's) is followed. The version we intend discussing later incorporates the following:

(a) problematizing teaching
(b) observing teaching and creating text
(c) confronting biography and history
(d) re-focusing and action

The collaborative, questioning and problem-posing possibilities fostered in the subsequent clinical supervision relationship, when pairs of teachers work together in establishing dialogical communities, are precisely the kind of arrangement that fosters fundamental changes in the pedagogical nature of teachers' work. Our central claim is that clinical supervision, conceived and enacted as we describe it here, can actually amount to a form of teacher resistance (Giroux, 1983) which confronts hierarchical and exploitative forms of teacher evaluation. While this result may be far from guaranteed, we believe that the particular view of clinical supervision discussed offers some hope for the re-construction of what has become a desultory practice. It is the discussion of those possibilities we want to turn to now.

Beginnings

Although clinical supervision, had its beginnings at Harvard University in the 1950s as a reputed form of teacher collaboration (and continues to be used in the USA, as well as in Australia, England and elsewhere), Anderson (1986) was not wrong when he said: 'adrenalin flows . . . in almost all discussions of clinical supervision, (p. 17). Looking back over the forty year history of clinical supervision it is hard not to regret that the choice of language had been different. In everyday usage the term 'clinical' conjures up pathological images because of its association with medical matters, and the feeling that at minimum there is a deficiency (or a disease) that has to be remedied. Much of the confusion and ambiguity surrounding the term dissipates when we accept that *in this context* it refers to the classroom-based process of teachers making sense of and beginning to challenge the complexity, contradictions and uncertainties that characterize teaching. Clinical supervision was clearly intended to empower teachers to engage one another in discussion, observation and analysis of teaching '. . . in the clinic of the classroom' (Wilhelms, 1973, p. ix). What Goldhammer (1964) was proposing was that teachers confront their distorted perceptions and inaccurate memories, along with those sources within the culture and from within themselves that tend to bias those perceptions (p. 26). In being sensitive to the limits and the potential of human autonomy, he proposed that we '. . . break away from [our] histories in order that [we] may have more viable futures . . . [What we need is] a revolution, through knowledge and study, of the influences that have shaped [us] and of [our] power to exercise rational control over them..' (p. 27). Goldhammer was in a sense arguing for a form of democratic practitioner research, based on 'educative' principles that were entrenched in 'reason'.

Problematizing Teaching

Goldhammer believed in the 'intellectual' and 'educative' nature of the teaching act, and of the way in which this should be reflected, not only in relationships with students but in the way teachers interact with one another and how they view teaching differently as a consequence. For him teaching is a tantalizing process of problem posing with on-going probing and questioning, such that new levels of understanding and action are always being sought.

To take an illustration (Smyth, 1987c) of what his notion of problematizing teaching might look like, we cite the example of two teachers who were using a clinical supervision relationship to focus on the actions of a 'quiet and withdrawn' student in the class. The text they created about this teaching revealed that this supposedly quiet child did a lot of muttering to herself. Curious about this muttering child who appeared to be engaged in work-related activities, they extended their observations to include a range of students across the ability range. The muttering was a prevalent practice, but there was a pattern to it. In the teacher's words:

> Our initial conclusions were that *able* students verbalized problems to clarify them; *not so able* students discuss their problems with a neighbour; and *weak* students rely almost entirely on the teacher for support and legitimation. For example:
> 'Six plus four *must* equal ten' (able student to self).
> 'Are you sure six plus four equals ten?' (less able student to neighbour).
> 'Miss, I think six plus four equals ten. Is that right?' (weak student to teacher).

Having engaged in this observation, analysis and dialogue, teacher and colleague issued a joint challenge to the widespread view that to be on-task students need to be silent. They said:

> If our theory is correct it has some very serious implications for teachers who demand total silence, or for remedial teachers who put struggling students in isolated situations so they won't interrupt, or cannot be interrupted by others . . . While the validity of our conclusion can be questioned, the increase in our own knowledge of how some students learn is supported by our evidence. (p. 47)

What this example highlights is something important about the relationship between reflection and practice, and how teachers can actively intervene in their own teaching so as to challenge the conventional wisdom of established practices. Their hunch about a 'withdrawn' student was quickly dismissed as they became involved in the wider question of what their observation told them about how young children learn, and how this contradicts general theories upon which teaching is often based. Most significant is the fact that their teaching led them to the point of suggesting alternative courses of action.

Implicit in Goldhammer's scheme was a particular view of the relationship between theory and practice in teaching. He was concerned with what Fay (1977, 1987) has more recently described as an 'educative' view, referred to earlier in this book. According to Fay (1977), to work in 'educative' ways is to have people recognize that repressive and frustrating social conditions exist ' . . . at least partly because people are systematically unclear about their needs and the nature of their social relationships' (p. 206). The claim is that by acquiring knowledge about themselves and their cultural domains, people are able to re-think the extent of their own implication in repressive and self-destructive practices and begin to see where more fulfilling changes might be possible. The intent is to aid people 'who are objects in the world, in transforming themselves into active subjects who are self-determining' (p. 210). This is in contrast to an instrumental conception of theory and practice which is 'rooted in the conviction that there are certain sets of naturally recurring general regularities which can be used to achieve one's purposes . . . ' (Fay, 1977, p. 203).

In his work with teachers, Goldhammer (1966) placed a high premium on 'intellectual engagement' (p. 50), by which he meant discouraging dependency and encouraging argumentation, disputation and 'reciprocity . . . such that the gaps in my logic, the faultiness in my thinking, is just as vulnerable to scholarly attack as those in yours' (p. 48). He summed up the kind of intellectualizing he wanted teachers to engage in with these words:

> The vast majority . . . of values and assumptions from which our . . . professional behaviour is governed are implicit. They're inarticulate, they're nebulous, they're buried someplace in our guts

and they're not always very accessible ... We can't always rationalize exactly what we're doing in a classroom as teacher. We can't always make explicit the justifications for the acts which we perpetrate in teaching. Now, I think that one hallmark of the kind of intellectual excellence that I'm talking about ... [is] the major effort [that] must be [made] to bring to conscious awareness the reasons that we have for doing the things that we do as teachers ... Only after these things have been made explicit, have been brought to the point where you can enunciate the damn things, can we begin to value those that seem to have some ... integrity and disregard those that seem to be inane. (1966, p. 49)

When the rhetoric is removed, clinical supervision amounts to ' ... close observation, detailed observational data, face-to-face interaction between ... teacher [and colleague(s)] ... ' (Goldhammer, 1969, p. 54), grounded in a view of the importance of 'inquiry', 'analysis', 'examination', and 'evaluation' that are 'self-initiated and self-regulated' (p. 55). It is a process that regards teaching problematically in that data, collected through observation by a teaching colleague, can be ' ... employed to authenticate the existence of certain problems, to make sure they are real, and as bases for articulating previously undefined problems' (Goldhammer, 1969, p. 62).

The kind of intellectual engagement with teaching that Goldhammer (1966) had in mind came in the form of 'process confrontation' (p. 78); that is to say, the opportunity for teachers, in their interactions with one another about their everyday teaching, to distil from events and patterns those salient characteristics they regard as being problematic. Teachers become involved in 'improvement', not by becoming 'better' but rather by becoming 'different' through ' ... abandon[ing] the comforts of well-worn intellectual and professional habits' (p. 63). In part, adopting a problem-posing stance towards teaching means that teachers obtain a more expansive view of what it means to control their own teaching. Control means self-control, in the sense of opening-up new lines of enquiry that force new issues and generate new directions in teaching: '[Control] is a condition that's in a state of becoming ... Control does not ... necessarily mean the closure of the issue or of relevant issues' (p. 94).

This view about the nature of control, and the ever-present power relationships implicit in teaching, emerges clearly in Goldhammer's views about the need for students themselves to be autonomous in their learning. Where the relationships between teachers and those to whom they are responsible are disabling, Goldhammer sees a strong likelihood of similar stifling pedagogical relationships between teachers and the way they interact with their students. As he put it:

One characteristic of a great many traditional classrooms is that so high a premium is placed upon the right answer to questions asked by the teacher or by the textbook ... that the child comes to live

in a world of answers where answers are sort of like dollar bills . . .
once you get them you've really got something . . . [There] seems
to be a universe of answers that tend to close off things in our lives
rather than to open them . . . [It] can almost be expressed by saying
that . . . in the act of having a question, you're alive. You're alive
because there is a reason for moving, a reason for looking, and that
maybe each time we get an answer we die a little bit because we're
closed off and [are] not impelled to move much. And maybe it
follows [if that's true] . . . that by putting so high a premium on
answers, for the kids, we tend to kill them in the schools . . . at
least intellectually. (p. 95)

Goldhammer does not suggest that the observation and data-gathering role
have to be enacted by a super-ordinate who is wiser, more experienced,
or of higher status than the teacher being observed. On the contrary, he
suggests that one of the intentions of clinical supervision is to enhance
symmetrical relationships between teaching colleagues so as to increase the
likelihood of autonomous teacher action emerging as a consequence of
informed conferral and dialogue. The kind of dependency implicit in
hierarchical relationships was antithetical to Goldhammer's mission. As
Goldhammer, Anderson and Krajewski (1980) put it, the role of the in-class
observer (or colleague) in all of this was:

. . . less a teacher of technique and . . . more a critical dialectician;
a mirror; an occasional collaborator in invention; a handmaiden,
primarily to the teacher's own strategies; a travelling companion
through whatever directions the teacher pursues. (p. 135)

Observing and Creating a Text about Teaching

The commitment of the colleague in clinical supervision is not, therefore,
primarily one of rating or passing judgment, but rather more like that of
a consultant. The role of the colleague is that of helping to create a narrative
or descriptive text about teaching, on the way to assisting the teacher to
penetrate the taken-for-grantedness that surrounds teaching. The colleague
does not come to this task with a tabula rasa to be inscribed with the teacher's
agenda. Both have different histories, assumptions and values about teaching
and the purposes of teaching, that need to be respected, articulated and
clarified in the course of their unpicking of one another's teaching. Built
into the philosophy of clinical supervision was a way of countering
hegemonic tendencies through the notion of reciprocity. What this mouth-
full amounts to in practice is a preparedness on the part of *both parties* to
have their teaching observed, critiqued and reconstructed, if necessary. The
function of text creator (or data-gatherer) is regularly reversed as colleagues
enact the respective role for one another. The presumption is that there

will be regular cycles (to be discussed in some detail below) such that at some times the teaching of one party will be observed, while the colleague acts as data-gatherer and 'critical friend' (Ingvarson, 1986), while on other separate occasions those roles will be switched or reversed. By this means it is possible to avoid what might otherwise be a double standard in preaching asymmetrical power relations, while in fact having what amounts to a hierarchical arrangement where the work of only one party is the object of analysis.

It is to be emphasized that if clinical supervision is to be fundamentally different from other hierarchical forms of evaluation, there must be a regular interchange of roles, such that:

Teacher A - engages in teaching, while -
Teacher B - observes, gathers data and creates text about A's teaching.

And later, on some other occasion:

Teacher B - engages in teaching, while -
Teacher A - observes, gathers data and creates text about B's teaching.

While the role of the observer (colleague) is akin to that of 'another pair of eyes', this is certainly not to suggest that the observer has any kind of monopoly over analyzing what the text means, or how it might be challenged or changed. Both teacher and colleague do that in a context that is characterized by reasoned dialogue. What is important to note is that this must emerge out of the reconstruction of the context of the teaching, that it happens in a convivial environment, and that it is not imposed as a consequence of administrative fiat in an attempt to arrive at some homogeneous standard of teaching. At the same time, questions about whose interests are being served by the process should be open to question and debate.

It is also important to understand that the 'two heads are better than one' notion need not necessarily lead to the parties simply reinforcing one another's professional ideologies and sharing their collective ignorance (Winter, 1987). Nor need it lead to action that is denigrating, or in which people feel they have to be harsh and derogatory about one another's practices. The aim is rather to raise questions about the ideas that sustain practice (Winter, 1987, p. 110), so that a reflective stance is adopted in which more self-evaluative ways of working become increasingly likely. In this sense, clinical supervision is a form of 'assisted self-evaluation' that acknowledges that leaving teachers to their own devices, somehow to mysteriously develop and flourish, is about as unhelpful as forms of close and sanction-ridden surveillance. Teachers need instead a form of collaboration that actively enables them to react intellectually to new ideas, rather than simply acquiescing to them as is so often the case.

The essence of clinical supervision is therefore a 'model' by which teachers can confer with one another in working towards breaking down the disabling isolation and alienation that has come to characterize teaching. But it is a lot more than just a way of promoting idle chatter, or fixing what is wrong in teaching. Because it focuses directly on *pedagogical practice* and on *creating a text* about that practice, it provides an avenue through which teachers can begin to raise pertinent questions about issues to do with equality, justice and morality in teaching and schooling and whose interests are really being served by particular organizational, pedagogical and administrative practices. To that extent, it is a process that is as much about questioning the culture and structure of schooling, as it is with raising questions about the practicalities of teaching. Ritualism, ceremony and habitual observances persist in our teaching and need to be continually scrutinized and questioned. Creating a narrative and generating a descriptive text about a particular shared enactment of teaching provide scope for *conferral* between colleagues focusing on the 'who', 'what' and 'when' of pedagogical practice (i.e., the practicalities of teaching) as well as how these came to be constructed (i.e., the wider culture and structure of schooling).

By way of support for the need to create a text about teaching as a central element to its analysis, Garman (1986) has found that the importance of a 'record of the scenario' or 'stable data' is a crucial pre-requisite in unmasking the agenda within teaching. Where teachers enter into such an analysis of teaching through clinical supervision, she found (Garman, 1983) that they were able to avoid the situation of having to rate one another's performance according to arbitrary criteria.

The Notion of Confrontation

Although he did not use the language of confrontation, Goldhammer was concerned with getting teachers to 'confront' their teaching. By that, we do not mean confrontation in the sense of aggressiveness or hostility—rather we refer to teachers coming face-to-face with the realities of their own teaching. It is the ideals, the practices and their heritage that are being confronted, challenged and questioned rather than the competence of individuals or their personalities. In suggesting that teachers confront themselves and how it is they have come to appropriate certain ideas about teaching, we are suggesting that they move beyond the habitual, the unquestioned and the ritualistic in a way that enables them to see better the social and historical nature of their practices. One way of developing the kind of self-confrontation necessary is to foster a process of systematic description, disclosure and discussion with a trusted colleague. This means that the teacher and colleague become involved in a process of asking questions both about her/himself, as well as about the process of teaching and how it came to be constructed the way it is.

As Goldhammer portrayed it, forms of in-class supervision that amounted to rating teachers ignored the importance of the historical, social and emotional aspects of being and becoming a teacher, because of an absence of 'educational' values. Existing strategies of unco-ordinated one-shot visits into classrooms by people who bore the labels of 'supervisors' were as ineffectual then as they have always been. They failed to get behind the superficialities and the habitualness of classroom practices and were preoccupied with shaping classroom practices according to pre-formulated images of the way teaching 'should be'. There was no sense of teaching developing according to defensible and debatable moral and ethical principles. What was needed instead were processes that transcended the 'economic watchdog' mentality of existing forms of supervision, to ones that acknowledged the importance of classroom-based face-to-face dialogue between teachers about the nature of their work and the social, political and economic conditions that sustain and frustrate it. This meant enhancing an understanding of the social nature of the teaching act, and of how it related to and was a part of much broader economic and political life. Because schooling is about shaping and controlling the lives of the young by those who wield power, then schooling is heavily imbued with economic and political agenda, disclosed or otherwise.

Goldhammer's vision was to free teachers from the threatening, hierarchical, autocratic and administratively-bound contexts of traditional forms of supervision, by enabling them to see, through reason and argument, how they might strive for more personally and professionally rewarding possibilities in teaching. He was as much concerned with the 'inner' turmoil in teachers' minds as he was with the 'outer' forces that manipulated and shaped them. Above all Goldhammer saw clinical supervision as a method for questioning and challenging the authoritarian and exploitative ways in which schools and classrooms were organized. He was concerned about stripping away the rituals and observances that posed such powerful barriers to understanding how teaching has come to be the way it is. On one occasion he put it in these words:

> Authoritative teaching and the content curriculum, to which it is handmaiden, result in certain advantages to the scholastic status quo, namely, the reduction of students to a condition of docility, dependency and ignorance: that is, a condition in which they are non-threatening. In such a system, the teacher is invariably king of the mountain; because the subject matter, the questions, the answers, the books, and the tests are his, and because the students are really in class by his sufferance, the teacher exists in a universe that is almost perfectly free, internally, from competition or attack . . . [It] would seem, schoolmen know that ritualism is one of the institution's most powerful means for ensuring conformity and obeisance, both of which are required for institutional stability and duration. One might isolate, as the school's crowning achievement, its almost absolute success in making so many people accept so much

> on faith, the parents and teachers no less than the learners. Collectively, the rituals of school life combine to form a penumbral mystique. (1969, p. 26)

In the kind of confrontation that is involved, teachers work with other teachers non-hierarchically, respecting the dignity and human worth of one another's perspective, while challenging the bases upon which one another's perspectives have been formed. In its original form, clinical supervision endorsed a quite deliberate set of values that regarded teachers as autonomous and knowledgeable, capable of working collaboratively to expose their own dilemmas and sense of the inconsistencies in their teaching, while tackling the incompleteness of their assumptions and beliefs about the wider possibilities inherent in the process of schooling.

In many ways what is being attempted here is akin to what Winter (1987) describes as combining 'the moment of practice with the contrasting moment of theoretical reflection, rather than merely oscillat[ing] between them' (p. 110). The argument is that in processes like clinical supervision reflection needs to join teaching in a dialectical relationship that does more than highlight inadequacies. The key to this is not to introduce new and different concepts from 'outside' ' . . . but to question the reflective basis on which practice is taking place and to *recall* the real possibilities which practice is choosing, on this occasion, to ignore' (p. 112). It is what is passed over in teaching and regarded as not deserving of a second thought that needs to be excavated and celebrated by processes like clinical supervision.

It should also be said that although it is a model that is solidly located in the practice of teaching, there has been much confusion (some of it mischievous), restricting the model to correcting deficiencies in the practicalities of teaching. Such a narrow view precludes clinical supervision being used to pursue wider moral, ethical and political questions to do with justice and equity within teaching. That the *means* rather than the *ends* towards which teaching is directed have tended in some quarters to be the focus of clinical supervision is more an indictment of the way in which the model has been distorted by others, than a fundamental flaw in the model itself. How to safeguard against that is a matter we shall come to shortly. Notwithstanding, what is clear is that the ideas that have come to be known as clinical supervision amount to: a *discursive and dialogical* way in which teachers can question their intentions and confer with one another before the teaching of one is observed; a way in which a *text can be created* about that teaching for further collaborative interrogation; and an opportunity for *a re-convening* after the observation to *reconstruct and confront* what has occurred. The opportunity exists as well for the participants periodically to review the efficacy of the process itself through post-conferral discussions.

None of this is to suggest that Goldhammer's conceptualization was without some quite severe problems and limitations. There is much that

Goldhammer said, as well as what he left unsaid, that is also deserving of challenge. In being less than deliberate, insistent and unequivocal about the nature of the power relationships, he hedged around the issue of whether teachers *can* act as informed and competent colleagues for one another. The consequence is that although he may have believed in the nature of egalitarian relationships, his equivocation leaves it open for those who wish to use clinical supervision in hierarchical, instrumental and exploitative ways. The result has been large numbers of teachers regarding clinical supervision as being so tainted as to be avoided at all costs. The reasons for this are clear enough, for as St Maurice (1987) put it, 'the gaze is asymmetrical: the subject-as-object may seem powerless to gaze back and question its majesty and authority' (p. 246). Where clinical supervision is 'done' to a teacher by someone in the administrative hierarchy what goes uncontested are the ethics and morality of a largely female workforce in schools being inspected and evaluated by a cadre of males—already existing gender imbalances in teaching and administration of schools are, therefore, solidified and reproduced.

Another legacy of Goldhammer's vision of clinical supervision that is proving especially difficult to dislodge is its behaviourist view of teaching. The psychological paradigm he worked within accepted unquestioningly the idea of individual deficits that had to be rectified by diagnosis and remediation. Such entrenched views of individualism and treatability obviously get in the way of teachers viewing their teaching in socially constructed terms. As long as this view remains dominant, teachers are trapped within a fault-finding mentality in which they are unable to see that problems in their teaching are the consequence of complex forces that lie considerably beyond their classroom walls. As we shall see shortly, this 'blame the victim' (Ryan, 1971) approach, that targets individual teachers as the cause of school and societal problems, puts quite severe constraints on wider dialogue within school communities. The 'two heads are better than one' approach (Winter, 1987) that can be so easily ascribed to clinical supervision is an exceedingly constricted and narrow view of collaboration, as we shall argue at some length later. In much the same vein, Goldhammer's emphases on 'objectivity', 'neutrality' and 'improvement' are also manifestations of a misguided view of the route by which teachers might gain control over their teaching—in reality, such notions serve to reinforce the status quo which is tilted severely against teachers and students in favour of dominant interests outside schools.

In considering the efficacy of these various criticisms, it should be borne in mind that they were ones that worried Goldhammer (1969) as well, and although he could not surmount them, he was sensitive to the possibility that things might be different in the future. In his words: 'Clinical supervision is begun, but not nearly completed. Its final form will differ substantially from its present ones, and I would be gratified for this writing to guide its transfiguration' (p. ix).

Distorting the Intention of Clinical Supervision

It seems that with the passing of time the meaning and intentions behind Goldhammer's (1969) *original* conception of clinical supervision have become lost. In its implementation, clinical supervision, seems to have taken on many of the features of a sinister, and in some cases, quite sophisticated form of teacher surveillance and inspection. Perhaps we need to acknowledge, as Garman (1984) does, that the habit of evaluating teaching by *prescribing what the teacher ought to do* is a 'ritual so deeply embedded in the culture of the school that we have become resigned to the inevitable' (p. 4). She suggests that:

> The present day versions of clinical supervision . . . have been widely interpreted by educators for their own situations. For the most part this is a welcome sign. The questionable part comes when educators begin to alter the basic tenets of the practice in order to fit their own rigid timeframes and mindsets. Clinical supervision is not warmed over ritual. It represents a drastically different form of professional development . . . (p. 3)

Guditus (1982), for example, denies the empowering possibilities of clinical supervision on cost-benefit grounds, while actively endorsing its potential as a way of rating the performance of teachers. In his words:

> Clinical supervision makes a lot of sense from a theoretical standpoint but it is never going to become standard practice in the schools . . . [School] administrators are already hard pressed for time and . . . they don't need the added time burden of the clinical approach to supervision . . . Without convincing evidence that the procedures used in clinical supervision are worth the time and energy involved, widespread acceptance of the clinical approach is highly unlikely.
>
> There are, however, a number of sound reasons for adopting clinical techniques in instructional supervision. Not the least of these is the potential of the clinical approach for increasing the reliability of teacher performance ratings. The unreliability of these ratings becomes a matter of increased concern as a result of the continuing clamour for greater accountability in education. (p. 7)

The basis of Guditus' argument is that the rhetoric of clinical supervision as a way of empowering teachers may be a fine ideal but it is better, however, as a way of evaluating the work of teachers so as to ensure conformity to established norms of teaching.

An even more blatant example is the Hunter (1980a) 'teaching skills' model which has widespread use in the USA and purports to use a variant of clinical supervision as a way of prescribing what should pass as teaching. Hunter's (1980a) manipulative intentions are clear when she says:

> Conferences designed to improve instruction must be both diagnostic and prescriptive and are more accurately labelled instructional conferences . . . The objective of an evaluative conference is that a teacher's placement on a continuum from 'unsatisfactory' to 'outstanding' will be established and the teacher will have the opportunity to examine the evidence used . . . [And] . . . the observer focuses only on those aspects of instruction that were effective and brings those decisions to the conscious awareness of the teacher. (pp. 408–12)

Hunter's (1985) 'version' of clinical supervision is really nothing of the kind—she calls it 'mastery supervision'—and in its removal of teacher choice over pedagogy it bears no resemblance at all to any process we have described in the preceding pages. In her own words: 'Our clinical supervision model is . . . derived from learning theory and the cause-effect relationship in teaching and learning' (Hunter, 1980b). In this, Hunter's work is clearly part of the current educational reform vanguard in the USA that believes in the back-to-the-basics, discipline-centred curricula, prescriptive teaching and sequential modular design-based instruction based on the authority of research. Hunter's model amounts to 'traditional instruction' '. . . [in the form of] large-scale, mandated implementation of a stripped-down, formula-like application of her principles . . .' (Slavin, 1987, p. 57). The movement derives its popularity from 'its relative simplicity and [the] claim that it is research based . . . [and capable of] being implemented to improve instruction and increase student achievement' (Ceroni, 1987, p. 2). In the current climate of simplistic solutions to protracted and complex economic problems, it is seen as an administratively expedient solution with which to force schools to strait-jacket the work of teachers, and make them responsive to producing a 'product' acceptable to narrow and sectional business interests. The result, according to Hazi (1987), is a form of 'teacher evaluation [i.e., performance appraisal] incognito' because of its high level of prescriptiveness about what should occur in teaching, and because of the process of checking for the presence of these attributes of 'acceptable' teaching. Pointing to the ridiculous extremes to which such folly can be carried, Slavin (1987) relates the incident of the physical education teacher in Texas who received an unsatisfactory appraisal 'because her explanation of volleyball rules didn't include all the steps of a Madeline Hunter lesson!' (p. 56). Another illustration of the oppressive and dehumanizing relationships that can be foisted on teachers becomes evident enough in the following memo from a school principal to his staff about the necessity for 'Statements of Learning', a notion that is central to the Hunter scheme.

College Square School
Beaver, Pa.

MEMORANDUM

To: College Square Staff
From: Albert Camp, Principal
Date: September 10, 1985
Subject: *Statements of Learning*

One of the items first mentioned at our first building meeting on Orientation Day, September 3rd, dealt with the importance of placing a Statement of Learning on the chalkboard prior to every lesson. In this manner everyone in the room would know why they were there and what the focus and direction would be for the lesson.

Yesterday, I visited nineteen (19) classrooms. Five (5) of the classrooms had no Statements of Learning on the board; the remaining fourteen (14) had Statements on the board or an oaktag that ranged from acceptable to the suspect which looked more like assignments than Statements.

In case those of us who may have forgotten over the summer, the following is offered:

1   If you have a chalkboard in your room, the chalkboard is to be used for the Statement of Learning. The Statement need not require much space and the chalkboard makes it convenient time-wise and location-wise to change the Statement when the lesson changes and easy for all to locate it.

2   The Statements are to be full sentences such as 'The learner will . . .' or 'The student will . . .'

3   Outlines, page numbers and short phrases are not appropriate Statements of Learning.

4   Placing a Statement of Learning on the chalkboard would take only a minute or so, provided prior planning for the lesson takes place.

Consider this memorandum a direct order. Non-compliance, that is, not having a Statement of Learning on the chalkboard or not doing it properly, will result in documentation of the incident. The documentation will be placed in the individual's file and may have a detrimental effect on the rating one receives.

By co-opting teachers as 'trainers' of other teachers, Hunter cynically capitalizes on the individualistic, upwardly mobile career aspirations of some teachers at the expense of their colleagues. What she creates is a cadre of 'accountability and efficiency experts' who see in the process a way of 'maintaining and enhancing their positions and paths to upward mobility' (Apple, 1987, p. 213). Not surprisingly, teachers regard the Hunter approach as 'rigid', 'mechanistic' and 'anti-intellectual' (Ceroni, 1987, p. 8) because of the way in which it increasingly treats them as unthinking technicians. Understandably, some teachers are opposed to what is involved here. Typical of such hostile reactions was the teacher who, after four days of training, recalled the experience as ' . . . the most anti-intellectual experience I ever encountered. What it felt like was anologous to bringing all the great chiefs of the world together and teaching them how to boil water' (Gondak, 1986, p. 4).

In the current climate of the swing to conservative educational politics it is not difficult to see how clinical supervision can be used in a particular form to provide a veneer of respectability for what amounts to an infantile treatment of teachers. Superficially, the Hunter process, with its classroom observation and collection of evidence, gives the appearance of being benign, neutral and value-free, especially when clothed with the authority of 'science' and 'research'. If all that lay behind the appropriation of clinical supervision were the substitution of 'different' words, matters would be relatively simple. However, by adopting the reformist language of 'improvement', the Hunter movement actually twists the meaning of that term, while gaining support for its purpose, which is that of controlling and constraining the work of teachers. Who in their right mind could possibly be against 'improvement'? By focusing exclusively on the means or the technicalities of teaching, the social ends and political purposes of that teaching go unquestioned. In actuality, of course, the Hunter approach to supervision (and teaching) is riddled with quite explicit values on what constitutes acceptable ways of working with teachers (and, in turn, teachers working with students)—it is hierarchical, judgmental, excessively proceduralized, measurement-oriented, and endorses individualistic relationships based on highly questionable claims to certainty. In sum, it is a narrow recipe approach to both teaching and supervision that is neither sustainable in terms of its alleged research basis (Gibboney, 1987; Costa, 1984), nor bears any resemblance to the ways teachers actually work in classrooms.

None of this technologization of clinical supervision occurred by accident. Versions of clinical supervision touted by people like Hunter (and the closing down of teacher-controlled forms of self-evaluation in England and Australia) came about because of what Shor (1986) claims was a concerted effort at the end of the 1960s, particularly in the USA (but followed closely in Australia, England and elsewhere), by conservatives to recapture and reassert what they saw as lost control over schools brought about as a result of the progressivism and permissiveness of the 1960s. The move was to re-establish control over school culture, the curriculum, the structure of authority and the language of debate about schooling (Smyth, 1987b).

According to Shor (1986), this reassertion was made possible by the economic downturn, and was driven by notions of career education and vocationalism which capitalized on the widespread fear of unemployment. It was also characterized by the much vaunted 'literacy crisis' and its accompanying call to 'get back to the basics'. The attempt was to restore the notion of authority which had been lost and to declare war on 'mediocrity', using the secret weapon of the push for (an undefined return to) 'excellence'.

According to Shor (1986), this 'rearmament' of conservative interests has taken the form, at least in the USA, of a concerted move 'to displace the wrong words' and to 'teach the right words'. Oppositional words like 'peace', 'open access', 'free schools', 'equal rights', 'anti-imperialism', 'civil rights', 'power to the people' (p. 11), were replaced by more conserving words like 'illiteracy', 'tests', 'accountability', 'competence', 'quality', 'excellence', 'basics', and the like (p. 11). As Apple (1987) put it, the terrain of the educational debate has been shifted 'from a concern with inequality and democratization' (no matter how weak) to the language of 'efficiency, standards and productivity' (p. 200). What we are, therefore, witnessing in the large number of national reports on education is an attempt to mouth the right language, and through that, orchestrate public opinion so as to create the kind of climate in which to standardize and control further the work of teachers. This amounts to a rehearsing of what Apple (1987) sees as a repetition of an older strategy: 'When larger economic and governmental crises erupt, export the crisis outside the economy and government onto other groups' (p. 210). Lack of competitiveness in the economy, increasing unemployment, unfavourable trading arrangements and the generally changing nature of labour market relations are blamed on the inadequacy of schools and teachers to meet the emerging needs.

It has been this orchestrated chorus by educationally conservative critics of schooling that has produced support for a narrow instrumental view of schooling and education, and resulted in processes like clinical supervision being seen as a convenient way of ensuring conformity to behaviourally determined indices of teacher competence. As St Maurice (1987) notes, for this reason critiques of clinical supervision have invariably tended to concentrate on its limitations as a technical process, not upon the power relationships implicit in its form. In the next section we take up the issue of how we might begin to reclaim the ground lost to the technical experts in teaching, by construing clinical supervision as a way of examining teaching in socially critical ways.

Becoming 'Critical' through Clinical Supervision

What is really at stake here is whether clinical supervision is to remain a way of controlling, disenfranchising and pushing teachers around, or whether it has other possibilities as an emancipatory process through which teachers are able to assist one another to gain control over their own professional lives and destinies. The issue is whether clinical supervision should be construed *only* in instrumental terms as a way of fine-tuning teaching, or whether it is a way for teachers to challenge and transform not only their teaching, but the social and cultural circumstances in which they do it. Technicist interpretations of clinical supervision amount to a conservative political process of perpetuating the status quo (Smyth, 1984a), in which the only change possible is that which occurs within the framework of existing practices and structures. Used in instrumental ways, clinical supervision can do no more than aid teachers to do better that which they were *already doing*; they try *harder* to apply established techniques and rationales, reasserting and continuing to endorse the same basic assumptions and practices. What remains uncontested are the ends of teaching. Means-oriented views like this fail to take account of the purposes to which teaching is directed, and of the moral, ethical and philosophical questions that are central to what teaching is about.

An example (adapted from Cooper and Meyenn, 1984) may make our point clearer. A teacher accepts an invitation to work with a colleague in clinical supervision to 'improve' her mathematics teaching technique. At the start of their collaborative clinical supervision project the observer, in casual conversation, draws attention to a 'bright-eyed' and eager five-year-old girl who, while performing well, appeared to be poorly dressed and come from an under-privileged family. At the end of the clinical supervision project, some six months later, the two teachers agreed that the process had indeed been successful in improving the teacher's mathematics teaching skills. Almost as an after-thought they noted that the child referred to earlier had become marginalized, with limited social contact with other students in the classroom—still poorly dressed, generally left out of activities and often waiting to be noticed, she had not been given any mathematics that would alter her life chances in the world; instead she had been given another lesson on her place in the world. Now, while the example may be caricatured somewhat, it serves to make the point that using clinical supervision to improve the technical efficiency of teaching precludes questions being asked about equity, access and how mathematics might be made more inclusive for certain categories of students.

On the other hand, as we have seen so far, clinical supervision can be a way of 'empowering' teachers by helping them to take charge of aspects of their lives over which they have hitherto been restrained, by social or political forces, from assuming such control (Fried, 1980). It involves abandoning a 'delivery of services' view of clinical supervision in which remediation is provided to targeted audiences of teachers deemed to be inexperienced, inefficient, incompetent or in need of re-skilling (Smyth, 1986b). But being critical in the sense that we use the term here does not mean being negative; it refers rather to enabling teachers to see their classroom actions in relation to the historical, social and cultural context in which their teaching is actually embedded. Acting critically involves individuals and groups in reflecting rationally upon their own action and using these reflections as a basis for practically altering things (Carr, 1987). This means creating conditions under which teachers, both individually and collectively, can view themselves and their teaching historically; to treat the contemporary events, practices and structures of teaching problematically (and not to take them for granted); and to examine the surface realities of institutionalized schooling in ways that enable them to clarify for themselves alternative courses of educational action that are open to them. Acting critically, therefore, refers to 'collaboration in marshalling intellectual capacity so as to focus upon analyzing, reflecting on and engaging in discourse about the nature and effects of practical aspects of teaching and how they might be altered' (Smyth, 1985, p. 9). Apple (1975) summed it up when he said of the socially critical perspective:

> It requires a painful process of radically examining our current positions and asking pointed questions about the relationship that exists between these positions and the social structure from which they arise. It also necessitates a serious in-depth search for alternatives to these almost unconscious lenses we employ and ability to cope with an unambiguous situation for which answers can now be only dimly seen and will not be easy to come by. (p. 127)

The interests being served are those that relate to 'the emancipation of individuals from lawlike rules and patterns of action . . . so that they can reflect and act on the dialectical process of creating and recreating themselves and their institutions' (Apple, 1975, p. 126).

In practical terms this means teachers engaging in systematic individual and social forms of investigation that examine the origins and consequences of everyday teaching behaviour so they come to see those factors that represent impediments to change. The intent is to overcome the fatalistic view that change in teaching is 'impossible for me', and seeing that circumstances can be different from what they are. It means moving from a 'passive . . . dependent, [and] adaptive' (Fay, 1977, p. 220) view of themselves and their potentialities, to one in which teachers are able to 'analyze and expose the hiatus between the actual and the possible, between the existing order of contradictions and a potential future state' (Held, 1980, p. 22). In short, it involves teachers becoming oriented to the development of an enhanced 'consciousness' of their own circumstances and a political involvement in working towards actively changing the frustrating and debilitating conditions that characterize the work lives of themselves and their students. This may involve, for example, teachers looking carefully at the source of the authority they have over students. If teachers see themselves as servants of the State, then they need to be clear as to their implication as part of *that* apparatus in pursuing the objectives laid down by the State. An unproblematic acceptance of the institution's objectives can mean that the school's authority becomes the teacher's authority (Tozer, 1985). This may lead, for instance, to a categorization of students according to 'low' and 'high' ability, with the teaching of vocational skills to the former, while preparing the latter for professional-class jobs. Endorsing the imposition of this kind of hegemony is something which schools and teachers must vigorously contest. Acting in ways that fail to challenge these forms of hegemony deeply implicates teachers in sustaining the inequities in the status quo, while depriving students of the capacity to 'form understandings of themselves and their society that are different from what the dominant class of society *want* them to understand' (Tozer, 1985, p. 150). The way in which teachers act in respect of their teaching and the structures of society within which it occurs obviously has implications for whether or not students are able to learn to question the dominant order of society.

What we are claiming, then, is that clinical supervision as we are portraying it has to be concerned with fostering forms of teaching that are 'critical of current practices and institutions in the sense of showing them to be frustrating [and] based on a false understanding of human need and possibility' (Fay, 1987). Fay (1987) would claim this means simultaneously *explaining* the social world, while *criticizing* it, and empowering its audience to transform it. It amounts to revealing how the social order works by showing how that constructed order is unsatisfactory to those who live in it, and '. . . to do both of those in such a manner that it itself becomes the moving force helping transform this order into something . . . different' (p. 23).

We want to turn now to the more concrete notion of clinical supervision being 'strategic' (Carr and Kemmis, 1986) in the sense that it involves teachers actively intervening in their 'life worlds' and asking pointed questions about the historical, social and political nature of what is that they do in teaching, and how they might operate differently. Questioning the veracity of things to which we have become habituated and accustomed is bound to be an anxiety-provoking and risky business. But it is only through the process of challenging what it is we do not yet know that there is any real chance for improvement. What is involved is teachers moving beyond accepting the limitations built into the traditions of their own teaching, to a position in which they are able to understand how the structures of schooling, within which they and their students work, are systematically and hierarchically distorted. At a practical level, the perspective we have developed so far in this chapter of an 'educative' or 'emancipatory' view of clinical supervision can fit within the broad framework of Goldhammer's (1969) original phases of teacher and colleague being involved in:

(i)   conferral prior to teaching (pre-observation conference)
(ii) observation and data collection
(iii) analysis of data

    (iv) conferral and disclosure of data about teaching (post-observation conference)

    (v) reviewing of the entire process (post-conference review).

While we believe that this general format (which is more like a spiral than a cycle) is useful, we want to avoid unnecessary confusion between Goldhammer's terminology and the particular new directions in which we have taken his work. We have devised our own descriptors which are more descriptive of what occurs in a critical approach to clinical supervision. Through this means we believe that it may be possible to re-visit the original intent of what clinical supervision was supposed to be about, while at the same time reversing the instrumentalism that has come to characterize the widespread use of the process. The aspects we have chosen to highlight below are those we alluded to at the start of this chapter:

    (a) problematizing teaching
    (b) observing and creating text about teaching
    (c) confronting biography and history
    (d) re-focusing and action.

Problematizing Teaching . . . revisited

At the moment we are witnessing what amounts to a major paradigm shift in teaching (Smyth, 1987a). As Schön (1983) has argued, across a range of professions, knowledge based on the 'problem solving' approach of the traditional disciplines is out of step with changing situations. He sees such knowledge as no longer being able to 'deliver' solutions on important and protracted social questions. In particular: 'The complexity, uncertainty, instability, uniqueness, and value conflicts which are increasingly perceived as central to the world of [current] practice . . .' (p. 14) are no longer able to be handled simply by recourse to existing bodies of knowledge or accepted ways of acquiring such knowledge. Rather than engaging in rational processes of resolving problems by choosing from available 'received' knowledge, teachers are raising questions about the relevance of such 'applied' approaches, and whose interests are being served by it anyway (Breinin, 1987). Practitioner-generated knowledge that is embedded in and emerges out of action is coming to be seen increasingly as the basis for a new and emerging paradigm in teaching (Smyth, 1987a). The emphasis has shifted from one of supposed universal certainties, to one of 'problem posing' or 'problem setting' in which the agenda is *problematizing* or bringing into question 'critical social analysis of the production, circulation and consumption of educational [knowledge]' (Smith, 1987, p. 48).

    Problematizing teaching within the collegial conferral framework of clinical supervision involves the teacher and an observer in using 'public space' (Greene, 1985), prior to actual teaching, deliberately to plan and rehearse with a colleague how to inject into teaching questions that normally go unasked about the *content of what we teach* so that students can begin to develop a sense of 'why things are the way they are' and 'how they got to be that way' (Simon, 1988). This amounts to working against what Freire (1972) labelled a 'banking' notion of education in which 'teachers make deposits of knowledge into the empty accounts of the students' minds' (Shor, 1980, p. 105). Adopting a problematizing approach to teaching, however, introduces into teaching a dimension that simultaneously denies and interrogates prescriptive forms of knowledge dictated to students. It opens-up for debate the pre-processed and pre-digested nature of such knowledge by questioning the way in which powerful and pervasive myths are 'instrumental in explaining events and situations that [prevent] the critical understanding of inequalities in society' (Benseman, 1978, p. 31). Shor (1986) argues that we should be striving continually to problematize our teaching so as to 'understand existing knowledge as an historical product deeply invested with the values of those who develop such knowledge . . .' (p. 420).

Here is an illustration of how two teachers working together within the clinical supervision model might go about problematizing the content of teaching. In discussing his plans to teach the geography of northern Peru to his year ten class, a high school teacher revealed to his colleague the view he held that poverty in the Third World was a historical fact caused by poor techniques and crop failures, along with climate and other natural disasters. Individuals in countries like Peru, he said, were the way they were basically because of an inadequate grasp of technological knowledge. In the pre-lesson conferral, his colleague raised the possibility that this view was perhaps a little too simplistic, and that perhaps there was a more complex explanation that took account of the nature of social inequality in Peru. The colleague went on to indicate that at the time of the horrendous earthquake of 1970 in northern Peru the annual income of the people from cattle raising was about $100 per annum. Indeed, the massive influx of foreign aid that followed the earthquake did nothing at all to change the basically unjust and exploitative economic system in Peru. He went on to point out that while the foreign aid could indeed be used to improve techniques—parasite control, vaccination of animals, and the like—this did nothing to tackle the real source of the problem. The problem lay in the production-marketing cycle in which the wealthy merchants who owned the land also controlled the markets and the prices the farmers were able to receive for their cattle. Because the merchants held the power to fix prices, the returns to farmers were unrelated to the amount of care they took or the work they put into raising their cattle. Not only that, the farmers bought their cattle from these same land-owning merchants, fattened the cattle and then sold them ten months later for a pitiful return on their labour. Herein, the colleague pointed out, lay the cause of the poverty—an oppressive and exploitative land tenure and marketing system. The poverty of the people of Peru had very little to do with poor agricultural techniques.

This example illustrates that when teachers, through open discussion with one another, adopt an enquiring and questioning approach to the content of what it is they believe they are about to teach *prior to that teaching*, then it is possible for them to arrive at alternative explanations to that of the 'received' (or textbook) view of knowledge. The added point to be taken from this example is that where teachers use an unproblematic pedagogy in transferring received knowledge to students (by preventing an exposure to the alternative way things might be), lessons are boring and students are treated in docile and subservient ways. But, more importantly, students are denied the opportunity of seeing that inequities are not natural and inevitable, but are socially constructed and morally regulated (Simon, 1988). Questioning 'why things are the way they are' and 'what conditions cause them to remain that way' is bound to expose the way in which we are systematically ignorant of how our social relationships are formed and sustained. As Shor and Freire (1987) argue, where the curriculum is presented as 'normative, neutral and benevolent', then 'inequality [and injustice] is presented as natural, just and earned', and the advantages that accrue to the elite continue to be hidden behind the myth of 'equal opportunity' (p. 123). Clearly, the way teachers choose (and are permitted) to treat the curriculum through curriculum frameworks, textbooks, testing and official forms of monitoring their work is closely reflected in the kind of intellectual activity (or passivity) among their students. Where there is rigid prescription and silence imposed upon teachers in these matters, along with an absence of teacher resistance, the consequence is what Bourdieu and Passeron (1977) label 'symbolic violence':

> It is symbolic because it is in the very order of things, not an actual physical beating, but an environment of rules, curriculum, tests, punishments, requirements, correction, remediation ... which establish the authorities as the ones in charge. (Shor and Freire, 1987, p. 123)

It is, therefore, in the actual process of conferral between teachers in clinical supervision prior to their teaching that a safeguard is built in whereby they are able to begin to develop the kind of resisting alliances necessary to reshape the nature of what it is they teach their students. It is here that the limits of the situation are sketched out, prior to being tested in the enactment of the lesson in concrete ways. Rather than feeling that they have 'to go it alone' in situations of curriculum exploration which are perplexing and confusing to them individually, it is here that teachers begin to develop solidarity with which to share progressively and collectively the problem of re-defining their teaching content. The dialogical relationships that emerge at this stage of clinical supervision enable teachers to see more clearly the 'political' nature of their teaching, and the disabling consequences that accompany bureaucratic intrusions into the classroom, like mandated curricula, prescribed textbooks and 'bench mark' testing.

Developing a political agenda within teaching during this problematizing phase is not to suggest that the other important aspects of the pre-lesson conferral (Goldhammer calls it the 'pre-observation conference') should go unattended. Indeed, unless these occur there is a risk that clinical supervision will lack the procedural clarity necessary to make it work. For example, it is important that both teacher and observer arrive at a shared understanding of what is to occur in the lesson to be observed. The conferral is a unique opportunity to begin the process of collaboratively and intellectually probing the teacher's intentions prior to their enactment. As in the traditional version of clinical supervision (Smyth, 1984c), there is no attempt on the part of the colleague to usurp the authority of the teacher or to call into question the competence or worth of the teacher. The attempt is rather to help the teacher to raise his/her consciousness as to why particular content is being taught, how it might be dealt with differently, as well as how and why particular teaching strategies are being pursued, and with what expected effect. It might be summarized as an exercise in mapping the domain, as it were, so that teacher and colleague have a shared basis upon which to continue to dialogue about the nature of concrete educative experiences.

Settling upon a 'focus' for the observation of the teaching that is to follow is an important part of the pre-lesson agenda, prior to its observation. Given what we know about the complexity of classrooms as social sites, and the often simultaneous, competing and unpredictable nature of occurrences in them, deciding upon an observational focus is not always easy. Experience has shown that it is best to be modest in terms of what is considered feasible to observe and collect data upon; we suggest a single focus. A way of handling the negotiation of an observational focus that respects the interests and wishes of the teacher is to allow the focus to emerge from discussion about the nature of the content to be taught, the manner in which students are expected to engage with it, and how students come to understand and experience the world in 'inclusive' rather than 'exclusive' ways. In other words, regardless of the content to be taught, or the way in which it is to be presented to students, the attempt should be for the focus to connect broadly with issues of justice, fairness and social change. The teacher and colleague might ask themselves questions along these lines:

- How does the proposed content of the lesson serve certain established interests, while denying or excluding others?
- How does the teacher intend to deal with the process of unmasking and de-mystifying those interests?
- What part does the particular teaching strategy itself play in endorsing or denying the interests of certain categories of students?

There is a host of other questions that might also be asked, but if questions like these can at least *begin* to inform and frame discussion as pairs of teachers meet to discuss proposed lesson content, teaching tactics and what might be observed during clinical supervision, then teachers will have begun the difficult process of problematizing their teaching. We believe that the scope for inserting this kind of social and cultural critique into teaching is just as possible in teaching the literary and social sciences as in mathematics and the natural sciences.

While we would hope that some form of social critique were able to commence in all pre-lesson conferrals, we are realistic enough to acknowledge that this might not be feasible or possible for all teachers at all stages in their career development. We are very mindful of the question of teacher 'ownership' of the focus, and of the importance of the teacher 'calling the shots' in selecting that focus. We are all at different points in our development as practitioners, and while some may warm readily to these forms of critique, for others it may be a more gradual process of starting at a somewhat different point. Starting with particular teaching skills to be improved or a problem to be solved may be more realistic. Examples of the latter might include:

> . . . the type and distribution of teacher's questions; the effect upon students of using new forms of group work; the way in which the teacher reacts to and handles classroom-control problems; the clarity with which the teacher provides directions to students about learning tasks; the reactions of students to co-operative group work activity; verbal interaction patterns between the teacher and students, and among students; the way the teacher provides individual praise or criticism; the way the teacher monitors which students contribute to class discussion; and, the effect of using some new teaching approach or idea. (Smyth, 1984c, p. 8)

On those occasions where teachers start out looking at 'technical' aspects of their teaching, it may be that through analyzing and dialoguing (at the confronting stage to be discussed shortly) they begin to see where other possibilities might lie. Tripp (1987) gives a nice example of how this might happen. He cites the instance of a teacher who started with a problem to be solved: 'John didn't finish his work again today. Must see he learns to complete what he has begun' (p. 28). Through dialogue and analysis this teacher was able to see the problem in a quite different light, and was prompted to ask further questions like:

- Why doesn't John finish his work?
- Why should he finish it?
- How does he see the tasks demanded of him?
- Are the tasks of the right kind, quality and quantity? (p. 29)

Rather than remaining with the question of 'how can I get John to finish his work?', she was able to see that the more important question was 'why must John finish his work before going onto the next task?' It was her own unquestioned professional history as a teacher that had prevented her from asking the 'why' questions—she had become fixated at the 'how' level. Why was it that she stopped John from starting anything new until the work he had begun was complete? As Tripp (1984) points out, she was 'teaching on autopilot'. In the case of John's unfinished work it can be argued that:

> In everyday life outside the classroom we continually leave unfinished what we have begun, so how is it that we are in a position of having to enforce upon . . . students the rule that they must finish one thing before they can go onto the next. Where did that rule come from, and when is it necessary? (Tripp, 1984, p. 28)

As Tripp points out, the issue on this occasion has more to do with the hidden curriculum of schooling. For reasons of orderliness and the general smooth running of the school, it was seen to be desirable that teachers have students complete tasks in a linear fashion—there was no educational rationale for this requirement.

In sum, the particular collegial process started during the pre-lesson conferral, with its declared political agenda, enables teachers to begin to exploit what Wirth (1987) has called the 'cracks and the openings' surrounding teaching, through which alternative teacher-driven democratic reforms in education will be possible.

Observing and Creating Text about Teaching . . . revisited

Creating a *written descriptive account* of what actually occurs during teaching (as distinct from one which is impressionistic or one done for purposes of rating) provides teachers themselves with an account *they* can use to dialogue and interrogate the critical relationship between what transpires in their teaching and their classrooms, and its relationship to the wider cultural and political life that shapes and informs schooling. Without that account, limited and selective though it may be, it is not possible to recall teaching in terms that enable the richness and complexity to be adequately addressed. Besides, description is an important starting point in teachers owning and analyzing their teaching. As Mishler (1986) put it, ' . . . one of the significant ways through which individuals give meaning to their experiences is [in] organiz[ing] them in narrative form' (p. 118). The rationale is that before teachers can confront themselves and their teaching in the sense of asking poignant questions about the nature, consequences and situatedness of their classroom practices, they first need to have a somewhat stable image (Garman, 1986) of what is occurring in respect of their teaching. Being clear about the elements (the 'who', 'what', 'when' and 'where') of their teaching means that they are more likely to have something concrete with which to enable them to dialogue about how their consciousness was formed in the first place, and what political conditions continue to limit and constrain them from working differently in the future.

In arguing for a descriptive retrieval of teaching in this way, we are especially mindful of the way in which observations of practice can degenerate into reductionist accounts of discrete bits of unrelated behaviour within teaching. This is not so much a problem of observation and recording of teaching per se, as it is an epistemological one of how to penetrate those accounts with the 'right' sort of questions. The intent should certainly not be one of seeking to objectify accounts of teaching in disinterested and allegedly neutral ways. Rather, the intent is to capture some kind of record or manifestation of the symbols, language and rituals of the enactment of teaching. The usefulness of this record lies in its capacity to open-up for contestation and debate the nature of hidden power relations in teaching. Greene (1985) expressed it in terms of what she termed the creation of 'public space', whereby teachers and others with an interest in schooling are able to break with their own enclaves and enter into dialogue with one another. In her words, such narratives should establish ' . . . a space, a site for dialogue about how . . . various meaning structures relate to one another and the way in which the cultural situation is understood' (p. 13).

It is through the creation of artefacts of this kind that 'name their world' (Freire, 1972) that teachers come to do what Giroux (1987) claims is vitally important for all who claim to be educators, namely, ' . . . shap[ing] collectively the ways in which time, space and knowledge organize everyday life in schools' (p. 7). For it is only by being articulate about 'what is' that teachers are able to be clear about 'what might be'. Such artefacts collected by teachers will not only help them to grapple with and understand the messages hidden in commercial textbooks and prescribed curricula, but it will also help them to uncover the nature of everyday classroom relations, teacher talk and alienation that are specifically supported by privileged groups both inside and outside schools.

At a practical level there are some pointers that can be taken into account in enacting the observation and creation of text. Observation is quite distressing for most teachers. The reasons for this are not hard to discern. It is generally not the observation per se that causes anxiety for most teachers, but the sanction-ridden and punitive ways in which information gleaned from such observations is used against teachers. The example below, cited by a professor of education (Eggleston, 1979) many years after his teaching had been observed by an inspector for evaluation purposes, makes the point about the malevolent intent:

I can still vividly recall after twenty-five years my first General Inspection. Form 5b were wrestling with the structure and physiology of the vertebrate eye. Vitreous humor flowed freely over the laboratory benches. At one point the class lapsed into a metaphysical exposition concerning the existence of the 'phantom' made visible by gently poking the inner corner of a closed eye. What my Inspector made of this activity was and remained beyond my ken. He uttered four words during forty-five minutes, 'good morning' and 'thank you'. There may be, lodged in the archives of the DES a more articulate report of the Inspector's observations, perceptions and judgments of the events of that possibly unique occasion. But any expectation I might have had that I would be the recipient of feedback rich in pedagogical insight was not realized. (p. 41)

Quite apart from the obvious involvement of the teacher in selecting the focus for observation and participation in the method of documentation to be used in creating a text of his/her own teaching, the way clinical supervision is construed here has the added inevitability of disclosure, compared with what occurs in traditional forms of teacher evaluation. Being able jointly to create and deconstruct the account of teaching is important primarily because of the way in which it works towards restoring the ideal of asymmetrical power relationships. We stress that this is an ideal to be strived for rather than an absolute state to be arrived at.

Arriving at a credible textual reconstruction of classroom phenomena requires a willingness at least *temporarily* to suspend judgment (about the desirability or otherwise) of the observed events. What the observer is trying to do is to render as 'descriptive' an account as possible, keeping in mind that we all observe through some kind of tinted perceptual lenses (beliefs, experiences, expectations, etc.). We are not suggesting that the process of 'fact gathering' is separate and isolated from the values, ethical and moral practices of teaching, or that such facts are endowed with any kind of 'prescriptive force' (Winter, 1987, p. 113)—clearly that is not the case, as we have been at some pains to point out at various places in this volume. Our argument centres on the claim that what participants in the clinical supervision process are doing is *temporarily* holding in abeyance ' . . . pragmatic interpretations of the job-at-hand' (Winter, 1987, p. 110) so that theoretical reflection becomes possible, rather than oscillating in what can be a random fashion between reflection and practice.

For example, a grade 4 teacher had her clinical supervision colleague record information about how children collaborated with one another in a language task, while the teacher 'taught' the remainder of the class. She was curious about the nature and extent of collaboration in a small group when she was absent from it. Excerpts of the children's dialogue were as follows:

'C'mon, let's get going . . . ' [student eager to get the group started]
[another student] 'You don't start a sentence with "and" '.
[one student to another] 'Why do you use that word?'
[student chastizing another] 'That's a common word. Let's find a better one'.

> [student to group when not sure of answer] 'Let's ask Miss . . . . No.
> Let's not go to the teacher'.
>
> 'She said to go onto the next one' [student negotiating with classmate].

When the teachers revisited the account of which these snippets of conversation were a part, they were able to discern instances in which students were harsh on one another, did not work in ways inclusive of the views of others, were domineering, and not open to possible alternative suggestions from others. Yet the teachers were also able to see in their account that at times the students had been self-sufficient, and were able to reason and justify to one another why they should work in certain ways. The data enabled the teacher to see more clearly that she was caught in a dilemma—while she wanted the children to help one another, when left to their own devices the children modelled adult forms of domination that were an unavoidable part of her own teaching, and which were built into the very fabric of teaching. Her way of seeking to resolve this dilemma, in consultation with her colleague, was to work towards making student collaboration a more regular and prominent feature of her teaching, as well as having the students see her collaborating with her colleague in teaching the class. They resolved to collect more information about how children react in these situations over time. They also concluded, as did Winter (1987), that descriptive accounts do indeed have a place in the dialectic between reflection and practice, as they explored a new idea they wanted to include in their pedagogical repertoire.

Confronting Biography and History . . . revisited

As the critical theorist Mead (1934) succinctly put it, we are all to some degree both the creators and the products our own history. What Mead was arguing was that on some occasions we have an important and dramatic effect on the way events unfold, while on other occasions we seem to be swept along and trapped by the course of events seemingly outside our control. In reality what this means is that we are continually struggling to survive in a world in which we have certain purposes, desires and needs, but our capacity to satisfy them is continually being shaped and re-shaped by the constraints within which we are required to work and live our lives. The challenge, therefore, is continually to be involved in the struggle of trying to 'disorient' (Berlak and Berlak, 1981, p. 230) ourselves so as to confront what is considered normal, natural or taken-for-granted. This is only possible when we are able to develop some distance from our teaching, and begin to locate ourselves in it. It involves adopting Greene's (1973) stance of 'teacher-as-stranger' and 'looking inquiringly and wonderingly on the world in which one lives' (p. 267). Put somewhat more expansively:

> It is like returning home from a long stay in some other place. The
> homecomer notices details and patterns in his environment he never

saw before. He finds that he has to think about local rituals and customs to make sense of them once more. For a time he feels quite separate from the person who is wholly at home in his in-group and takes the familiar world for granted. Such a person . . . ordinarily 'accepts the ready-made standardized scheme of the cultural pattern handed down to him . . . as an unquestionable guide in all the situations which normally occur within the social world'. . . . The homecomer may even have been such a person. Now, looking through new eyes, he cannot take the cultural pattern for granted. It may seem arbitrary to him or incoherent or deficient in some way. To make it meaningful again, he must interpret and re-order what he sees in the light of his changed experience. He must consciously engage in inquiry. (pp. 267–8)

We alluded at the beginning of this chapter to Goldhammer's sensitivity to the need to struggle against our own personal as well as our professional histories. We want to return to that notion here, and suggest that it is when teachers begin to ask a number of questions of themselves and what they do, based on the text they have created about their teaching, that they engage in unravelling their own histories and seeing what has 'caused' them to become the type of teacher they are. While, as Fay (1987) points out, this process of knowing ourselves can never reach any finality because it is always unfolding and continually being revised, any ideal which denies this fails to take account of the way people change themselves. In his words, because we are all ' . . . pressured to behave in particular ways by [our] physical environment and by the structures of power in [our] social arrangements, it is [we] who change [*ourselves*] by internalizing new conceptions of self and society, new possibilities of action, and by incorporating these in social practices and relations' (Fay, 1987, p. 52). In Fay's terms, it is the limits to clarity and autonomy that have to be continually challenged and worked against. At a practical level this might mean teacher and colleague asking the following kinds of questions in the post-lesson conferrals, as they engage with the data they have collected about teaching:

- Where do these practices come from historically?
- Whose interests are served and denied by these practices?
- What conditions sustain and preserve these practices?
- What power relationships among teachers, students and parents are expressed in them?
- What structural, organizational and cultural factors are likely to prevent teachers from engaging students in alternative ways?
- Indeed, what alternatives are available? (Smyth, 1986c, p. 3).

It is when teacher and colleague pursue questions which impinge upon whose knowledge is accepted as appropriate in the classroom; whose values infiltrate the curriculum; and in what ways the very notion of curriculum itself is tied to technical control, that they begin the process of unravelling the text they have created about teaching. For example, they will probably have begun to confront such fundamental questions as:

- Why do we insist on external rewards and punishments to make kids learn?
- Why do we define the 'good' kids as the 'quiet' kids?
- Why do we insist on equating 'workbook work' with 'reading'?
- Why do we regard 'on-task time' as synonymous with 'learning'?
- Why do we accept that 'getting through the material' should be the prime goal of teaching?
- Indeed, where did this notion come from, and how is it related to efficiency in factories? (Smyth, 1986c, p. 8).

It is questions like these that put the focus on the 'why' of teaching, that enable teachers to uncover the awesome extent of the habitual in teaching. There is so much in teaching that is deeply embedded in the mythology of the work that goes unquestioned. Williamson (1985), for example, found in her own teaching that when she gave students space to think and talk, the unexpected happened. The rebellious kids were the most talkative and the most perceptively critical, and the kids we label the 'good kids' were the most reluctant to participate. Perhaps, she concluded, this speaks eloquently to the enculturation process that goes on in schooling generally that teaches some students that it pays to be quiet even when invited to be openly critical.

Teacher and colleague in their post-lesson conferral might also ask themselves questions about such practices as 'ability grouping', if they use it, and whether they are using it as a utilitarian way of more efficiently handling diverse student skills and abilities; they might question their awareness of the way in which such practices actually stigmatize kids. If they have a concern about the allocation of time among students, they might pose the kind of questions that Berlak and Berlak (1981) suggest:

- What difference does it make if one gives equal time to each reading group or more time to the 'low' group?
- Why do I allocate my time this way?
- Is this pattern really a response to [central office] policy—especially when others allocate time differently?

If teachers insist upon 'quietness' in the classroom, is this because they believe that there are sound pedagogical reasons why pupils work better on their own, or is it because this approach fits better with school policy and the smooth general running of the school as an organization? Are they aware, for example, that:

We often make children do things that no one would expect adults to do in their jobs. Most adults get to talk to each other when they do work, but not kids. Most adults also don't like being told exactly what to do, where to go, how to think, or what to think every minute of the day, but this is exactly what we expect from kids in school. (Goodman, 1984, p. 16)

Some of these are notions that have widespread and unquestioned status in teaching. Teachers rarely bother to explore or challenge their veracity, and as Rudduck (1985) claims, if there is anything that teaching is vulnerable to ' . . . it is the flattening effect of habit' (p. 124). This is where the challenge of the post-lesson conferral implicit in a critical approach to clinical supervision can elevate teaching to the level of an examined activity. Habitual and unquestioned activity is seductive to the extent that it is ' . . . soothing, non-productive and anxiety-free' (p. 124). Rudduck's claim is that what is needed most in teaching at the moment are ways of rescuing at least part of teaching from the predictability of routine.

What this involves, of course, is an element of discomfort, even threat. Reality for most of us is that unless we feel uncomfortable, shaken, or forced to look at ourselves and our circumstances, then there is little likelihood of change. It is far easier to accept our current conditions and adopt the line of least resistance. This point is made in the following example, from Lampert (1985). Although this example is one of a teacher reflecting on her own teaching in an individualistic way, and to that extent may not have the benefits to be expected from collaborative confrontation with a colleague, it is nevertheless useful to illustrate the point about the way personal/professional histories need to be confronted and penetrated. Lambert has reached a point in the analysis of her teaching where she has encountered quite perplexing 'pedagogical problems', as she calls them. She has been socialized over many years into accepting that teaching occurs in certain ways, but when she examines the descriptive text of her teaching (the who, the what, the when and the where), she finds that there are aspects of the situation that severely constrain and limit her actions. It is in these very structural constraints themselves that she sees need for change. Lampert (1985) has come to the realization that teachers enact the role of brokers of contradictory interests. Paradoxical though it may seem, it is in locating such knowledge in the relations and discourses of teaching itself that the greatest prospects lie for teachers to redeem their work from the imposition of experts (Smith and Zantiotis, 1988). It is teachers who have control through the practical moral judgments they exercise on a daily basis. Keep in mind also as you read the example that although Lampert (1985) has unpicked the text of her own teaching on this occasion, we are suggesting that it may be easier when teaching colleagues collaborate in helping one another to 'see' what is happening:

In the classroom where I teach fourth-, fifth-, and sixth-grade mathematics, there are two chalkboards on opposite walls. The students sit at two tables and a few desks, facing in all directions. I rarely sit down when I am teaching except momentarily to offer individual help. Thus the room does not have a stationary 'front' towards which the students can reliably look for directions or lessons from their teacher. Nevertheless, an orientation toward one side of the room did develop recently in the fifth-grade class and became the source of some pedagogical problems.

The children in my classroom seem to be allergic to their peers of the opposite sex. Girls rarely choose to be anywhere near a boy, and the boys actively reject the girls whenever possible. This has meant that the boys sit together at the table near one of the blackboards and the girls at the table near the other.

The fifth-grade boys are particularly enthusiastic and boisterous. They engage in discussions of math problems with the same intensity they bring to football. They are talented and work productively under close supervision, but if left to their own devices, their behaviour deteriorates and they bully one another, tell loud and silly jokes, and fool around with the math materials. Without making an obvious response to their misbehaviour, I developed a habit of routinely curtailing these distractions from the lesson by teaching at the blackboard on the boys' end of the classroom. This enabled me to address the problem of maintaining classroom order by my physical presence; a cool stare or a touch on the shoulder reminded the boys to give their attention to directions for an activity or to the content of a lesson, and there was no need to interrupt my teaching.

But my presence near the boys had inadvertently put the girls in 'the back' of the room. One of the more outspoken girls impatiently pointed out that she had been trying to get my attention and thought I was ignoring her. She made me aware that my problem-solving strategy, devised to keep the boys' attention, had caused another, quite different problem. The boys could see and hear more easily than the girls, and I noticed their questions more readily. Now what was to be done?

I felt that I faced a forced choice between equally undesirable alternatives. If I continued to use the blackboard near the boys, I might be less aware of and less encouraging toward the more well-behaved girls. Yet, if I switched my position to the girls' side of the room, I would be less able to help the boys focus on their work. Whether I chose to promote *classroom order* or *equal opportunity*, it seemed that either the boys or the girls would miss something I wanted them to learn. (pp. 178–9)

A key point to be taken from this is Lampert's (1985) implicit message that teaching-as-text is not something that can or should be treated as 'given'. It is, after all, only in the 'reading' of this text (that is to say, in its deconstruction and the extraction of its message systems) that the contradictory discourses that plague teachers' lives become evident. It is as teachers struggle to 'extraordinarily re-experience the ordinary' (Shor, 1980) that they come to see the entrenched and oppressive nature of the social forces that produce the contradictions in their teaching. It is in demystifying the wider social forces operating in teaching that teachers begin to construct a 'new' text more of their own making whereby the social relations are both more educative and democratic.

While Lampert could have benefited from exploring with other teachers how her isolation has made her the way she is, and why it is that she regards 'equal opportunity' and 'order' as being simultaneously important, what is clear is that *even* experienced teachers need to be continually working at 'overcoming the limits of experience' (Buchmann and Schwille, 1983). Put another way, the constructions of reality that our senses tell us are happening around us need to be subjected to continual refutation and question. Immersion in the concrete and practical can too readily mean an unquestioning acceptance of matters at face value, just as 'learning from experience means learning to adhere to practices and standards that remain unchallenged' (Buchmann and Schwille, 1983, p. 38) or as Bourdieu (1971) labelled it the 'paradox of finitude'. He claimed:

> The individual who attains an immediate, concrete understanding of the familiar world, of the native atmosphere in which and for which he has been brought up, is thereby deprived of the possibility of appropriating immediately and fully the world that lies outside.
> (p. 205)

Part of the problem has to do with the isolation of teachers from one another and the burden this imposes on exchanging interpretations and making sense of experience. As Lipsky (1980) put it, teachers become ' . . . highly subject to street-level bureaucrats' definition of the situation' (p. 53) because of the difficulty of comparing their situations with those of colleagues. It is only through conferral about concrete examples of teaching, made possible through clinical supervision, that the kind of constraints and limitations alluded to here can be addressed and overcome.

Re-focusing and Action

The preceding discussion has sought to show that teaching is 'framed' by certain notions of the 'practicality ethic' (Doyle and Ponder, 1977) and the 'public servant' role (Bullough, Gitlin and Goldstein, 1984). Such frames 'define an operational space for planning and subsequent actions taken by teachers and students' (Smith and Zantiotis, 1988, p. 9), and rather than teachers being always at the exigencies of external forces, it is in the confrontation of their work that they become invested with the freedom to act autonomously. This does not mean that it is sufficient for them to have merely reflected in a speculative way about the oppressive and disabling nature of classrooms, learning, and teachers' work—there must be an actual commitment to changing those circumstances.

We have alluded to the way in which action needs to be seen as a natural follow-on from reflection. To be a truly reflexive process, clinical supervision must also engage the participants in looking enquiringly at the process of clinical supervision itself. While we intend to leave detailed discussion of that until the next chapter, there are some questions that can be kept in mind. We pose these questions not in any definitive way but as suggestions of the type of questions that participants might engage one another with as they work with clinical supervision:

*To what extent are the practices of clinical supervision **just** in treating teachers as capable of participating fully in the determination of their own destiny?*

- Who is clinical supervision appropriate for? Who is it supposed to benefit?
- What does it mean when a teacher continues to react defensively and shows signs of anxiety during clinical supervision?
- Does the teacher *have* to admit to having problems for clinical supervision to work?
- Should teachers who 'really need' clinical supervision be coerced into using the process?
- Should clinical supervision be used as a way of 'rating' teachers or teacher effectiveness?
- How much authenticity does the colleague have to display in disclosing his or her values, biases, beliefs and experiences about teaching? How aware does the colleague have to be of these, and how important are they to the success of clinical supervision?
- How can clinical supervision work where there are status, experiential, and subject matter content differences between teacher and colleague?
- What can be done to avoid clinical supervision becoming a ritualistic process?

*To what extent is the process of clinical supervision **practical** in enabling teachers to discover aspects of their own teaching through action?*

- Can inexperienced teachers work with other inexperienced teachers in clinical supervision? What part, if any, does experience play?
- How can teachers tell if clinical supervision is of benefit to them?
- Is it necessary that the teacher feels that clinical supervision is useful to him or her directly in teaching?
- Can clinical supervision work when teacher and colleague have fundamentally different values about education and what it is designed to do for children?

*To what extent is clinical supervision **realistic** in acknowledging the nature of school and classroom life?*

- How can teacher and colleague develop the kind of collegial relationship necessary to clinical supervision? Is this something that precedes or accompanies clinical supervision?
- What should others not directly involved in the inter-visitation aspects of clinical supervision be told about what is happening?
- How can networks of pairs of teachers involved in clinical supervision be developed?
- What is the critical mass of teachers in any one school that need to be involved if clinical supervision is to be self-sustaining?
- How can clinical supervision be extended to involve other teachers?
- What resources does a school have to be prepared to make available if clinical supervision is to have a chance of working? Can it work without these resources? (Smyth, 1984c, pp. 47–8).

Note

1 We acknowledge the help given by Noreen Garman in thinking through some of the issues in this chapter, and her assistance in locating some of the unpublished works of Robert Goldhammer. Her efforts enabled us to see much more clearly how his ideas have subsequently been distorted by others.

Chapter 7

'Lived Experiences' in a Critical Approach to Clinical Supervision[1]

Introduction

In the previous chapter we discussed something of the legacy of clinical supervision, the conceptual roots of the process, and how wider social and political forces have moved clinical supervision in a particular direction. It was clear too, that while the original ideas of clinical supervision have been misappropriated, it *can* be construed as an alternative to dominating forms of teacher evaluation. In part this rested on adopting a particular view of teaching that is at the same time *political, historical* and *theoretical*. In this chapter we want to carry that analysis further by looking at the lived experiences of teachers who have used clinical supervision as a way of critically analyzing their teaching. These teachers have come to see it as having fourfold merit:

confronting managerialism;
pursuing the 'critical' in teaching;
untying personal and theoretical histories;
building dialogical relations.

Before discussing the lived experiences, the particular view of teaching noted above requires further discussion. Our claim that teaching is an inherently *political* process rests on the view that it serves certain interests in demonstrable ways, while actively denying others. Speaking about the context of school and classroom struggle, St Maurice (1987) made the point about the long-standing politicized nature of teaching when he said:

... the history of the American teaching 'profession' is a story of labourers whose skills were defined entirely by management, in markets controlled by management, struggling for power in classrooms under the eye of supervisors empowered to describe and judge every aspect of their work. (p. 252)

Clearly, the way in which managerial issues (like supervision and teacher evaluation) intrude into classrooms has political implications in the sense that they reduce the scope for teacher and student choice over what is learned and how that learning takes place. What goes largely unacknowledged at the moment is that teaching involves 'social and political projects of one sort or another, whether that is consciously recognized or not' (Lawn and Grace, 1987, p. ix), and that teachers reclaiming pedagogical choice is at the heart of political teaching. Managerialism of the kind St Maurice (1987) refers to imposes quite severe limits and constraints on personal and collective choice. While there is much rhetoric in the school reform movements of various countries at the moment about schools developing the capacity for critical thinking (Swartz, 1986), such views are limited to the notion of *individual* autonomy and self-development and fail to embrace the *social* emancipation of categories of people whose lives can only be improved by an exposure to the models of authority that support the system. When we speak in terms of social emancipation, we mean allowing groups of people who have been silenced to acquire or regain a voice (Smyth, 1986b). It is clear that teachers and students are a group who have been progressively silenced through centrally-driven bureaucratic decrees (along with more subtle ideological processes that have the same effect), about 'the way teaching should be'. As Greene (1973) put it, emancipated people do not 'pretend to share the cultural pieties and conventional visions . . . [of] their less conscious fellow citizens . . . [They] are ready to wonder and question: and it is in wonder and questioning that learning begins' (p. 268). For Aronowitz (1977), this meant that: ' . . . the capacity of humans to distance themselves from the object in order to gain a critical perspective upon their social world can no longer be taken for granted' (p. 768).

Being open about the political agenda implicit in schooling means developing a concern about ' . . . the structure of power in society and its wide distribution to all social classes' (Aronowitz, 1977, p. 770), a process that is only possible where schools develop in students the capacity ' . . . to make inferences, to offer arguments, to develop explanations of social events that may counter those that are considered authoritative' (p. 771). The structures of schooling do not, by and large, do this because they perpetuate a 'banking' approach to education, one that says more about the oppressive structures of schooling than it does about the teachers and students that are trapped within these structural constraints. Quite explicit values, and hence a political viewpoint, are contained in what it is that teachers are required to do through this banking approach. Characteristic features include:

1   The teacher teaches and the students are taught.
2   The teacher knows everything and the students know nothing.
3   The teacher thinks and the students are thought about.
4   The teacher talks and the students listen—meekly.

5   The teacher disciplines and the students are disciplined.

6   The teacher chooses and enforces his choice, and the students comply.

7   The teacher acts and the students have the illusion of acting through the action of the teacher.

8   The teacher chooses the programme content, and the students (who were not consulted) adapt to it.

9   The teacher confuses the authority of knowledge with his own professional knowledge, which he sets in opposition to the freedom of the students.

10 The teacher is the subject of the learning process, while the pupils are the mere objects. (Freire, 1972, pp. 46–7)

As in any other view of the teaching/learning process, none of the above occurs within structures of schooling that are in any way value-neutral relationships—they all represent expressions of quite specific (even if undisclosed sets of) interests.

Closely linked to our claim that schools and classrooms are political sites is our second claim that teaching is also an *historical* process. We alluded to the long-standing, deep-seated unwillingness and/or inability of many teachers to question where particular curricular content and teaching practices came from, and the apparently opaque mind-set that characterizes so much of teaching and learning. What tends to prevail in situations where teaching actions are regarded as 'natural' or 'commonsense' is a form of structured silence that amounts to a failure to acknowledge that both curriculum and the way it is implemented are not accidental at all, but are a constructed response to wider social agenda. Unless we understand how teaching processes have come to be formulated, we wind up denying the power relationships that exist, and unwittingly become involved in perpetrating agendas decided by others outside schools. In this we are in accord with Berlak and Berlak (1975) that 'schooling acts'—by which they mean 'the everyday things teachers do as they teach reading, collect lunch money, admonish or comfort a child' (p. 11)—are social in nature. These acts, and many of the other mundane actions of teachers, can only properly be understood if regarded as 'part of the ongoing stream of life of teacher and child' (p. 11). They must be viewed in terms of the 'antecedents' that led to them, and the 'consequences' to society that flow from them. What goes on in schools, therefore, needs to be seen as part of a wider economic and political structure that has always intruded into schools and involves the exercise of power through 'controlling or shaping of the lives of individuals in directions consistent with the perspectives on the social world or the interests of those who wield power' (p. 11). As we indicated in the previous chapter, unless teachers are able to acquire a sense of where the practices they use come from, then they will be doomed to reproducing those practices in unthinking ways. Benseman (1978) put it more sharply when he said, people are only able to 'become makers of [their own] history [and] become involved in the historical process when they realize they are the objects of it' (p. 35). For teachers the importance of the intersection of politics and history is an issue that has gone largely unnoticed, but it is a crucial one if teachers are to begin to understand the nature of their own entrapment within the wider political structures and see the way in which their own actions continue to maintain the existing state of affairs. Although this may sound like an unduly pessimistic scenario, it highlights the importance of clinical supervision (and processes like it) as crucial ways of enabling teachers both to resist and develop the counter-discourse with which to 'demystify classroom structures, processes, forms and ideologies' (Carlson, 1983, p. 152).

Our final claim, although expressed somewhat differently in the previous chapter, is that when teaching is penetrated by processes like clinical supervision, then it becomes a decidedly *theoretical* activity. By problematizing teaching through systematic textual-based dialogue with one another, teachers are not only able to challenge the habitual and the taken-for-granted, but in the process they come to formulate theories or explanations about how and why the educative process is the way it is. This enables teachers to see how the current management rhetoric about teaching and schooling has been created and is sustained by the language, customs and the rituals that people 'outside' teaching have come to attach to teaching. When teachers grasp the fact that the norms, interactions and customs of teaching are frequently given their form and substance by the way teaching is described by non-teachers, then they have begun the process of seeing how those same constructed conventions can be resisted, deconstructed and replaced with ones of their own making. Construed in this way, teachers are theorizing; not in the limited sense of 'this is what works for me on Monday mornings', but in the wider sense of seeing that schooling is the way it is because it is shaped and directed by particular undisclosed political agenda. In Stevens' (1987) words:

> Contemporary educational theory and practice . . . are formulated within a position of political commitment despite claims to neutrality and balance, but [within a context in which] political commitment is for the most part undeclared (p. 82).

Not only are teachers prevented in the normal course of events from theorizing about their work, but this exclusion has a decidedly gendered bias to it. Steedman (1982) put it that:

> Teaching is an example of a work situation that preserves in its organizational hierarchy the division between those who evolve theories and map out schemata for operation and those who are supposed to be minor and admiring partners in the theoretical process. Other examples of this kind of work are nursing and

> policing, where the passive absorption of large-scale theoretical constructs (those of medicine and the law) is deemed necessary for operation on the ward and on the street. (p. 5)

The problem is that this exclusion amounts to a deliberately constructed situation in which a largely female workforce is deemed incapable of the heavy intellectual work required for the kind of theorizing that is necessary. While women are often considered inadequate through their upbringing, so the argument goes, their life conditioning has prepared them for the 'caring' function of sensitively attending to other people's needs and problems, particularly in situations of psychological and cultural turmoil (Williamson, 1985). In some cultural contexts, males, too, who enact a classroom function, are at least officially regarded as having a limited function in terms of choice. Clinical supervision, as we have construed it here, is largely about giving teachers a way of being able to reassert the right to choose.

The evidence we draw upon to exemplify the above three themes, as well as those of confronting managerialism, challenging the habitual, and working to build dialogical communities, emerges out of almost a decade of personal associations with literally hundreds of teachers who have 'experimented' with clinical supervision (albeit in an Australian context). The teachers whom we cite are of widely differing abilities, ages, sex, length of teaching experience, hierarchical status, grade levels, subject-matter specialisms and the like. We make no pretensions about the representativeness of the group we worked with, nor do we claim any absence of bias. On the contrary, what we do is present a pastiche of the 'lived experiences' of some teachers who have tried to work with clinical supervision in a 'critical' way. The views expressed all came from full-time teachers—some who we encountered in graduate studies (and who kept a journal/diary of their experiences), and others who were just curious to learn about clinical supervision at first-hand through non-credit in service courses. Regardless of background, then, all of the comments have one important thing in common—they come out of the hard-won struggle of having tried clinical supervision and learned something about teaching and about this form of educative evaluation. Our portrayals try to give some substance to the claim that *these* teachers have begun to engage in a reconstruction of their teaching and social relationships. Sometimes we even get glimpses of the 'downside' circumstances in which potentially educative processes like clinical supervision do not work. What is undeniable in all cases is that these teachers have begun to develop a 'voice'.

Confronting Managerialism

If we look at the history of teaching, it becomes clear that the ideas and practices of hierarchically ordered supervision had religious origins. Indeed, it was the religious dominance within early forms of schooling that led to the establishment of power regimes that were so easily transferrable when one form of bureaucracy (the State) replaced another (the Church) as the official provider of education. The difficulty was that as overt religious dominance waned it was replaced by an institutionalized and more covert form of bureaucratic control operating under the guise of benevolent managerialism. As far as teaching was concerned, the waters became muddied. Notions of humanism veneered over the basically exploitative social relationships in which teachers were evaluated by a cadre of experts in the form of inspectors and superintendents. According to St Maurice (1987), the attempt to professionalize teaching through processes like supervision that dressed-up the evaluative intent with the caring and curative ethos of the medical profession was destined to fail. Within the instrumentalist view of clinical supervision we looked at in the last chapter were intentions that had been misappropriated to manipulative ends:

> The teacher is asked to interact, but as a reclining patient in submission to the power of words, symbols and tools that examine and claim to cure what may or may not be simply seen and felt. By first dissecting instruction into behaviours, then diagnozing the causes and treatments for events lived by the teacher and students, the clinical supervisor exercises an exclusive authority to name what goes on in the classroom. A face-to-face encounter with these clinicians is stacked in favour of the face that claims expert knowledge, its own language and system of symbols, and tools that convey the power of truth ... The offer of assistance and improvement is cloaked in symbols of power. These symbols confer super-human capabilities on the clinician, to the benefit of the clinic and the regimes it serves. (p. 246)

His point is that where the notion of 'expertise' continues to remain separate, and is seen as being apart from the actual work processes and lives of teachers, it is the outside clinician who becomes enpowered, not the teacher. But need it be this way? What of the situation where a teaching colleague from across the corridor agrees to enact a service to a teacher, and he or she agrees to reciprocate? Surely where this occurs, even though there may be tensions because of different organizational roles and structural requirements, the scope nevertheless exists for a different kind of social relationship from that sketched above?

Let us take an example of a teacher of some ten years' experience, and who was the head of an English department in a small rural Australian high school. While the official expectations and role definitions of the corporate structure of which he was a part dictated one way of interacting with a junior and less experienced colleague about her teaching, clinical supervision was challenging him to think not only about that impositional relationship, but also about the way he interacted with his students. In both cases, the effect was hard to live with, as his journal entry below shows:

> Clinical supervision created an 'inner conflict' and 'uncertainty' for me both as a teacher, and as head of department responsible for the administration and professional development of a faculty. As a teacher it demanded that I re-examine my teaching practices. My actions in the classroom, which had for so long gone on without question or scrutiny were now the focus of close investigation and analysis. The consequence of such an investigation demanded that I change what had been secure and comfortable ways of operating in the classroom. It demanded that I surrender a [teaching] role which brought together power, knowledge and security . . . Who and what I am is defined, at least professionally, in my position of exercising power. I derive my identity [as a teacher], at least in part, from my sense of power and greater knowledge over students . . . [What was being asked of me was that I] . . . surrender that power which I exercised and enjoyed.

He goes on to point out that being required not only to observe a junior colleague teach, but also to have his *own* teaching observed by that neophyte was an especially troublesome notion. In the official scheme of things, his chosen colleague was 'only a first year probationary teacher', and he was her officially designated 'supervising teacher'. Even though his junior colleague had 'volunteered' to trial the clinical supervision process with him and was in no sense coerced into it, gender and status played their own indisputable part in engendering cooperation. By starting out with the most junior person observing the more senior, the tables had unexpectedly been turned. In the post-lesson conferral that followed the first occasion on which his colleague visited his classroom to observe him teaching English, the head admitted to feeling considerable discomfort at her revelation that sections of his class had been prevented from involvement in the class discussion because of his questioning strategy:

> I was a little uncomfortable . . . [After all] it was the head teacher being shown how to 'improve' by a first-year-out teacher. My initial reaction was 'what the hell does she know'. Thankfully, the feeling was only momentary . . . I think the lesson to be learned is that all of us at different times emerge to take on a leadership role. It takes courage to step back and listen to what others have to say.

Distancing himself from the situation, he was able to see that it was the organizational structure that had made him the 'expert', and his own complicity in willingly accepting that role even though he knew better. As the experience with clinical supervision developed he admitted to feeling 'less threatened' by the situation, and even feeling a 'sense of liberation' at being able finally to develop a more democratic way of working with a colleague. What was interesting about this particular case was that his colleague echoed similar sentiments and feelings about the way in which clinical supervision had opened-up new possibilities for her in her teaching too.

On other occasions, clinical supervision acted as a kind of lens through which school people were able progressively to re-focus on what was occurring around them and to see the wider political agenda occurring in and around their teaching. Working in a small, remote, racially mixed, low socio-economic primary school, with teachers who were experiencing classroom discipline problems, a teaching principal (of twenty-five years classroom experience) was able to see matters much more clearly. For the first time, as he began to focus on these issues, the bureaucratic edicts and prescribed ways of doing things emanating from head office seemed remote, distant and irrelevant to him, his teachers and their students. Speaking as a principal who had to accept and implement policies developed (managerially) beyond his school, as well as live with the (pedagogical) realities of trying to understand and implement those distant policies as a classroom teacher, this principal/teacher articulated his unease about his loss of control over teaching matters in these words: '. . . more and more I am feeling the influence of the accountant mentality of 'politicians'. More and more decisions are being made about schooling by people who are not part of the schooling scene'. Being able to see and experience how clinical supervision gave teachers control over teaching was a stark contrast to the forms of remote control he was forced to endure.

In yet another instance, the principal of a primary school (who was responsible for the professional development and conduct of his staff) was able to see the educative intent of clinical supervision, as he contrasted his personal clinical supervision experience with traditional ways of working with teachers. In his words:

> Clinical supervision has changed my whole thinking about the supervision of my staff. The most significant change I feel is my change of focus. Previously my observations tended to focus on what I wanted to see in classrooms, whereas clinical supervision assists me to work alongside the person being observed and towards the collection of data owned by the observed person . . . [even if] at times, the starting point may be educationally distant from the goals of the supervisor.

None of these instances of 'turning the supervisory world on its head', as it were, was without its own set of unique difficulties as participants struggled hard genuinely to acknowledge the worth and integrity of their teaching colleagues. There were difficult questions of competing values to be sorted out, and the risk of feeling to be still operating in impositional ways. The observational role generated a lot of sensitive soul searching by those involved. One Grade 5/6 teacher in his eleventh year of teaching put it this way:

> Working intimately with a colleague to address their terms of
> reference is a complex and demanding exercise. It involves much
> time, communication, sensitivity, energy, analysis and thought. At
> times I wondered about my own skill level and at times had doubts
> about how I was managing the process. I do however feel confident
> enough to say that the results and changes, as they mounted, proved
> the exercise to be a great success.

This clinical supervision participant found that it was possible to build in
safeguards to ensure that the communicative relationships were as equal as
possible. The kind of safeguard being referred to is that discussed in Chapter
6, where teacher and observer are able systematically to reconstruct the
context and elements of a teaching situation (i.e., the text) so as to have
a basis upon which to analyze it for the less obvious meanings. By penetrating
the descriptive accounts of teaching, instead of having to pass judgments
about the correctness according to preformulated standards (like those
contained in the check-lists used in traditional styles of evaluation), teacher
and colleague are able to use reason, argument and debate in place of external
authority. Having a descriptive account enables the discussion to start in
a way in which the artefacts of teaching, rather than the actions or
personality of the teacher, become the object (but not necessarily the end)
of the focus. As the colleague/observer in the above instance put it:

> At times I had difficulty in suspending judgments or comments . . .
> This was particularly so when my own values were being tugged
> at, or when I felt some responsibility to effect change in K [his
> teaching colleague]. I discussed this with K . . . [It] was an issue for
> me at various stages. It would be very easy to take an 'all knowing'
> stance, particularly if your colleague is [prepared to allow you to
> be] that way.

This relates closely to the issue of ownership, or who 'calls the shots' in
clinical supervision. There clearly needs to be a feeling that both parties
have an equal stake in the venture.

Attending to and redressing inequitable power relationships in
evaluative relationships are important, but so too is ensuring that the teacher
derives a real sense of control over his/her teaching through the discovery
of knowledge. Reflecting on what had happened to him as a result of inviting
a colleague to observe his Year 10 history class, one teacher put it this way:

> The lesson seemed to go well . . . until I saw the data. In the post-
> conference we reached the conclusion that the real issue was the
> intensity of the lesson. The whole lesson was filled with my attempt
> to 'teach' the lesson. I am wondering if the level of cognitive
> application I expect from the students is too great. Is there a need
> for me to back away? Yet, all of my teaching experiences have led
> me to believe that I must be totally in control.

The point being made here is that clinical supervision *can* be conceived as a way of actively working against exploitative power relationships. In Chapter 2 we went to some lengths to discredit the separation between those who teach, and those who are deemed fit to know about and pass judgments on teachers. As long as that separation is allowed to continue, based as it is on a differentiation between 'conception' and 'execution', so too will the attendant 'cold war' (Blumberg, 1980) as teachers and supervisors eye one another off across the widening chasm. At the same time, there is a more optimistic scenario which regards teaching less definitively, and as an enterprise that can only be unravelled as a consequence of the joint enquiries of concerned practitioners. This is a kind of knowing that is inextricably linked to the notion of teacher empowerment.

From the evidence of working with teachers trying out clinical supervision, if there is a single aspect that works against the traditional sanction-ridden way in which teachers are treated within a management model of evaluation, then it has to be the notion of role reversal. At issue is the view that expertise in teaching does not necessarily reside hierarchically, nor is it solely invested in those who have escaped the classroom. Authoritative statements about what it means to be engaged in teaching need to be informed and chastened by reflection upon personal experience—a process which is harder to do the further one is from personal and collective involvement in classroom action.

Repeatedly, participants in clinical supervision have told us (see, for example, Smyth, Henry and Martin, 1982) that reciprocity is fundamental. It is only when one person opts out, by reason of 'authority' or 'status', and is not prepared to teach and thus have his/her teaching observed, that hierarchy and its associated problems become a real issue. Reducing the tension that can exist between relative strangers, in the way schools are organized and conducted, can only occur when both parties concerned with the analysis of teaching are prepared to accept equality of treatment, despite any real status differences that might exist. As one teacher involved with clinical supervision put it: 'The reversal of roles could well prove [to be] the vital step in this regard'.

Pursuing the 'Critical' in Teaching

In the previous chapter, and elsewhere in this book, we have argued that teaching is a decidedly political activity—that is to say, political in the classical Greek sense in which 'questions which concern the society as a whole' (Berlak, 1970, p. 262) are raised for consideration. As Hartnett and Naish (1986) put it, teaching (and education in the wider sense) is political in that it is located in 'particular political theories about how a society should be organized so as to yield to its citizens the possibility of living lives that they find valuable and satisfying' (p. 13). Any teaching worth its salt, these writers argue, must raise issues about 'social justice and fairness and whose conceptions should be institutionalized' (p. 13) and legitimated. This holds important consequences, as White and White (1987) point out, for the way teachers regard their work, since:

> . . . both teachers and, as they become capable of understanding the issues involved, also pupils, have the moral right to know how a particular curriculum content . . . fits into the wider political plan, and the moral duty not blindly to accept this plan and its constituent parts, but to reflect on its moral acceptability. (p. 173)

According to this view, teachers: '. . . should not be ashamed of being branded political activists. It is when they try to *disclaim* a political dimension to their work that their attitude becomes suspect' (p. 180). Whether they are prepared to admit it or not, their work *does* have a political dimension to it.

The curious paradox is that while teachers are increasingly being required by educational bureaucrats to work in reputedly objectivist ways and thus to keep subjectivity out of schools and classrooms (see, for example, US Department of Education, 1986), they are being required at the same time to accept increasing political interference in schools in the form of financial cutbacks, imposed curricula, demands for vocationally-oriented courses, and greater centralized control of their work. Not surprisingly, 'those who protest most loudly when teachers introduce progressive initiatives into the curriculum or act collectively within their organisations to combat class, race or gender prejudices, seek nevertheless to impose their own political choices' (Stevens, 1987, p. 75). Berlak and Berlak (1981) put it that teaching:

> . . . is political in that it either encourages persons to develop and use their critical capacities to examine the prevailing political, social and cultural arrangements and the part their own acts . . . play in sustaining or changing these arrangements. If [teaching] . . . fails to encourage critical inquiry into everyday problems of teaching and learning, a *de facto* political position has been taken. (p. 253)

According to Williamson (1985), the point at which educational politics becomes more concrete is at the classroom level, yet:

> . . . this is the most neglected end of the educational debate because it is the hardest to generalize about. But the silence in which actual classroom experiences are shrouded comes partly from the distance between theorists and teachers . . . Theories on education not only have to sound good in the rhetoric of the wider political debate— they have to *work*. (p. 94)

It is in putting teachers back into this debate as *active theorists*, able to construct and test out the 'larger' theories of teaching, that will be the ultimate yardstick as to whether a critical perspective is possible for clinical supervision, and indeed for teaching. Our claim is that clinical supervision not only has the potential to assist teachers to make sense of the complexity of teaching and learning, and thereby provide a basis for growing and developing, but it also has the capacity fundamentally to transform the nature of the way they go about that teaching. The journal entry of one clinical supervision teacher put it rather eloquently when he said that he, and other teachers like him, were working in a context that:

> . . . subtly works against the promotion and development of dignity and self-worth, where there is little or no systematic recognition, where feedback is unfocused and *ad hoc*, where there is little opportunity to share and work collegially, and where teachers are dependent upon a hierarchically organized leadership structure.

This same participant went on to note that a critical approach to clinical supervision is, therefore, necessary. In his words:

> . . . any observation and analysis of teaching must occur within a critical self-reflective perspective . . . Clinical supervision must have an unashamed value orientation toward exposing myths, constraints and practices that perpetrate domination, inequality and powerlessness. Therefore, clinical supervision should aim to enlighten teachers about their practices within a cultural, political and ideological framework as well as in a technical sense. In this way meaningful change and understanding may occur in both a practical and social sense.

The impetus for examining one's teaching (either alone or with the aid of a colleague) in a socially critical way comes from some perplexing incident that emerges as a feeling of unease. Coming from the earlier cited case of the high school head of the English department (who was also a classroom teacher) and his neophyte colleague, an incident arose that is informative. He had long been troubled by the seeming irrelevance to 16-year-olds of centrally provided (but suggested) curricula. In an earlier clinical supervision discussion, he and colleague had isolated 'irrevelance' as the perceived reason for student non-engagement with ideas. Put simply, what was occurring in class was failing to touch in any meaningful way the lives of students. In trying to grapple with how to introduce what he described as 'relevance' into teaching his Year 11 pupils, the head and his colleague uncovered issues that went beyond merely making material 'more interesting'. They were able to see how schooling, their view of authority and their own teaching generally fail to connect at all with the out-of-school experiences of students. In the journal he was keeping as a way of reflecting, the head wrote about a classroom incident (and the subsequent clinical supervision discussion) in the following terms:

> Today in my Modern History class I was struck with the ongoing problem of making the material as relevant as I can to the experiences of the students. We had been looking at primary source material on the preparation for the war on the Western Front in World War I. The material included extracts from the training manuals and a letter from Field Marshall Kitchener about the way the troops should behave in the field.

> I struggled to make this material relevant to the students and engage them with the material. Today I was able to lock onto the idea of society and authority. I asked [them] the question, 'Would you go to war out of patriotism?' We discussed the ways in which today we have less respect for authority. We are much more sceptical of 'motives' and we tend to question and doubt those in authority, such as parents, schools, governments, etc. This seemed to form at least a partial bridge between the material and the experiences of the students.

The instigating event here, or the unsettling trigger, was the head teacher's feelings of inadequacy in dealing with the relevance of what he was required to teach his history students. It would have been easy, he says, 'to have covered the material and dismissed the students as being intellectually incapable of dealing with it'. But instead, looking back over the incident, both he and his colleague could see that the struggle to make issues and concepts more relevant in fact led them to question the view they both held about the utility of knowledge to students, and how textbook knowledge can be used in ways that begin to intersect with students' lives. It was this search for new 'strategies' (a problem to be solved) that ultimately led them to the joint conclusion that students need to be able to make connections between received forms of knowledge and everyday reality.

On other occasions, teachers seem to be much less clear about where the impetus for a social analysis of their teaching comes from—perhaps from a 'gut feeling' that they could be implicated somehow in unjust educational practices. One teacher in his eleventh year as a classroom practitioner came to the realization in his combined Year 5/6 class that many of his pupils appeared to have racist and sexist attitudes, and indeed quite distorted views of society:

> It appears that [they] do have some sense of fairness, but little or no analytical skills to discern among competing values . . . [They] lack the interpersonal and thinking skills that enable a serious consideration of alternatives . . . [What I want to do in my teaching] is to explore ways in which [I] can not only facilitate the development of children's technical skills, but how to apply them to enhance socially just values and practices . . . [Coupled with this I am] interested in building an understanding of how we operate as practitioners in either enhancing or constraining children's

freedom and enlightenment, and in particular the degree to which [I] assist in the perpetuation of the status quo through [my] teaching methods.

This teacher was able to give further expression to this in the form of the suspicion he had that 'the Year 5 boys made more contribution to class discussion, and the Year 5 girls were very passive'. As a first step, he had to obtain some confirmation of his hunch. Classroom observational data collected by his colleague, showing who spoke to whom in class and for how long, enabled them to confirm the following:

(1) that boys did indeed dominate class . . . time, at the expense of the Year 5 girls in particular.
(2) that boys spend a lot of time 'goofing off' when not supervised.
(3) that children do not encourage one another except when forced to by the teacher.
(4) that the boys appeared to lack interpersonal skills, while the girls lacked assertiveness.
(5) that I [as teacher] dominated the [class] time far too much—over 60 per cent.

While it is obviously a matter of some conjecture and personal preference as to how much teacher 'domination' is too much, for this teach the issue revealed by the data he collected was the need to redress what he considered two forms of imbalance—his teacher-centred approach, and his allowing boys to dominate proceedings in class. In returning the favour to his colleague, by helping him to construct a text about his own teaching, the teacher noted that:

> . . . the Year 5 girls [in your class] seemed much more at ease discussing their thoughts in a large group situation . . . One factor that I believe aided you in your ability to elicit an equal number of responses from each gender, was that you allowed thinking time for each question and weren't put off by silence. When this happens to me, I tend to launch into a series of explanatory statements such that the resultant answer I'm looking for becomes either very closed or redundant. One of my aims in future cycles then, will be to ask more open questions, and to allow thinking and explanation time. In association with this, I want to reduce *my* . . . time in class discussion to under 40 per cent. The effect this will have on the four groups will be most interesting to observe.

What started out as a gender issue in class, as a result of dialogue, became part of a larger question of how teachers might hand over increasing power to students to learn. Rapid-fire question and answer sessions have built into them the presumption that the interests of classroom efficiency are more important than shared learning. The issue for this teacher was more than acquiring an effective teaching 'strategy'. What he uncovered was a personal theory of teaching that said, in effect, reflective discussion in class has to be slow paced and contain sustained silences. When he interrupted these silences he was, as Stenhouse (1983) put it, 'breaking under the strain rather than [making] a real contribution to the task of the group' (p. 213). By giving way under the inevitable strain of silence, and by talking, his students were using ' . . . silence as a weapon to make him take over the task they should face as a group' (p. 213). The students were engaging him in a game in which they were able effectively to avoid having to confront their own feelings of intolerance, and dealing with them in an open way. The teacher's premature intervention served further to entrench the socially unjust practices he wanted the students to confront. As he and his colleague talked this through further, they could see that this situation was not something entirely of their own making (attributable to personal failings)—rather, it was an artefact of the fast-paced and superficial way in which the 'system', of which they were a part, required them as teachers to act. What they were coming around to seeing was that the way much of our schooling is organized and enacted, with externally determined curricula aimed at vocationally-oriented programmes, is a form of pedagogy that concentrates more on 'arid nonsense' and is 'connected with the real world [only] by the most tenuous of threads' (Goodman, O'Hehi and O'Shea, 1977, p. 12). In large measure, what went on in his classroom not only produced no alternative action on the part of the students, but led instead to the continuation of the form of oppression he was opposed to. Reflecting in his journal on what clinical supervision had meant in terms of teaching and collegial relationships, he recorded the following:

> My overall feelings, then, were a mixture of discomfort (with identifying points of concern in my practice), of support (at having a close colleague there with whom to plan, postulate and share), confusion (at where to head in order to meet challenges), and enlightenment (at seeing data supporting my beliefs, and offering up new possibilities), excitement (at the growth that I know is occurring in my professional relationship with a colleague), and optimism (at what I see possible in the future).

For both teacher and colleague, it seemed that the most rewarding part of their three month involvement together in clinical supervision was the discussions in which they focused 'on specific data, travelled the universe, reached the depths of despair, returned and glowed with enthusiasm'. The most tangible result was the noticeable change that occurred in his classroom. According to his colleague, there was 'a buzz of excitement in [his] class when [he] managed to reduce his air time and increase the children's interactions . . . '.

On the issue of the potency of the data and how it helps teachers to re-think and reshape their practice in different ways, one primary teacher who used clinical supervision put it in these words:

> Clinical supervision data is not really particularly significant in itself, but it is the act of interpretation and analysis that is significant. Two people with a basically liberal orientation are likely to be interested in one another's world view and construction of reality. The data provides a springboard for the discussion and sharing of that construction.

He and his colleague were able to see, through the data, that critically examining teaching can uncover the relationship between power and knowledge. They could see how this has important implications for the way in which teachers encourage students to have the confidence, the courage and the skills to question, to challenge and to change. Moreover, analyzing teaching in this manner enabled the teacher to arrive at the important conclusion that ' . . . [students] are less likely to surrender their autonomy if they know what it means'. To illustrate what he meant by this, he related a clinical supervision encounter in which he and a colleague explored how the Grade 6 students in his class reacted to role-playing a local community issue involving a multi-national mining company. As he recounted the instance:

> Most of the children come from farming backgrounds, but there are a small number of other occupations. I asked the children to take on their parents' adult roles, to pretend that they were their parents. I then got them to line their chairs up in rows at the front of the room in the manner of a public meeting, and I enlisted three of the students as my assistants. I introduced myself and my three assistants as executives of a mining company who had just discovered a mineral in the surrounding district. I explained the nature of the mineral and the great wealth that could flow from mining it. The students quickly assumed the roles of adults with disconcerting verisimilitude. Their initial enthusiasm for the mining project waned when it became clear that their properties would need to be taken over by the company and the top six inches of the top soil stripped off, rendering the land useless for agriculture forever. I explained that they would be compensated at present market rates and deliberately attempted to divide the group by offering a small number of them jobs in the mine. The children's questions became more and more pointed and their reactions to my responses, and the assurances of my assistants, became progressively more hostile. The three boys who showed some interest in working for the mining company came under unbearable pressure to maintain solidarity, and they withdrew their interest. The children's performances as outraged rural adults were so authentic that I found it difficult not

to laugh out loud. Their behaviour mirrored exactly the behaviour of angry parents at a public meeting that I had attended a few weeks previously.

The point of the lesson had been to engage students to learn to defend themselves and their interests, and to establish and defend a point of view. This was clearly not possible by merely explaining the workings of a multi-national company, because these 'workings' are themselves situated in broader social and economic agenda. What this teacher was trying to do was to get his students to see that mining companies are not benign entities that acquire land, employ people and extract minerals. He wanted his students to explore beyond the 'blinkers of their own experiences' and see that in the kind of societies in which we live there are interests whose power is 'invisible' and who 'hide away knowledge because it is power' (Williamson, 1985, p. 94).

At the same time as he was trying to engage his students in critique, this teacher was using the dialogue and reflection made possible through clinical supervision to struggle with some large issues in respect of his own teaching. He was required to adopt a questioning and enquiring stance towards what had become a comfortable way of life. In the next section we want to give an enlarged dimension to that by looking at how aspects of both personal biography and collective professional history are important.

Untying Personal and Theoretical History

We would be less than honest if we did not say that developing the critical perspective we are speaking about is difficult, if not impossible, for some teachers. Through clinical supervision some teachers are able quite adequately to arrive at a description of their teaching, but even with collegial assistance they are unable to 'untie the text' (Young, 1981) in a way that makes much sense—they never really get to the root causes that lie behind their actions. The action remains locked in the realm of the mystical, caused as it were, by some vague magical forces that they neither understand nor control.

An indication of what we mean by this can be seen in the example of the teacher cited earlier who used the mining company role play. For the first time in many years of successful teaching, involvement in clinical supervision had unsettled him to the extent of requiring him to confront his educational ideas and ask where they had come from. In trying to make sense of what he did pedagogically on a daily basis he could see that he was caught up in a complex web of forces in which he was making his own history, but not under circumstances of his own choosing (as Marx put it). Looking back at his involvement in various social 'causes' in the 1960s, he could see that the acquisitive and competitive society, of which he had become a part, had twisted and tarnished many of his original ideals:

All of [the] social phenomena [at the time] seemed to me to indicate that something was wrong with the traditional authority structures. This, combined with my school experience (rigid, hierarchical, privileged, private school) . . . [caused me to leave] the place angry and rebellious, and made me an enthusiastic radical. [But now] I am part of the structure that I once daubed with slogans; survival has become a priority . . . .

Having reached what was a sophisticated stage in the analysis of his teaching in terms of its social, political and cultural origins, it was an unfortunate reflection on what he thought he had achieved at the end of three months of clinical supervision that this same teacher claimed to have ' . . . found it difficult to achieve the level of political analysis called for . . . ' and of having ' . . . struggled without much success to identify the nature of the ideological domination at work in the school'. Like many teachers who labour under the burden of a poor public image, he had clearly made much greater progress in evaluating his teaching than he was able to give himself credit for.

As long as teachers remain preoccupied with examining their teaching at the level of technical in-class skills, then they and their students will be denied a comprehensive understanding of how their lives are being shaped. Here is an example to illustrate our point. Although it arose as something of an aside in a conferral with his clinical supervision colleague, the following excerpt of dialogue illustrates the personalistic (and ultimately unhelpful) way in which some teachers tend to portray and analyze their problems:

Yesterday was Friday again! Friday bloody Friday. It's the third Friday that I've *had* those Year 7s—emphasis on the *had* . . . I am the [teaching] principal of a primary school of 150 kids. I've just come from a smaller school of fifty kids; had been there for five years. Kids were beautiful . . . independent, reliable, self-directed, self-motivated. Great. Now, after twenty years of teaching I meet twenty-one Year 7s, half of whom act like caged bastards. God I've been angry . . . [Took] them for a lesson intending to get to know them and do some social learning activities. I told them to work in small groups on a task—read a story and answer some questions. They did everything but. Roamed around, talked about everything else, annoyed the class next door, drew and coloured-in . . . I couldn't believe it. I'd been so used to asking Year 7s in previous years to do so and so, and they would; but not this mob.

Using my theory of social learning and group development as a guide, I tried to explain my *modus operandi* and why I was doing it this way. Half of them wouldn't even listen. I asked them several times to sit down. Because I didn't know them by name, I walked over to the offenders and said: 'Excuse me, but I would like you to sit down so I can tell you what I would like you to do'. Some

> complied with my request. After almost pleading for cooperation,
> I did my block and yelled at them. That got their attention, but it
> is not the way I tend to operate.

For this teacher, he found that he was trying to put into effect a theory about teaching and learning that says: learning cannot occur unless students are paying attention so they can hear directions. He was prepared to pursue that theory to the point of verbal violence, if necessary. The students, on the other hand, seemed to be displaying a different set of values and beliefs (a theory) about learning; namely, that they had the right to communicate with one another and dictate what went on in class, and the teacher was powerless to change that. It could be argued that the narrowness of the teacher's learning theory generated a student reaction. To put another interpretation upon it, what the students were expressing by ignoring the teacher was a form of opposition and resistance to what they saw as the teacher's institutional exercise of hierarchical control, despite his claim to be doing otherwise.

It is always difficult to make inferences on the basis of behaviour alone, and in the particular case cited above, the actions of the students could be construed as simply disruptive. Another interpretation, however, could be that this example shows some of the signs of the teacher's inability to see how his own actions were inextricably bound-up in perpetuating a particular power relationship with his students, despite the fact that he thought he was actually divesting power to students. He was also unable to see student opposition in a different light—as a possible expression of their unwillingness to submit to what they saw as a thinly veiled authoritarian form of control, dressed-up as democratic intent. As his words below indicate, while this teacher had some success in seeing the more general point about the historical domination of students by teachers, he was still blind to the contradiction in his own practice:

> It seems to me that it's always been the practice for teachers to 'bark' orders at students, just as if they were in the army . . . It's the way teachers have spoken to students ever since schools began; it's never been questioned . . . I believe that asking students for cooperation . . . goes hand in hand with an explanation of why the request is being made. This gives children more information to go on when they make their choices about cooperating or not . . .

> [And later] . . . it seems I am the person with the power in that I have decided what the class is going to do, but I am willing to 'give the power away' to the students by negotiating what I intend to do. What I am saying is that I hold the power, because I am making decisions about how I want the students to behave while I tell them my intentions for the lesson. But *then*, they have the power to re-negotiate the activities.

The difficulty facing this teacher (albeit, a teaching principal) is that his cultural upbringing has led him to accept that schools and what transpires within them occur according to some rational and hierarchically sanctioned rules. This can be a difficult view to dislodge, especially in a context where it is being continually reinforced and massaged by a 'scientific' and management pedagogy (Giroux, 1985 a) view of schooling. Because the notion of social critique is so foreign to teachers, what they sometimes end up doing is either of two things: either they (metaphorically) turn the blowtorch on themselves in quite self-denigrating ways that reveal enormous guilt feelings at the way they do things, or they seek to rationalize and justify their practices on the basis of what they consider to be the perceived needs of children or the communities which schools exist to serve. In both cases the result is the same: an unwillingness to confront the systematic way in which their teaching has been dictated to them by others.

What we see exemplified in the instance just referred to is a kind of conforming and acquiescent failure to challenge the trajectory of history—it amounts to a fatalistic throwing up of the hands, that says, 'things have always been this way'. This particular teacher has not become empowered because he has been unable to elicit or respect ' . . . the integrity of the cultural informant's [own] constructs' (Anderson, 1987, p. 5), in this case that of his students. Had he been able to understand the Year 7s on their terms, he would have been able to see that their ' . . . behaviour takes on a certain rationality [even predictability]' (p. 5), where 'social learning' means genuinely democratic relationships among students, not some version of social engineering that teachers try to engender. But, to be fair to the teacher, there is also a rationality to his apparently irrational behaviour. What we can see here is the difficulty teachers encounter in trying to sort out the overlapping complexities of Willis' (1977) school norms—the 'official' (what the institution says are its statements of purposes), the 'pragmatic' (how teachers deal with day-to-day problems relating to social control), and the 'cultural' (how they speak about both of the others in the staff room and with colleagues). As Anderson (1987) put it, the interpenetration of these presents teachers with an ' . . . inchoate social reality from which he or she must extract a rationale for his or her actions. The practitioner, then, cannot be blamed for possessing contradictory goals and rationales which he or she uses in different contexts' (pp. 11–12). What has to be remembered, however, is that it is not the monumental strides that are important so much as the beginnings of a changed orientation towards thinking and acting with respect to teaching. It is really a matter of teachers moving from a situation in which they think and act as if they have no other alternative than to follow the 'invisible hand' that seems to be controlling them, to a circumstance in which they are able to see that a wider social reality not only constrains and enables their action, but that there are measures they can adopt.

Progress is indeed possible where teachers are able to bring together small pieces of evidence that amount to examples of how ' . . . taking the circumstances of their own life and materials to hand, people can, without the benefit of theory or the expectations of others, critically confront the way things are and dimly imagine, out of those very circumstances, the way they might be' (Steedman, 1982, p. 157).

Our earlier claim that to politicize their work teachers need to start with the concrete lived reality is not based on convenience; rather, by starting with reality, we are able to work on it, see its limits, and hence begin to overcome it (Shor and Freire, 1987, p. 107). Because of the way our culture accommodates us to working in unthinking and unquestioning ways, and because we have come to accept as 'natural' the ways we teach and the social relationships we develop with our students, we tend to accept as bearable forces around us which are really quite intolerable. This happens because of the way in which teaching is construed as being a technical process that only requires fine-tuning in order to achieve pre-determined educational objectives. Viewed in this light, teaching actually denies questions about the ends towards which actions are directed and the interests being served. It is possible to envisage teaching in a way that involves contesting the variables that govern the way we teach, and opens-up for contestation and debate crucial issues about the politics, the ethics and the morality of that teaching. Part of the difficulty in uncovering these alternative courses of action is that they are shrouded by such complex networks of forces that they are not always easily penetrable.

Below is an example of a teacher in a private secondary school who used clinical supervision as a way of untying his personal, institutional and theoretical history. Through the collection of data about his teaching, he and his colleague were able to begin to problematize his teaching by speculating about the courses of action he needed to adopt in order to change some of the educational structures that surrounded him. He relates an incident in which he called the class to attention, gave them permission to proceed with a 'set' assignment, and what happened when a student came to him with a 'puzzled look' on his face:

S: Mr . . . What's the answer to number five?
T: [referring to the question] What is meant by the texture of the soil?
S: I don't know, that's why I'm asking you.
T: Well, . . . you should be able to find the answer to this question. Have you read the information sheets I gave you when the assignment was handed out?
S: No.
T: What about searching through your notes on soil texture? Have you done that?
S: No.
T: Well you should refer to your notes first, read them through and then if you don't understand something come and see me
  [student left still looking puzzled].

Largely on his own, but using his colleague as a sympathetic ear, he proceeded to analyze what had happened, his aspirations as a teacher, and his own unwitting implication in the preservation of a form of teaching and learning that he was unhappy with. In the comment made below we can see that the assignment/worksheet style of teaching he was using is geared more to students covering content for examinations than it is to any meaningful learning about the interrelationship between ideas and the world:

Why do I maintain a situation where student participation, negotiation and reconstruction of learning is minimized? Why do I continue with non-negotiable forms of teaching and learning processes? If I expect my students to assume increasing levels of responsibility for their own learning, then surely I must begin to allow them to participate in deciding how they are expected to learn.

His explanation carried him into pursuing questions he had not even thought about in his teaching. Certainly his thinking about his school underwent a major reconstruction, and we would imagine this to be a prelude to actions he might adopt. By not analyzing his teaching in terms of personal or individual shortcomings, he is able to develop with some broader avenues for action. As he put it:

. . . the school's current practice of rank ordering students through competitive assessment means that some students are locked out of future life options. Those who succeed are being rewarded for their compliance in following the rules which have been laid down by the community and endorsed by the school. My school demands that the quality of a student's work be judged. Why then do I allow such a requirement to pervade classroom life in such a manner that it discourages learning for some of the students I teach?

. . . my practices are constrained within the philosophical constraints laid down by the . . . values of the school. One of the goals of the school is to provide an ordered, structured environment so that learning and willingness to apply effort to worthwhile tasks is facilitated. I may ask myself, who decided which tasks are worthwhile? Why do I expect the full attention of students when addressing them? Why do I demonstrate to the students my ultimate power over the classroom? The answer is becoming more and more apparent. The accepted political order within the school makes it that way.

The established political order of the school dictates the curriculum. It decides what is taught and where resources are allocated, even down to the timetable allocations. The same political order restricts students from being involved in any meaningful decision-making within the school.
Why are the students excluded from decision-making?

What kinds of decisions should they be involved in?
Why do I expect my students to gracefully accept decisions being
handed down to them?
Why are students precluded from possessing an effective power
within this school?.

Analysis of this kind enabled him to see how particular aspects of his
geography lesson that were troublesome to him were not isolated or
unconnected fragments; they were part of a broader agenda in which he
was implicated in his school. Locating the micro aspect of the classroom
in the macro scene of the school and society enabled him to see more clearly
how the limited nature of his pedagogy was shaped by forces that required
subordination of students, rank-ordering of students and accompanying
forms of competitive assessment—compliance being ensured by means of
official forms of patronage that accompany the selective allocation of
resources.

Building Dialogical Relations

It is interesting how intentions can be mischievously misconstrued. In
Australia recently, schools in Victoria were invited by the Minister of
Education to share with one another 'good news' about practices that
worked well for them (*Melbourne Age*, 23 May 1988). That a sharing of
successful teaching ideas could produce a cry of 'propaganda' from the political
opposition party says something unfortunate about the cellular and insular ways
in which teachers are *supposed* to operate in schools. Clearly, in some
quarters, dialogical relations are regarded as akin to a form of subversion.
   Notwithstanding, one of the major potential limitations of clinical
supervision, even when construed 'critically', is that it can remain in the
realm of the individualistic; that is to say, it can be a process in which pairs
of teachers act reflectively, but they never involve a wider community of
teachers or others interested and involved in schooling. Merely having
teachers develop dyadic relationships, even if they are reflecting critically
on their teaching, can amount to no more than an extension of already well-
entrenched individualistic ways of viewing teaching. Although there are the
beginnings of dialogical relationships (of a type) in clinical supervision, what
is missing is the wider collaboration and sharing of viewpoints that are only
possible when teachers gather in groups beyond the classroom to consider
the intersection of classroom practices and other social forces. In C. Wright
Mills' (1959) terms, there is a need for a 'sociological imagination' that
enables us 'to grasp history and biography and the relations between the
two within society' (pp. 6–7), and to dialogue in such a way that we are
able to see the relations between the two.

The educational literature, as well as in the documented and anecdotal experiences of teachers (Raphael, 1985; Herndon, 1985; Palonsky, 1986; Shann, 1987; Ashton-Warner, 1958; Wigginton, 1985), suggests that where teachers *have* dialogical relations with one another, then schools are much more vibrant and reflective places in which to live and work. Freedman, Jackson and Boles (1983) captured the mood by describing teaching as 'an imperilled profession' which, under normal circumstances, structures silences between teachers through individualistic, 'blame the victim' approaches to evaluation. Their research found that teaching was largely founded on the false premise that being a 'good' teacher involved 'facing the issues alone' (p. 298). In their words:

> This approach defines the problem as an aggregate of disaffected or incapable teachers whose deficiencies are seen as personal, rather than a reflection of a failure of the educational system to grapple with and confront . . . contradictory demands. We . . . need to look at the institutional nature of schools and how the structure of schools creates such contradictions and prevents their resolution. (p. 263)

If clinical supervision as a process is to escape its unfortunate history of preaching 'collegiality', 'trust' and 'open mindedness', while actually being enacted in some quarters as a sophisticated system of human relations and teacher surveillance (St Maurice, 1987), then there needs to be ways in which teachers, along with parents and students, are able to reflect upon the clinical supervision process itself and its relationship to schooling and society. If clinical supervision is to be more than collegiality for collegiality's sake, then teachers need to see how the process enables them to break through the silence and 'claim power on the basis of knowledge gained in teaching practice' (McDonald, 1986, p. 357). Greene (1986) expressed this notion of teachers raising their 'voice' as a way of developing much needed 'public space' in schools, whereby people are able to ask critical and creative questions. By rejecting the 'mystifications of the system' and challenging the 'inexorability of the system', Greene (1985) argues that teachers in concert are able to arrive at a critical understanding that 'schools like other institutions, are fabricated by human beings' (p. 13), and to that extent represent particular cognitive and political interests that can and must be confronted. This amounts to engaging others in describing, unveiling and explaining the contradictions between what people actually experience in the world of schooling and the ways in which they are required to live their lives in schools. Differences, according to Greene (1986), have to be resolved 'rationally, authentically, politically' (p. 6) so that a variety of voices is heard and so that new forms of collaboration can emerge that are founded less on single standards and more on a questioning of the way socio-economic arrangements dictate current forms of schooling.

The notion of collaboration being pursued here through clinical supervision is oriented towards teachers using the sharing process they have begun through intervisitation and problematizing their teaching, to extend those discussions into the wider school community to involve administrators, other teachers, curriculum/in-service consultants, parents, members of the surrounding community, as well as students. Where teachers have begun to be articulate about what it is they do, why and with what effects, they are able to see how these relate to the structural factors that facilitate and constrain their work.

Having teachers publicly share and dialogue with others about what they have discovered about themselves, the contexts and the structures within which they teach is one of the more exciting possibilities that has yet to be fully explored for clinical supervision. Our experience in working with clinical supervision has been that when teachers from within, as well as across schools, come together in a workshop, seminar or forum, then important shared understandings about what it means to develop empowering relationships within schools begin to become a reality. They come to see that exchanging experiences on what it means to penetrate their teaching through face-to-face discussions with another colleague, that constructing accounts of that teaching through the collection of data, and asking searching questions about where habitual teaching processes come from and whose interests they serve, are all actions that are more sustainable when the results of doing that are shared. It is also true that participants in clinical supervision dyads cannot always see the merits of extending and building individual knowledge about teaching into a socially shared dimension. One teacher who came along to a reflective workshop, after having tried clinical supervision, summed up both aspects when she said:

> I really came to the workshop feeling that listening to each other would be repetitive. I was pleasantly surprised to find that there was a variety of situations. I was very interested to hear others' experiences and impressions . . .
>
> This was an intimate session where I felt I could speak honestly and without being embarrassed. I was really surprised at how comfortable I felt when it was my turn to speak. These situations are usually pretty tense for me . . .
>
> I thought this was an excellent day. I realized that nearly all the other teachers faced the same sort of problems we did . . . Just to hear how other teachers used clinical supervision, gave me many ideas about my own teaching . . .
>
> It gave me an indication of many varied and different ways clinical supervision can be used. It also illustrated that all teachers have areas of concern, not just me, and that clinical supervision is not just for poor teachers. (Smyth and Henry, 1985, p. 9)

The idea of reflective workshops, in which teachers build the kind of collaborative and supportive alliances necessary for sustaining and maintaining clinical supervision as a teacher-controlled form of evaluation, extends clinical supervision beyond what might otherwise be an isolated and individualistic process. The notion is quite simply that teachers who have agreed voluntarily to work with a colleague on clinical supervision agree to come together after about two months of having tried the process, to share their thoughts on what happened and to act as a support network of critical friends in sustaining and extending the process in their schools. Our experiences have been (Smyth and Henry, 1985) that this is crucial to the success of clinical supervision, especially in the early and formative stages. Not to have this supportive forum in which teachers share lived experiences (while hearing of the problems, successes and achievements of others) is seriously to under-rate the importance of the support, encouragement and the critical perspective teachers can provide for each other when trying out new ideas.

In articulating their thoughts and feelings about clinical supervision as a way of problematizing their teaching, teachers often arrive at what appear on the surface to be obvious enough insights. For example, one group who came together several weeks after having commenced clinical supervision in their schools were most apologetic to one another for the limited amount of clinical supervision they were able to report upon. What was surprising was that these teachers actually had expectations that in their already crowded schedules it was possible for them to have achieved more than they had done. This in itself was a sobering experience for many, but as a result of their joint efforts they were able to come to a collective realization that engaging in reflection of the kind implicit in clinical supervision takes substantial amounts of time. Without additional resources, the limitations on what was possible became glaringly obvious—it provoked heated discussion about the relative merits and priorities of what is considered important about teaching and schooling, and who it is that makes these decisions. Two comments representative of many made by teachers on this theme of resource constraints were: 'Clinical supervision has been fascinating; my only regret is that there was not enough time . . . Here perhaps is a message for our administrators—to do the job properly requires more than a few hours here and there'. And from another teacher: 'Overall, I found clinical supervision very demanding. While it was refreshing and professionally enriching, it was frustrating in trying to find time . . .'.

When teachers arrive at understandings like these about the importance of collective knowledge and the way school structures and ideological dispositions impede their aspirations to work with one another in more educative ways, then these are not insubstantial discoveries. What we can see here are the beginnings of the power of collective reflection as teachers come to see more clearly the oppressive circumstances in which they work. But as Giroux (1985b) has noted, the struggle is still considerable:

At the present time, teachers labour in the public schools under organizational constraints and ideological conditions that leave them little room for collective work and critical pursuits. Their teaching

> hours are long, they are generally isolated in cellular structures and have few opportunities to teach with others . . . Moreover they operate under class loads and within an industrial timetable that is oppressive . . . By fighting for conditions that support joint teaching, collective writing and research, and democratic planning, teachers will make in-roads into opening up new spaces for creative and reflective discourse and action. The importance of such discourse cannot be overstressed. (pp. 95–6)

Possibly the most tangible benefit to emerge out of the teacher-to-teacher exchanges when teachers dialogue about clinical supervision is the mutual encouragement and support. As one teacher put it: 'I really appreciated the personal contributions of other teachers—being able to listen to their doubts and concerns and find that they often matched mine' (Smyth and Henry, 1985, p. 8). At its most practical level, the experience of actually reconstructing the events of how they used clinical supervision, the context in which it occurred, and with what effect, provided a neat series of case studies for other participants in the workshop to think about in comparison to their own situations. The fact that other teachers had tried ideas *and found them to work* was an important piece of information. As well as promoting a clearer understanding of the advantages of collaborative learning and mutual support, the reflective workshop on clinical supervision represented something of a breakthrough in converting ideas into action. In contrast to the common and often disappointing experience of many school reform efforts, where good ideas are presented and applauded but never actually materialize in teachers' practices, it became clear on this occasion that new ideas had been tested in practice. The immensely difficult task of overcoming personal and social inertia and concretely changing personal and institutional practices had begun. As teachers discussed their experiences, there was an increased realization of the strategic value of constructing circumstances that require practical action rather than mere speculation.

Learning that clinical supervision is possible in secondary schools as well as in a range of situations in elementary schools; that it had uses in social situations outside classrooms (such as faculty meetings); that it made unexpected demands on personal and interpersonal resources; that it sometimes required learning about data-gathering skills; that it is often dependent on altering timetables and schedules; and that it involved adding more tasks to already crowded work schedules—were all inescapable lessons that emerged from the experiences of teachers who experimented with clinical supervision (see Smyth, Henry, Marcus, Logan and Meadows, 1982). Not all such experiences were endearing, it was true. Some experiences were trying, others unpleasant, still others frustrating and disappointing. But regardless of impact, the crucial factor was that participants were able to convey to each other personal knowledge gained through participation in clinical supervision. The ideas canvassed were ones that had been tested in practice. Moving beyond the stage of talking or speculating about what clinical supervision would add up to when tried gave a great deal of credibility to the teacher-to-teacher exchanges that took place in the reflection workshop. Personal impressions, chastened by comparison with others' experiences, were powerful means of confirming the reliability of each person's contribution. Authentic and believable insights depended to a large extent on the capacity of teachers to present to each other 'true to life' experiences.

In summary, clinical supervision as we have described it here amounts to a commitment to develop a discourse among teachers which creates the opportunity for the exploration of different ways of enacting values in schools. It is a form of evaluation that requires teachers to engage themselves in a critical analysis of evidence about ideas and practices, and in the process to create dialectical forms of communication and exchange. The ultimate commitment is to the creation of a style of discourse that is not only directed towards the problematic, but one which is also educative and capable of enabling participants genuinely to 'hear' one another.

Note

1 We express our gratitude to the teachers who allowed us to draw so intimately on their experiences in this chapter. They were colleagues in the true sense of that term.

Chapter 8

The 'Other Face' of Teacher Evaluation

Introduction

If we accept that the evaluation of teaching is not simply an ephemeral and isolated technical act done to teachers in classrooms, but rather a way of both constructing and deconstructing the social experience of schooling; and if we acknowledge that teacher evaluation is not about bureaucratically controlling teacher behaviour, but a means for rendering problematic taken-for-granted habits, practices and institutional norms—then viewed in this way, teacher evaluation amounts to a way of contesting and developing a counter-discourse of schooling. Like Frank Smith in his *Insult to Intelligence: Bureaucratic Invasion of Our Classrooms* (1986), we believe that dominant and inspectorial forms of evaluation are simply forms of surveillance dressed-up as 'fiscal tools' in the hands of those who claim to be acting out their own infallability through the possession of truth (Freire, 1985, p. 23).

Much of the argument in this volume has centred on explicating the characteristics, features and forms of two antagonistic and competing views of what it means to be involved in evaluation (of teaching, in particular). What we labelled the dominant view was shown to be impregnated with the undisclosed agenda of entrenchment, oppression and submissiveness, and the overwhelming concern to promote only superficial change through ensuring the maintenance of existing exploitative relationships. Historically this has been possible because of the contrived and orchestrated process of progressively removing teachers (but also students and their parents) from the political, historical and theoretical traditions of schooling. By inserting, sustaining and maintaining a managerial ethos rather than a pedagogical one, in schools during periods of economic crisis, it has been possible to legitimate dominant forms of evaluation on spurious grounds of accountability. The net effect of this depressing scenario is that decisions about the nature of schooling, what counts as knowledge and what kind of pedagogical relationships are sanctioned are formulated on the basis of beliefs, assumptions and values that are at best anti-educational.

Missing from the instrumental and technicist ways of evaluating teaching, are the kinds of educative relationships that permit the asking of moral, ethical and political questions about the 'rightness' of actions. When based upon educative (as distinct from managerial) relations, evaluative practices become concerned with breaking down structured silences and narrow prejudices. Striving for dialogical (compared with monological) relationships was seen to be based on values of reason, argument, debate and persuasion, and opening-up questions about the relationships between schooling and society. This ability to make transparent what had previously been opaque and impenetrable, to disclose what had previously been hidden and off the agenda—is what gives a critical perspective on evaluation its political and ethical potency. Socially constructed hierarchies (of race, class and gender), which have always served the interests of the privileged, are flattened as teachers and others in schools, who had previously been silenced, are able to develop a voice.

The tension between the two major competing paradigms (and we acknowledge that there are others too that we have not discussed here), is thus seen to be based largely upon a silent struggle between ideological forces that espouse surveillance, hierarchy and bureaucracy, and the contesting forces of reflection, collegiality and educative relations. The contestation takes the form of a private cold war in which the posture of the dominant technological mode of evaluation is posited as if it were natural and commonsense. The rightfulness of that position and the view of schooling it encapsulates is far from settled.

Historical Perspective

A look at the historical development of the teacher evaluation processes in the USA, UK and Australia shows that those responsible for making decisions about schooling have long held a misguided faith in the capacity of 'science' (of a particular kind) to deliver definitive knowledge about the nature of teaching. For almost a century, the search has proceeded unabated for the indicators of efficiency and effectiveness in teaching. Even though this quest has been to no avail, the faith is as unshakable today as it ever was. What these early beginnings of teacher evaluation point to is the unquestioned right of the State to determine and control schools bureaucratically. But just as the elite exercised what they saw as their right to control, teachers and students exercised their reciprocal right to contest and resist those forms of imposition.

The other thing that our historical sketch pointed to was (whether rightly or not) that schools have always been a prominent force in shaping society. Efforts aimed at so-called 'educational reform' have been the mechanism by which schools have been required both to reflect, and at the same time to shape society—and teacher evaluation has been an important ingredient in all of this. Keeping the ends towards which schooling is directed off the agenda, and, therefore, in a sense unquestioned, has been a major achievement of the teacher evaluation movement. As long as evaluation can be contained to a limited technical process of assessing the extent to which schools, teachers and students meet up to pre-specified ends, then the more contestable aspects can be kept under wraps. It thus becomes relatively easy to justify the separation and the widening gulf between those who 'know about' teaching from those who 'do' the teaching. Overlooked, of course, are a number of major issues—the largely gendered basis of that separation; the fact that teachers' work does not lend itself to quasi-rational conceptualizations; and, that school people are continually resisting, contesting and re-shaping schools in the light of political bargains, compromises and understandings. Such authoritarian and commodified views of evaluation flow into the ways teachers are expected to discharge their responsibilities to students, but above all there is an abiding presumption that the evaluation of teaching must focus upon the presumed deficits of individuals. Ignored in all of this are the social and relational aspects of teaching and the ways in which these are constructed, contested and reformulated in light of the specific ways in which teachers and others choose to live out their lives at particular historical moments.

What we are witnessing at the moment with moves to intensify control over teachers by insisting upon authoritarian pedagogical styles is wrong-headed. The aim is to separate even further those who lay claim to 'scientific' knowledge about teaching from those who labour in the fields of the classrooms. This constructed separation is only sustainable as long as the major players and their 'minders' are prepared to believe in its efficacy. If teachers, for example, think and act in ways that deny such forms of subservience, then the dichotomy begins to break down. Dissolving the basis of this division of labour not only requires a clear conception of the way things are, and an understanding on the part of teachers as to how the current situation came about historically (and of their part in it), but an equally strong feeling for the struggles and resistances that have mediated and contested that dominant viewpoint.

Clearly, there needs to be frontal attack on the prevalent but indefensible view that 'science' (of the limited kind we have alluded to here) can be relied upon to generate valid conceptualizations of what constitutes 'good' teaching. In part this will mean exposing the fragmentary and behaviouristic nature of such accounts which are demonstrably at odds with the more robust ways in which teachers, students and parents experience the realities of schooling. At another level, the way in which 'science' trumpets neutrality and disinterest, while encapsulating a well-defined but undisclosed political agenda of the way teaching *should* be, needs to be continually exposed. The touchstone needs to be the total absence of mutuality and exchange that has long dogged the scientific view of teaching. We need vigorously to challenge the dogmatism that has come to characterize teacher evaluation and which is used to give legitimacy to certain forms of teaching over others. Likewise, we need to be harsh and uncompromising in terms of the non-relational view of teaching and evaluation that is contained within claims to objectivity and universality. Where the rationality of technique is eulogized as the *sine qua non* of evaluation, we need to be insistent in asking annoying questions about the moral, ethical and educational worth of what is not measured (as well as what is measured) by these fragmentary procedures. Whenever alternative values are denied and excluded through evaluation procedures, but especially where pre-specified criteria and formulae are used, then we should be troubled. The alleged supremacy of technique within evaluation should be seen for what it is—a means of portraying a false consensus about the ends of teaching, and a denial of the debate that should ensue about what the nature of those desired goals might be.

Where we require teachers to adopt the stance sketched out above, and require them to work under conditions that either metaphorically or physically cut them off from discussions about the ideas that inform their classroom practice, then we endorse a form of social amnesia in which teachers' professional history is effectively expunged. Remaining trapped within the constrained limits of the habitual means that teachers are forced to accept as natural and commonsense a narrow psychologistic view of teaching. Problem situations are diagnosed as personal inadequacies in a situation in which the structural and ideological categories that give rise to such circumstances are considered off limits.

It is no mere coincidence either that dominant forms of evaluation reinforce these forms of disembodiment through monological relations between teachers and evaluators. An obvious manifestation is the way in which teachers are not involved in determining who their evaluators are, what criteria are to be employed, or what the focus of the observation will be. As if this is not enough, they are further silenced by the yawning chasm between the 'expert' and the 'inexpert'. Relationships are inquisitorial, with proclamations about what is 'wrong' (or right) about teaching being followed by transfusions about how inadequacies can be corrected and monitored. Purged is any attempt to introduce debate, reason or argumentation in a scheme that seems primarily designed to bolster individualistic and competitive norms, rather than foster social and collaborative ones. What becomes lost is the notion that schools can exist as self-correcting communities that understand what they are doing, and know perfectly well how to pursue forms of discourse that enable them to ascertain and attach worth to what it is they do.

The Educative Approach

We see educative approaches to teacher evaluation as part of a long-term process of establishing such self-correcting communities. Hierarchical arrangements which allow one group to control and dictate the work of another give way to more egalitarian and democratic relations in which reason is the prime informant of decision-making. A technocratic view of schooling which focuses attention solely on 'how to' questions, is replaced by a critical orientation that links 'what ought to be' with 'how to' concerns. As Jonathan (n.d.) put it recently:

> Recent obsession with the curriculum—what should be taught, who should decide, how learning might best be effected and assessed—has diverted attention from the logically prior question of what purpose the whole educational apparatus ought to serve . . . In entering into substantive discussion we may well risk falling off philosophy's greasy pole into the mud of ethical commitment, but no fundamental inquiry into the task of education can take either our current educational practice or our present social arrangements as given, nor avoid evaluating both in the light of rationally defensible normative principles. (p. 6)

Achieving this radical restructuring of the way we regard schooling cannot occur simply by inserting educative models of teacher evaluation into schools. Even when educative innovations actually contest the nature of schooling in substantive ways, these impulses need to be bolstered by educative structures if change is to be enduring. Transforming schooling, therefore, requires fundamental and corresponding changes in dominant ideological views. Because the beliefs teachers and the community in general hold are deeply entrenched, any school change that hopes to be educative must penetrate the ideologies and the structures that often reinforce and support limited notions of schooling.

We have argued that a technical emphasis on teaching actually obscures the political, ethical and moral underpinnings of the enterprise, while denying teachers a voice in the determination of purposes. By silencing teachers, this technologization of teachers' work legitimates oppressive and alienating school hierarchies. Textbooks, the core curriculum (of a certain kind), national student testing schemes and various kinds of rationalized curriculum have all played a part in narrowing the teacher's role. While these structures might be designed with the very best of intentions to eliminate incompetent teachers, what they end up doing is reinforcing the notion that teachers are not experts, that educational hierarchies are necessary and just, and that teachers do not have to enter into educative dialogue with one another about their work.

In part the problem is one in which the distorted and constrained image of what teachers do (and should do) has acted to produce and sustain an oppressive technical role for vast numbers of teachers. Breaking the public service ideal which has come to characterize the work of teachers requires a strong assertion by them that they are no longer prepared to tolerate the forms of isolation that cut them off from one another as members of a critical community and from dialogue about the moral and ethical worth of teaching. Countering the cellular nature of the way schools are organized is one aspect, but there are others too. For instance, there is the need to be vociferous about the individually competitive reward structures (called 'career ladders' in the USA) that further alienate and separate teachers from one another. Rather than the dialogical and the educational aspects of what teachers do being allowed to be relegated to the realm of an 'add-on' and, therefore, subservient to the technical aspect of passing on knowledge to students, teachers need to develop a voice in asserting the primacy of the educative as a recognized, legitimate and appropriately rewarded part of teaching.

A Place for Horizontal Evaluation

Horizontal evaluation was offered as one exemplar of an educative approach to teacher evaluation. Based on communicative reason, we have argued that this dialogical process enables teachers to re-think fundamental assumptions about schooling and act on this understanding to reshape educational processes. As opposed to dominant schemes which attempt to control what teachers do, this approach fosters change by empowering teachers to see classroom practice and schooling in different ways. This shift from control to empowerment not only strengthens teachers' voices but makes them less dependent on supposed experts, better able to dialogue with parents, students and others about what they do and why they do it. They are able to go considerably beyond a technical orientation that limits their role to that of facilitating educational ends determined by others. Empowerment of this type is not only important for teachers, but it is also a necessary part of contesting the taken-for-granted role of schooling.

Schooling changes all the time. Unfortunately, the political implications of schooling remain hidden and are rarely considered or acted upon, thereby leaving largely uncontested the role of schools in reproducing inequalities. Among other reasons, because those who interact most directly with students are silenced, questions about schooling are limited to 'how to' concerns, and school structures which shape educational experiences in important ways are ignored. Because educative forms of evaluation actively contest this oppressive and limited teacher role, they have the potential to put the political back onto the educational agenda and give teachers a say in these important debates.

The lived experiences of teachers using horizontal evaluation indicated that they started such a process. They did so by shifting the focus from finding solutions to technical problems to posing problems that take into consideration the political implications of schooling, by expanding the range of problems addressed, by assessing deeply entrenched and authoritarian practices, and by rethinking prejudgments including those that act in concert with school structures to shape educational practices in hierarchical ways. This understanding of schooling enabled teachers to act on school practices that shape the values individuals hold and the relations found in society.

While these results are promising, there is much more that needs to occur if teachers are to be at the forefront of educative school change. Missing in the teacher dialogue, for example, was any mention of class, race or gender. Teachers went beyond the technical but did not address a number of central political issues. Also absent was a historical analysis of school problems and practices. Teachers were locked within the confines of a presentist perspective and could not always see how their understanding of schooling comes out of a particular history or living tradition. Finally, although teachers broke down barriers with parents, much more needs to be done if change is to be guided by the strongest arguments of those with a legitimate interest in education. To take the process further these questions and related concerns need to be part of an ongoing dialogue on teacher evaluation that shifts from finding ways of controlling teacher behaviour to empowering them to understand schooling more fully and act on that understanding to transform destructive school patterns.

A Different Role for Clinical Supervision

Clinical supervision, construed in a 'critical' way, was proffered as a further exemplar of an educative way of going about teacher evaluation. From its largely humanistic origins, we have argued that this collaborative process has many of the ingredients necessary to enable teachers to begin the job of reclaiming their teaching from those who would have them remain beholden to a hierarchical view of how it should be conceived and enacted. What has prematurely frustrated the extended development of clinical supervision as a powerful means of teacher-to-teacher dialogue has been the prevailing view that clinical supervision should remain in the hands of a cadre of experts who know best about teaching, and whose function it is to diagnose, recommend and tender to the personal pedagogical inadequacies of teachers.

We believe that the way in which we have chosen to reconstruct the principles and the practices of clinical supervision, so as to bring out the problematic, the communicative and the dialogical in teaching, is consistent with the pioneering work of Goldhammer before his untimely death in 1968. Using clinical supervision in a problematizing way means that teachers are able to dialogue, analyze, deconstruct and reformulate their teaching in practical ways that lead to a rebuilding of fragmented school communities. As a well articulated form of teacher resistance to dominant modes of teacher evaluation, clinical supervision clearly holds the potential to enable teachers systematically to pose problems about teaching, but to do so in a way that actively implicates the wider social, economic and political structures that bear down so heavily on what normally occurs in teaching. Our claim is that processes like clinical supervision, when construed 'critically', have the philosophical and conceptual potency to supplant less informed dominant modes of teacher evaluation. The free-ranging 'problem-posing' (as distinct from the constrained 'problem-solving') aspect of clinical supervision, as we have discussed it, enables teachers to construct an overt agenda of challenging the established practices of teaching, theorizing about that teaching, making judgments about its moral worth, and in the light of reasoned argument adopting better informed and more just alternatives. This systematic rethinking of the aims of teaching (both disclosed and undisclosed), along with the internal and external contexts that accompany teaching, amounts to a way of re-assessing and continuously re-focusing the aims of teaching that takes account of participants' own experiences and viewpoints. Starting with participants' own texts, created about their teaching, provides for dialogue, reason and re-focusing that would otherwise be impossible. The kind of distortion that usually occurs where evaluation involves checking-up on another person dissolves. The more egalitarian relationship engendered where pre-defined criteria of 'good' teaching are not an issue enables teachers to dispense with ritualistic encounters and instead begin to pose and answer difficult questions like: why do I teach the way I do? how did I come to believe in this way of teaching? who says this is the 'best' way to teach, and why do they say that? when I have the interests of my students uppermost, how might I do things differently? why is it that other forces stop me from doing that? who in the end is morally right? The clear intent is to tilt the balance away from policy directives that originate outside classrooms, and to place authority in the hands of teachers, where it rightfully belongs. To become critical through clinical supervision is to have the unashamed political agenda of placing control over the message systems of curriculum, pedagogy and evaluation in the hands of teachers—no matter how unfashionable it may be to espouse that view in some quarters.

End Piece

We can do no more than close this volume with a simple but powerful invitation. We invite all associated with schools in whatever capacity to join together in the debate about the nature of evaluation so that the dominant mode no longer continues to be regarded as natural or irreplaceable. For the survival of our schools as vibrant, questioning and democratic communities it is imperative that we begin to explore forms of teacher evaluation that represent more genuinely educative possibilities.

References

ANDERSON, G. 'Towards a critical ethnography of educational administration'. Paper to annual meeting of American Educational Research Association, Washington D.C., 1987.

ANDERSON, R. 'The genesis of clinical supervision', in SMYTH, J. (ed.), *Learning about Teaching through Clinical Supervision*, London: Croom Helm, 1986.

APPLE, M. 'Scientific interests and the nature of educational institutions', in PINAR, W. (ed.), *Curriculum Theorizing*, Berkeley: McCutcheon, 1975, pp. 120–30.

APPLE, M. *Education and Power*, Boston: Routledge and Kegan Paul, 1982.

APPLE, M. *Teachers and Texts: A Political Economy of Class and Gender Relations in Education*, Boston: Routledge and Kegan Paul, 1986.

APPLE, M. 'Producing inequality: Ideology and economy in the national reports on education', *Educational Studies* (USA), **18**, (2), 1987, pp. 195–220.

APPLE, M. and BEYER, L. 'Social evaluation of curriculum', *Educational Evaluation and Policy Analysis,* **5**, (4), 1983, pp. 425–34.

ARONOWITZ, S. 'Mass culture and the eclipse of reason: The implications for pedagogy', *College English*, April 1977, pp. 768–74.

ASHENDEN, D. 'Information and inequality: A systematic approach to increasing educational equity'. Paper prepared for the State Board of Education, Victoria, September 1987.

ASHTON-WARNER, S. *Spinster*, London: Virago, 1958.

AUSTIN, A. *Australian Education, 1788–1900: Church, State and Public Education in Colonial Australia*, Melbourne: Pitman, 1961 and 1965.

BAGLEY, W. *Classroom Management: Its Principles and Techniques*, New York: Macmillan, 1907.

BAGLEY, W. *Craftmanship in Teaching*, New York: Macmillan, 1911.

BAKER, R. 'Whither bureaucracy'. Occasional Paper Series: University of New South Wales, 1977.

BENSEMAN, J. 'Paulo Freire: A revolutionary alternative', *Delta,* **23**, November 1978, pp. 29–53.

BERLAK, H. 'Values, goals, public policy and educational evaluation', *Review of Educational Research,* **40**, (2), 1970, pp. 261–78.

BERLAK, A. and BERLAK, H. 'Towards a political and psychological theory of schooling: An analysis and interpretation of English informal primary schools', *Interchange,* **6**, (3), 1975, pp. 11–22.

BERLAK, A. and BERLAK, H. *Dilemmas of Schooling: Teaching and Social Change*, London: Methuen, 1981.

References

BERNSTEIN, R. *Beyond Objectivism and Relativism: Science, Hermeneutics and Praxis*, Philadelphia: University of Pennsylvania Press, 1983.

BEYER, L. 'Educational reform: The political roots of national risk', *Curriculum Inquiry,* **15,** Spring 1985, pp. 37–56.

BLAND, P. 'No man's friend?' *Quest*, May 1975.

BLUMBERG, A. *Supervisors and Teachers: A Private Cold War*, Berkeley, Ca: McCutcheon, 2nd ed., 1980.

BLUMBERG, A. 'Where we came from: Notes on supervision in the 1840s'. Paper to Annual Meeting of American Educational Research Association, New Orleans, 1984.

BOOMER, G. (ed.) *Negotiating the Curriculum: A Teacher Student Partnership*, Sydney: Ashton Scholastic, 1982.

BOOMER, G. 'Deciphering the teaching code', *Education News,* **19,** (1), 1984, pp. 22–26.

BORICH, G. (ed.) *The Appraisal of Teaching: Concepts and Process*, Reading, Mass: Addison-Wesley, 1977.

BOURDIEU, P. *Outline of a Theory of Practice*, Cambridge: Cambridge University Press, 1977.

BOURDIEU, P. 'Systems of education and systems of thought', in YOUNG, M.F.D. (ed.), *Knowledge and Control*, London: Collier-Macmillan, 1971.

BOURDIEU, P. and PASSERON, J. *Reproduction in Education, Society and Culture*, Beverley Hills: Sage, 1977.

BOYER, E., and the Carnegie Foundation for the Advancement of Teaching, *High School: A Report on Secondary Education in America*, New York: Harper and Row, 1983.

BRAVERMAN, H. *Labour and Monopoly Capital*, New York: Monthly Review Press, 1975.

BREININ, C. 'A complaint and a prediction', *Phi Delta Kappan*, September 1987, pp. 15–16.

BRIDGES, E. *The Incompetent Teacher*, Lewes: Falmer, 1986.

BROADFOOT, T. 'Towards a sociology of assessment', in BARTON, L. and WALKER, S. (eds.), *Schools, Teachers and Teaching,* London: Falmer, 1981.

BUCHMANN, M. 'The use of research knowledge in teacher education and teaching', *American Journal of Education,* **92,** (4), 1984, pp. 421–39.

BUCHMANN, M. and SCHWILLE, J. 'Education: The overcoming of experience', *American Journal of Education,* **92,** 1983, pp. 30–51.

BULLOUGH, R. and GITLIN, A. 'Schooling and change: A view from the lower rung', *Teachers College Record,* **87,** (2), Winter, 1985, pp. 219–37.

BULLOUGH, R. and GITLIN, A. 'Limits of teacher autonomy: Decision-making, ideology and reproduction of role', *New Education,* **8,** (1), 1986, pp. 25–34.

BULLOUGH, R., GOLDSTEIN, S. and HOLT, L. *Human Interests in the Curriculum: Teaching and Learning in a Technological Society*, New York: Teachers College Press, 1984.

BULLOUGH, R., GITLIN, A., and GOLDSTEIN, S. 'Ideology, teacher role, and resistance', *Teachers College Record,* **86,** (2), 1984, pp. 339–58.

BUROS, O. 'Fifty years in testing: Some reminiscences, criticisms and suggestions', *Educational Researcher,* **6,** (7), 1977, pp. 9–15.

BUTTON, W. 'A history of supervision in the public schools 1870–1950'. Unpublished Ph.D., Washington University, St. Louis, Missouri, 1961.

CANTER, L. 'Assertive discipline: A take charge approach for today's educator', Los Angeles: Canter Associates Inc., 1979.

CARLSON, D. 'Of capital, labor and teachers', *Journal of Curriculum Theorizing,* **5,** (3), 1983, pp. 148–57.

CARR, W. 'Critical theory and educational studies', *Journal of Philosophy of Education*, **21**, (2), 1987, pp. 287–95.

CARR, W. and KEMMIS, S. *Becoming Critical: Education, Knowledge and Action Research*, Geelong, Australia: Deakin University Press, 1986.

CERONI, K. 'The Madeline Hunter phenomenon: Questions bothering a trainer'. Paper to American Educational Research Association, Washington D.C., 1987.

CONNELL, R. , ASHENDEN, D., KESSLER, S., and DOWSETT, G. *Making the Difference: Schools, Families and Social Division*, Sydney: George Allen, 1982.

COOPER, T. and MEYENN, B. 'A school based project and educational change'. Paper to the annual meeting of the Australian Association for Research in Education, Perth 1984.

COSTA, A. 'A reaction to Hunter's knowing, teaching, and supervising', in HOSFORD, P., (ed.), *Using What We Know about Teaching*, Alexandria, Va: Association for Supervision and Curriculum Development, 1984, pp. 196–203.

COX, I. 'Report of the review of superintendents in the Education Department of South Australia', Adelaide, S.A., 1987.

CUBBERLEY, E. *Public School Administration*, New York: Houghton Mifflin, 1922.

DARLING-HAMMOND, L., WISE, A., and PEASE, S. 'Teacher evaluation in the organizational context: A review of the literature', *Review of Educational Research*, **53**, (3), 1983, pp. 285–328.

DEAKIN UNIVERSITY. *The Action Research Reader*, Geelong, Australia: Deakin University 1982.

DEAR, K. 'Payment by results and the status of teachers in Victoria 1862–1872'. Melbourne Studies in Education, in MURRAY-SMITH, S. (ed.), Melbourne University Press, 1975.

DEYOUNG, A. 'Educational "excellence" versus teacher "professionalism": Towards some conceptual clarity', *The Urban Review*, **18**, (1), 1986, pp. 71–84.

DOYLE, W. 'Interpreting teaching effectiveness research', *Viewpoints in Teaching and Learning*, **54**, (4), 1978, pp. 141–53.

DOYLE, W. and PONDER, G. 'The practicality ethic in teacher decision-making', *Interchange*, **8**, (3), 1977, pp. 1–12.

EGGLESTON, J. 'Evaluating teachers or teaching?' *Forum*, **21**, (2), 1979, pp. 40–42.

ELLIOTT, J. 'Knowledge, power and teacher appraisal'. Paper to annual meeting of the British Educational Research Association, Manchester, 1987.

EVERHART, R. *Reading, Writing and Resistance*, Oxford: Routledge and Kegan Paul, 1983.

FAY, B. 'How people change themselves: The relationship between critical theory and its audience', in BALL, T., (ed.), *Political Theory and Praxis: New Perspectives*, Minneapolis: University of Minnesota Press, 1977, pp. 200–33.

FAY, B. *Critical Social Science: Liberation and its Limits*, Oxford, Polity Press, 1987.

FLORIDA COALITION FOR THE DEVELOPMENT OF PERFORMANCE MEASUREMENT SYSTEM, *Domains: Knowledge Base of the Florida Performance Measurement System*. Tallahassee, Florida: Office of Teacher Education and In-Service Staff Development, 1983.

FOUCAULT, M. *Power/Knowledge: Selected Interviews and Other Writings*. Gordon, C. (ed. and trans.), New York: Pantheon, 1980.

FREEDMAN, S., JACKSON, J. and BOLES, K. (The Boston Women's Teachers' Group) 'Teaching: An imperilled "profession"', in SHULMAN, L. and SYKES, G., (eds), *Handbook of Teaching and Policy*, New York: Longmans, 1983, pp. 261–99.

FREEDMAN, S., JACKSON, J. and BOLES, K. (The Boston Women's Teachers' Group) 'The other end of the corridor: The effect of teaching on teachers', *The Radical Teacher*, **23**, (3), 1983, pp. 2–23.

References

FREEDMAN, S., JACKSON, J. and BOLES, K. (The Boston Women's Teachers' Group) *The Effect of Teaching on Teachers*. North Dakota Study Group on Evaluation, Center for Teaching and Learning: University of North Dakota, Grand Forks, 1986.

FREIRE, P. *Pedagogy of the Oppressed*, Harmondsworth: Penguin, 1972.

FREIRE, P. *The Politics of Education: Culture, Power and Liberation*, South Hadley, MA: Bergin and Garvey, 1985.

FRIED, R. *Empowerment vs Delivery of Services*, Concord, NH: New Hampshire Department of Education, 1980.

GADAMER, H. *Truth and Method*. Translated by BARDEN, G. and CUMMINGS, J., New York: Seaburg Press, 1975.

GADAMER, H. *Reason in the Age of Science*, Cambridge: MIT Press, 1984.

GARMAN, N. 'The mousetrap study: Stable data in clinical supervision'. Unpublished manuscript, University of Pittsburgh, 1983.

GARMAN, N. 'Clinical supervision: Quackery or remedy for professional development'. Paper to the annual meeting of the Association for Supervision and Curriculum Development, New York, 1984.

GARMAN, N. 'Reflection, the heart of clinical supervision: A modern rationale for professional practice', *Journal of Curriculum and Supervision*, 2, (1), 1986, pp. 1–24.

GEERTZ, C. *The Interpretation of Cultures*, New York: Basic Books, 1973.

GIBBONEY, R. 'A critique of Madeline Hunter's teaching model from Dewey's perspective', *Educational Leadership*, February, 1987, pp. 46–50.

GIDDENS, A. *Central Problems in Social Theory*, Berkeley: University of California Press, 1979.

GIROUX, H. *Theory and Resistance in Education: A Pedagogy for the Opposition*, South Hadley, MA: Bergin and Garvey, 1983.

GIROUX, H. 'Teachers as transformative intellectuals', *Social Education*, 49, May 1985a, pp. 376–9.

GIROUX, H. 'Critical pedagogy and the resisting intellectual, part II', *Phenomenology and Pedagogy*, 3, (2), 1985b, pp. 84–97.

GIROUX, H. 'Educational reform and the politics of teacher empowerment', *New Education*, 9, (1 and 2), 1987, pp. 3–13.

GITLIN, A. 'Understanding the work of teachers'. Unpublished doctoral dissertation, University of Wisconsin, Madison, 1980.

GITLIN, A. 'School structure and teachers' work', in APPLE, M. and WEIS, L. (eds), *Ideology and Practice in Schooling*, Philadelphia: Temple University Press, 1983, pp. 193–212.

GITLIN, A. and BULLOUGH, R. 'Teacher evaluation and empowerment: Challenging the taken-for-granted view of teaching', *Educational Policy*, 1, (2), 1987, pp. 229–47.

GITLIN, A. and GOLDSTEIN, S. 'A dialogical approach to understanding: Horizontal evaluation', *Educational Theory*, 37, (1), 1987, pp. 17–27.

GOLDHAMMER, R. 'Observations on observation and observations on observations on observation'. Unpublished Ms, 1964.

GOLDHAMMER, R. 'A critical analysis of supervision of instruction in the Harvard-Lexington summer program'. Unpublished doctoral dissertation, Harvard University, 1966.

GOLDHAMMER, R. *Clinical Supervision: Special Methods for the Supervision of Teachers*, New York: Holt, Rinehart and Winston, 1969.

GOLDHAMMER, R., ANDERSON, R. and KRAJEWSKI, R. *Clinical Supervision: Special Methods for the Supervision of Teachers*, New York: Holt, Rinehart and Winston, 2nd ed., 1980.

GONDAK, D. 'Madeline Hunter/Clinical supervision sweeps the state', *The Mideasterner,* **8,** (1), Spring 1986.

GOODMAN, B., O'HEHI, R. and O'SHEA, J. 'Really useful knowledge', *Secondary Teacher,* **9,** 1977.

GOODMAN, J. 'Reflection and teacher education: A case study and theoretical analysis', *Interchange,* **19,** 1984, pp. 9–26.

GRACE, G. 'Judging teachers: The social and political context of teacher evaluation', *British Journal of Sociology of Education,* **6,** (1), 1985, pp. 3–16.

GRACE, G. *Teachers, Ideology and Control: A Study in Urban Education,* Henley: Routledge and Kegan Paul, 1978.

GREENE, M. *Teacher as Stranger: Educational Philosophy for the Modern Age,* Belmont, CA: Wadsworth, 1973, pp. 267–302.

GREENE, M. 'Teacher as project: Choice, perspective, and the public space'. Paper to the Summer Institute of Teaching, Teachers College Columbia University, July 1985.

GREENE, M. 'In search of a critical pedagogy', *Harvard Educational Review,* **56,** (4), 1986, pp. 427–41.

GUBA, E. and LINCOLN, Y., *Effective Evaluation,* San Francisco: Jossey-Bass, 1982.

GUDITUS, C. 'The pre-observation conference; Is it worth the effort?' *Wingspan. The Pedamorphosis Communique,* **1,** (1), 1982.

HABERMAS, J. *Legitimation Crisis,* London: Heinemann, 1976a.

HABERMAS, J. *Communication and the Evolution of Society,* Boston: Beacon Press, 1976b.

HABERMAS, J. 'Review of Gadamer's truth and method', in DALLMAYR, F. and McCARTHY, T. (eds), *Understanding and Social Inquiry,* Indiana: University of Notre Dame Press, 1977, pp. 335–64.

HANDFORD, S. and HERBERG, M. *Langenscheidt's Shorter Latin Dictionary,* UK: Hodder and Stoughton, 1977.

HANNAN, W. 'Has school-based curriculum worked?' *Education Victoria,* May 1986, p. 16.

HARRIS, B. *Supervisory Behavior in Education,* New Jersey: Prentice Hall, 1985.

HARRIS, K. *Education and Knowledge: The Structured Misrepresentation of Knowledge,* London: Routledge and Kegan Paul, 1979.

HARTNETT, A. and NAISH, M. 'Conceptions of education and social change in a democratic society', in HARTNETT, A. and NAISH, M. (eds), *Education and Society Today,* Lewes: Falmer, 1986.

HAZI, H. 'Teacher evaluation incognito: The Madeline Hunter movement and school reform'. Paper to the annual meeting of American Educational Research Association, Washington D.C., 1987.

HAZI, H. and GARMAN, N. 'Legalizing scientism through teacher evaluation'. Unpublished manuscript, West Virginia University, 1988.

HELD, D. *Introduction to Critical Theory: Horkheimer to Habermas,* London: Hutchinson, 1980.

HERNDON, J. *Notes from a School Teacher,* N.Y.: Simon and Schuster, 1985.

HEXTALL, I. and SARUP, M. 'School knowledge: Evaluation and alienation', in WHITTY, G. and YOUNG, M. (eds), *Society, State and Schooling,* Lewes: Falmer, 1977.

HUNTER, M. 'Six types of supervisory conferences', *Educational Leadership,* **37,** (5), 1980a, pp. 408–412.

HUNTER, M. 'Personal communication, 1980b.

HUNTER, M. 'What's wrong with Madeline Hunter?' *Educational Leadership,* **42,** (5), 1985, pp. 57–60.

INGVARSON, L. 'With critical friends, who needs enemies', in FENSHAM, P. *et al.,* *Alienation from Schooling,* London: Routledge and Kegan Paul, 1986.

JACKSON, P. *Life in Classrooms*, New York: Holt, Rinehart and Winston, 1968.

JOHNSON, R. 'Educational policy and social control in early Victorian England', *Past and Present,* **49,** 1970, pp. 96–119.

JONATHAN, R. 'The manpower service model of education'. Unpublished manuscript, nd.

JONCICH, G. *The Sane Positivist: A Biography of Edward L. Thorndike*, Middletown, Conn: Wesleyan University Press, 1968.

JONES, A. 'The inspector at the crossroads', *Journal of Educational Administration,* **11,** (1), 1973.

KARIER, C. 'Supervision in historic perspective', in SERGIOVANNI, T. (ed.), *Supervision of Teaching*, Alexandria, Va: Association for Supervision and Curriculum Development, 1982, pp. 2–15.

KEMMIS, S. 'Action research and the politics of reflection', in BOUD, D., KEOGH, R. and WALKER, D., (eds), *Reflection: Turning Experience into Learning*, London: Kogan Page, 1984.

KLAUSMEIR, H. 'Individually guided education, 1966–80', *Journal of Teacher Education,* **27,** 1976.

KLIEBARD, H. 'Bureaucracy and curriculum theory', in PINAR, W. (ed.), *Curriculum Theorizing: The Reconceptualists*, Berkeley, CA: McCutcheon, 1975.

KOHL, H. 'Examining closely what we do', *Learning,* **12,** (1), 1983, pp. 28–30.

LAKOFF, G. and JOHNSON, M., *Metaphors We Live By*, Chicago: University of Chicago Press, 1980.

LAMPERT, M. 'How do teachers manage to teach? Perspectives on problems in practice', *Harvard Educational Review,* **55,** (2), 1985, pp. 178–94.

LANDRY, C. et al., *What a Way to Run a Railroad*, London: Comedia, 1985.

LASCH, C. *The Minimal Self*, New York: Norton, 1984.

LAWN, M. and GRACE, G. (eds) *Teachers: The Culture and Politics of Work*, Lewes: Falmer Press, 1987.

LEVY, T. 'A hired hand responds', *Social Education*, May 1985, pp. 366–7.

LICHTMAN, R. *The Production of Desire: The Integration of Psychoanalysis into Marxist Theory*, New York: The Free Press, 1982.

LIPSKY, M. *Street-level Bureaucracy*, New York: Russell Sage Foundation, 1980.

LORTIE, D. *School Teacher: A Sociological Study*, Chicago: University of Chicago Press, 1975.

LUNDGREN, U. *Between Hope and Happening : Text and Context in Curriculum*, Geelong, Australia: Deakin University Press, 1983.

McDONALD, J. 'Raising the teacher's voice and the ironic role of theory', *Harvard Educational Review,* **56,** (4), 1986, pp. 355–78.

McDONALD, J. 'Curriculum, consciousness, and social change', in PINAR, W. (ed.), *Contemporary Curriculum Discourses*, Scottsdale, AZ: Gorsuch Scarisbrick, 1988, pp. 156–200.

McLAREN, P. 'The ritual dimensions of resistance: Clowning and symbolic inversion', *Journal of Education,* **167,** (2), 1985, pp. 84–97.

McLAREN, P. 'Education as counter-discourse: Toward a critical pedagogy of hope', *The Review of Education,* **13,** (1), 1987, pp. 58–68.

McLAREN, P. 'Language, social structure and the production of subjectivity', *Critical Pedagogy Networker,* **1,** (2 and 3), 1988.

McROBBIE, A. *Feminism for Girls: An Adventure Story*, Boston: Routledge and Kegan Paul, 1981.

MEAD, G. *Mind, Self and Society*, Chicago: University of Chicago Press, 1934.

MELBOURNE AGE, 'Hogg promoting propaganda, says opposition', *The Age*, 23 May 1988, p. 15.

MILLMAN, J. (ed.), *Handbook of Teacher Evaluation*, Beverley Hills, CA: Sage, 1981.

MILLS, C. WRIGHT *The Sociological Imagination*, Harmondsworth: Penguin, 1959.

MISHLER, E. 'Meaning in context and the empowerment of respondents', in MISHLER, E., *Research Interviewing: Context and Narrative*, Cambridge, MA: Harvard University Press, 1986.

MOORE, T. and NEAL, W. 'The evaluation of teaching performance', *Journal of Educational Administration*, **8**, (2), October 1969, pp. 127–36.

NAY, W. *Quality Education—Teacher Efficiency Review*, New South Wales Department of Education, Sydney, 1985.

NICASTRO, G. 'Teacher professionalism and support groups', Unpublished Masters Thesis, University of Utah, Salt Lake City, 1986.

PAGANO, J. 'The schools we deserve. Review of Goodlad's, "A Place Called School"', *Curriculum Inquiry*, **17**, (1), 1987, pp. 107–22.

PALONSKY, S. *900 Shows a Year: A Look at Teaching from the Teacher's Side of the Desk*, New York: Random House, 1986.

PATEMAN, T. 'Accountability, values and schooling', in DALE, R., ESLAND, G., FERGUSSON, R., and MACDONALD, M. (eds), *Politics, Patriarchy and Practice*, Lewes: Falmer Press, 1981.

PATON, K. *The Great Brain Robbery*, London: Moss Side Press, 1973.

PIERCE, C. *Collected Papers on Charles Sanders Pierce*, Charles Hartshorne and Paul Weiss, eds, Cambridge, Mass: Harvard University Press, 1931–5.

POPKEWITZ, T. *Paradigm and Ideology in Educational Research,* Lewes: Falmer Press, 1984.

PRESTON, B. 'Teacher evaluation: Contextual issues and policy development'. Paper to the Australian Council for Educational Research forum 'Teacher appraisal: An emerging issue in Australian education', Melbourne, August 1987.

RAPHAEL, R. *The Teacher's Voice: A Sense of Who We Are*, Portsmouth, NH: Heinemann, 1985.

RIZVI, F. 'Ethnicity, class and multi-cultural education', Geelong: Deakin University Press, 1986.

ROSENSHINE, B. 'The master teacher and the master developer'. Paper to the Invisible College of Researchers on Teaching, University of California, Los Angeles, April 1981.

RUDDUCK, J. 'The improvement of the art of teaching through research', *Cambridge Journal of Education,* **15**, (3), 1985, pp. 123–7.

RYAN, W. *Blaming the Victim*, New York: Pantheon, 1971.

SARASON, S. *The Culture of the School and the Problem of Change*, Boston: Allyn and Bacon, 1982.

SCHÖN, D. *The Reflective Practitioner: How Professionals Think in Action*, New York: Basic Books, 1983.

SCHÖN, D. 'Leadership as reflection-in-action', in SERGIOVANNI, T. and CORBALLY, J. (eds), *Leadership and Organizational Culture: New Perspectives on Administrative Theory and Practice*, Urbana: University of Illinois Press, 1984, pp. 36–63.

SCHÖN, D. *Educating the Reflective Practitioner*, San Francisco: Jossey Bass, 1987.

SHANN, S. *School Portrait*, Fitzroy/Ringwood: McPhee Gribble/Penguin Books Australia, 1987.

SHOR, I. *Critical Teaching and Everyday Life*, Boston: South End Press, 1980.

SHOR, I. *Culture Wars, School and Society in the Conservative Restoration 1969–84*, New York: Routledge and Kegan Paul, 1986.

SHOR, I. 'Equality is excellence: Transforming teacher education and the learning process', *Harvard Educational Review,* **56**, (4), 1986, pp. 406–26.

SHOR, I. and FREIRE, P. *A Pedagogy for Liberation: Dialogues on Transforming Education*, South Hadley, MA: Bergin and Garvey, 1987.

References

SILBERMAN, C. *Crisis in the Classroom*, New York: Random House, 1970.

SIMON, R. 'Signposts for a critical pedagogy: A review of Henry Giroux's "Theory and Resistance in Education"', *Educational Theory,* **34,** (4), 1984, pp. 379–88.

SIMON, R. 'For a pedagogy of possibility', *Critical Pedagogy Networker,* **1,** (1), 1988.

SIZER, T. *Horace's Compromise: The Dilemma of the American High School,* Boston: Houghton Mifflin, 1984.

SLAVIN, R. 'The Hunterization of America's schools', *Instructor,* **96,** (8), 1987, April, pp. 56–60.

SMART, D. 'The status of the teacher in the penal and early colonial New South Wales society, 1799–1848', in SPAULL, A. (ed.), *Australian Teachers: From Colonial Schoomasters to Militant Professionals,* Melbourne: Macmillan, 1977, pp. 22–15.

SMITH, F. *Insult to Intelligence: Bureaucratic Invasion of Our Classrooms,* New York: Arbor House,1986.

SMITH, R. 'Becoming more self-reflexive in educational research', *Australian Educational Researcher,* **14,** (3), Sept. 1987, pp. 47–56.

SMITH, R. and ZANTIOTIS, A. 'Practical teacher education and the avant garde', *Journal of Curiculum Theorizing,* **8,** 1988, (in press).

SMYTH, J. 'Toward a "critical consicousness" in the instructional supervision of experienced teachers', *Curriculum Inquiry,* **14,** (4), 1984a, pp. 425–36.

SMYTH, J. (ed.), *Case Studies in Clinical Supervision,* Geelong, Australia: Deakin University, 1984b.

SMYTH, J. *Clinical Supervision—Collaborative Learning about Teaching, A Handbook,* Geelong, Australia: Deakin University Press, 1984c.

SMYTH, J. 'Developing a critical practice of clinical supervision', *Journal of Curriculum Studies,* **17,** (1), 1985, pp. 1–15.

SMYTH, J. 'Clinical supervision: Technocratic mindedness, or emancipatory learning', *Journal of Curriculum and Supervision,* **1,** (4), 1986a, pp. 331–40.

SMYTH, J. 'Towards a collaborative, reflective and critical mode of clinical supervision', in SMYTH, J. (ed.). *Learning about Teaching through Clinical Supervision.* London: Croom Helm, 1986b.

SMYTH, J. 'Using clinical supervison to develop a critical perspective towards teaching', Paper presented to a colloquium at Teachers College, Columbia University, New York, 1986c.

SMYTH, J. (ed.), *Educating Teachers: Changing the Nature of Pedagogical Knowledge,* Lewes: Falmer Press, 1987a.

SMYTH, J. 'Teachers-as-intellectuals in a critical pedagogy and schooling', *Education of Society,* **5** (1 & 2), 1987b, pp. 11–28.

SMYTH, J. *Rationale for Teachers' Critical Pedagogy: A Handbook,* Geelong: Deakin University Press, 1987c.

SMYTH, J. *A 'Critical' Pedagogy of Teacher Evaluation,* Geelong, Australia: Deakin University Press, 1988.

SMYTH, J. and HENRY, C. 'Case study experience of a collaborative and responsive form of professional development for teachers', *The Australian Journal of Teacher Education,* **10,** (1), 1985, pp. 1–17.

SMYTH, J., HENRY, C., MARTIN, J. 'Clinical supervision: Evidence of a viable strategy for teacher development', *The Australian Administrator,* **3,** (5), 1982, pp. 1–4.

SMYTH, J., HENRY, C. MARCUS, A., LOGAN, T. and MEADOWS, M. 'Follow-through case study of clinical supervision'. Deakin University, Report to the Educational Research and Development Committee, Canberra, Australia, 1982, pp. 1–57.

ST. MAURICE, H. 'Clinical supervision and power: Regimes of instructional management', in POPKEWITZ, T. (ed.), *Critical Studies in Teacher Education: Its Folklore, Theory and Practices,* New York: Falmer Press, 1987.

STATE BOARD of EDUCATION, 'Monitoring the achievements of schools', *Working Paper No. 1,* Ministry of Education, Victoria, December 1987.

STEEDMAN, C. *The Tidy House,* London: Virago, 1982.

STENHOUSE, L. 'The relevance of theory to practice', *Theory into Practice,* **22,** (30), 1983, pp. 211–5.

STEVENS, P. 'Political education and political teachers', *Journal of Philosophy of Education,* **21,** (1), 1987, pp. 75–83.

SUFFOLK EDUCATION DEPARTMENT, *Those Having Torches. . . Teacher Appraisal: A Study,* Suffolk: Department of Education and Science, 1985.

SURKES, S. '''Assess schools by behaviour'', says DES', *Times Educational Supplement,* 28 August 1987, pp. 1 and 5.

SWARTZ, R. 'Restructuring curriculum for critical thinking', *Educational Leadership,* **43,** (8), 1986, pp. 43–5.

TAYLOR, F. *The Principles of Scientific Management,* New York: Holt, Rinehart and Winston, 1911.

The Republic of Plato, translated by CORNFORD, F. W. London: Oxford University Press, 1941.

THOMAS, D. 'About teaching and teachers: The torpedo's touch', *Harvard Educational Review,* **55,** (2), 1985, pp. 220–22.

THOMAS, E. 'Criteria employed by high school principals in evaluating teachers in Victoria', *Journal of Educational Administration,* **10,** (1), 1972.

TOZER, S. 'Dominant ideology and the teacher's authority', *Contemporary Education,* **56,** 1985, pp. 148–53.

TRIPP, D. 'From autopilot to critical consciousness: Problematizing successful teaching'. Revision of a paper presented to the Sixth Curriculum Theory and Practice Conference, Bergamo, Ohio, November 1984.

TRIPP, D. 'Teachers, journals and collaborative research', in SMYTH, J. (ed.), *Educating Teachers: Changing the Nature of Pedagogical Knowledge,* Lewes: Falmer Press, 1987, pp. 179–92.

TRONC, K. 'The district inspector: Educational missionary or ogre?' *The Practising Administrator,* **9,** (2), 1987, pp. 30–3.

TRONC, K. and HARRIS, H. 'Victims of history: The establishment and growth of the Australian inspectorate', *Practising Administrator,* **7,** (1), 1985, pp. 43–8.

UTAH STATE BOARD OF EDUCATION, *Elementary and Secondary Core Curriculum,* Salt Lake City, Utah, 1987.

US Department of Education, *What Works:Research aout Teaching and Learning,* Washington, 1986.

WALSH, K. 'The politics of teacher appraisal', in LAWN, and GRACE, G. (eds).*Teachers: The Culture and Politics of Work,* Lewes: Falmer, 1987.

WEIS, L. *Between Two Worlds: Black Students in an Urban Community College,* Boston: Routledge and Kegan Paul, 1985.

WHITE, J. and WHITE, P. 'Teachers as political activists', in HARTNETT, A. and NAISH, M. (eds), *Education and Society Today,* Lewes: Falmer, 1987.

WHITEHEAD, J. and LOMAX, P. 'Action research and the politics of educational knowledge', *British Educational Research Journal,* **13,** (2), 1987, pp. 175–190.

WIGGINTON, E. *Sometimes a Shining Moment: The Foxfire Experience,* New York, Anchor, 1985.

WILHELMS, F. *Foreword to Clinical Supervision by M. Cogan.* Boston: Houghton Mifflin, 1973.

WILLIAMSON, J. 'Is there anyone here from a classroom?' *Screen,* **26,** (1), 1985, pp. 90–5.

WILLIS, P. *Learning to Labour: How Working Class Kids Get Working Class Jobs,*

Westmead, England, 1977.

WINTER, R. 'Collaboration? The dialectics of practice and reflection in action research', *Classroom Action Research Network,* Bulletin, No. 8, Cambridge Institute of Education, 1987, pp. 109–16.

WIRTH, A. 'Review of Ira Shor's "Culture Wars"', *Educational Studies,* **18,** (1), 1987, pp. 175–82.

WORTHEN, B. and SANDERS, J. *Educational Evaluation: Theory and Practice,* Belmont, CA: Wadsworth, 1973.

YOUNG, R. (ed.), *Untying the Text,* Boston: Routledge and Kegan Paul, 1981.

Index

and technocratic rationality ix,
21-2, 23-4, 68-9
and technologization 164-5
and textbooks, *see* textbooks
and texts about teaching 98,
102-4, 116, 121-4, 140, 145
and theoretical histories 152-3
and theory and practice 87-93,
100
and understanding 61-75, 77-96
views of evaluation of 78-81
teaching
see also schooling; teachers
and craft orientation 42-3, 64-5
as cultural politics 33-4
gender in 69, 107, 135-6, 144-6
habitual activities in 126-7
as historical process 134-5
as individualistic 154-5, 157
and industrialization 34-5
and managerialism 9-10, 12, 132,
135-41, 160-1
and moral issues 113, 152, 164-5,
107
and mutual understanding 30-1
political agenda in 118-19, 132-4,
141-2
power relations in 122, 134
problematizing of 98, 99-102,
116-21
and public servant ideology x,
49-51, 79, 129
religious origins of 136-7
social context of 113-14, 127-9,
151-2, 162
and social justice 142
social nature of 104-7
social relations in 127-9
as technical 43, 44-9
textbooks and 43, 44-9
as theoretical activity 135-6
theory and practice in 87-93, 100
and uniform standards 45-46
unquestioning nature of 152

technocratic mindedness 81-93
technocratic rationality ix, 21-2,
23-4, 68-9, 163
textbooks 43, 44-9, 91, 164
Thomas, D. 48-9

understanding
and human potential 62-3
levels of 62
and teacher evaluation 61, 62-3
transformative potential of 62
United Kingdom (UK)
national testing proposed in 45
performance indicators in 46-7
responsibility for teacher evaluation
in 16
teacher evaluation in 8, 12-17,
161
United States of America (USA)
accountability in 46-7
Common Schools in 10
core curriculum in 44
educational reform in 108-9
horizontal evaluation in 77-96
rationalized curriculum in 45-6
supervision in 9-11
teacher evaluation in 8, 9-12, 22,
161
teacher evaluation and military
supremacy in 22
'teacher proofing' of curriculum
in 45-6
textbooks and teaching in 43,
44-9
universal pragmatics 65, 69-71

Victoria
educational practices in 154
inspectors and teachers in 18-19
teacher evaluation in 20, 21
teacher militancy in 20
teachers and promotion in 20

Wilkins, W. 17-18